MILTON STUDIES
III

MILTON STUDIES

STUDIES

III &ə *Edited by*

James D. Simmonds

UNIVERSITY OF PITTSBURGH PRESS

MILTON STUDIES

is published annually by the University of Pittsburgh Press as a forum for Milton scholarship and criticism. Articles submitted for publication may be biographical; they may interpret some aspect of Milton's writings; or they may define literary, intellectual, or historical contexts—by studying the work of his contemporaries, the traditions which affected his thought and art, contemporary political and religious movements, his influence on other writers, or the history of critical response to his work.

Manuscripts should be from 3000 to 8000 words in length and should conform to the *MLA Style Sheet*. They will be returned only if sufficient postage is enclosed (overseas contributors enclose international reply coupons). Manuscripts and editorial correspondence should be addressed to James D. Simmonds, Department of English, University of Pittsburgh, Pa. 15213.

Milton Studies does not review books.

Within the United States, *Milton Studies* may be ordered from the University of Pittsburgh Press, Pittsburgh, Pa. 15213.

Overseas orders should be addressed to Henry M. Snyder & Co., Inc., 440 Park Avenue South, New York, New York, 10016, U.S.A.

Library of Congress Catalog Card Number 69–12335

ISBN 0–8229–3174–5 (Volume I)

ISBN 0–8229–3194–x (Volume II)

ISBN 0–8229–3128–0 (Volume III)

Copyright © 1971, University of Pittsburgh Press

Henry M. Snyder & Co., Inc., London

Manufactured in the United States of America

E. L. Marilla, 1900–1970

M Y T A S K of preparing this volume for the press has been saddened, and delayed, by the death of E. L. Marilla last May. Since 1958, when I traveled from Australia to Louisiana State University to work on Henry Vaughan under his supervision, Esmond had been my closest personal friend and closest professional associate. He was, naturally, one of the first people whose advice I sought after conceiving the notion of founding *Milton Studies*, and, just as naturally, he became a member of the original Editorial Board. He regarded this as an honor, and, through a long and painful illness, continued to read manuscripts and evaluate them with the meticulous and impartial thoroughness which marked all of his work. He lived to see the second volume, and to see the page proof of the *festschrift* commemorating his contributions to Milton and seventeenth-century scholarship. *Milton Studies*, and Milton studies, will miss him; and so will I.

J. D. S.

April 11, 1971

CONTENTS

DONALD M. FRIEDMAN   *Lycidas:* The Swain's Paideia   3

STEWART A. BAKER   Milton's Uncouth Swain   35

G. STANLEY KOEHLER   Milton's Use of Color and Light   55

ALBERT R. CIRILLO   Tasso's *Il Mondo Creato:* Providence and the Created Universe   83

LEE A. JACOBUS   Self-Knowledge in *Paradise Lost:* Conscience and Contemplation   103

THOMAS H. BLACKBURN   "Uncloister'd Virtue": Adam and Eve in Milton's Paradise   119

SISTER MARY BRIAN DURKIN   Iterative Figures and Images in *Paradise Lost,* XI–XII   139

KITTY COHEN   Milton's God in Council and War   159

SAMUEL S. STOLLMAN   Milton's Samson and the Jewish Tradition   185

BARBARA BREASTED   *Comus* and the Castlehaven Scandal   201

MILTON STUDIES

III

LYCIDAS:
THE SWAIN'S PAIDEIA

Donald M. Friedman

Lycidas is an embodiment of the long process of education
Milton underwent for the task of writing epic. The experience
of its speaker, the "uncouth swain," is primarily that of struggle. Milton believed that man fails to see truth partly because
he fights actively against it. The swain tries to shield himself
against the pain of reality by casting his experience in the
modes of pastoral convention. But each attempt to substitute
idealized memory or symbolic analogy for actuality is defeated,
in part because the language of pastoral itself points toward
a transcendent redefinition of its meaning. The swain's view of
his poetic vocation changes during the poem, and when he at
last abandons his attempts to surround Lycidas' death with
literary artifice, he is granted a vision of Lycidas' true state. In
the "consolation passage" the poet speaks for the first time to a
human audience, and takes on the double burden of knowledge
and pastoral responsibility. The psychological pattern of resistance and acceptance is reflected in the recurrent conflict
Milton records between his eagerness to attain and use full
poetic powers and his willed submission to God's providence.
In *Lycidas* this battle is fought out in the form of discovery of
the true meaning of "shepherd"; the language of the passage of
consolation leads directly to the new shepherd who prays for
inspiration at the beginning of *Paradise Lost.*

WHATEVER the quality of Milton's friendship with Edward
King, no particularly subtle insight is needed to see that the
shock he sustained at King's death resonated to the depths of his conscious commitment to the life of art. That shock reached even to his
willed belief that time and the will of heaven were "leading" him to
the fulfillment he was trying to merit. And Milton was always too

3

ruthlessly honest to hold that belief complacently. Sonnet VII was composed when he was twenty-four, and neither its mood nor its statement seems strange in a young, serious, and ambitious poet; but when Milton was nearing fifty, blind and burdened by a conviction of unfruitfulness, he still imagined a personified patience counseling him that "they also serve who only stand and wait." How much more poignant, then, must have been his feeling of uncertainty, how much stronger the temptation to despair, in a man nearing thirty, alive to the forces of political and social disintegration crowding in upon that country by whose "instruction" he hoped to win "God's glory," a man who had probably already given up the hope of a priestly career in favor of the equally self-denying calling of poetry, which he fervently believed to be

of power beside the office of a pulpit, to imbreed and cherish in a great people the seeds of vertu, and publick civility, to allay the perturbations of the mind, and set the affections in right tune, to celebrate in glorious and lofty Hymns the throne and equipage of Gods Almightinesse, and what he works, and what he suffers to be wrought with high providence in his Church, to sing the victorious agonies of Martyrs and Saints, the deeds and triumphs of just and pious Nations doing valiantly through faith against the enemies of Christ, to deplore the general relapses of Kingdoms and States from justice and Gods true worship.[1]

The grandeur of the concept is a way to gauge the pain and the cost of the act of self-examination Milton performs in *Lycidas*. His situation is in many respects like that of Marvell in the *Horatian Ode*, who, as he also approaches his thirtieth year, is forced by the disruptive events of history to consider the place of poetry in that history and the question of poetry's intrinsic worth. But Marvell's poem is truly Horatian in that the initially modest gesture of forsaking the "Muses dear" and "Numbers languishing" is transformed as the poet's mind moves on to the more majestic planes of historical dialectic, transformed into the monitory, moral voice of civilized judgment that reminds the conqueror of the costs of conquest. Marvell, in short, finds a new place to stand in the course of the poem, and the "Numbers languishing" are made to seem well left.

In *Lycidas*, however, the transformation is not worked so easily, nor is the leave-taking so painlessly accomplished. This is not simply a consequence of the poem's adhering so strictly to its occasion, or to the parochial boundaries of the pastoral or the collegiate epicedium. It is, rather, a harsh and deliberate choice; Milton forces himself to confront all the implications of the event he is ostensibly to commemorate, and he will allow himself no escape into history, metaphysics, or any previously prepared literary role. This last statement may seem odd, in view of the fact that Milton chose a pastoral *persona* through which to speak *Lycidas;* but the shepherd character is in no sense a disguise or a device for "distancing" in this poem; on the contrary, it is the most pitilessly precise figure Milton could have chosen to express the attitude of *questioning* that is at the heart of the poem.

Lycidas has provoked debates and disagreements because so many of the questions it asks remain unanswered or receive inadequate or irrelevant answers; the experience of reading *Lycidas* is, I suspect, more like Milton's in writing it than is the case with most other poems. And it is an important part of Milton's central conception of his pastoral *persona* to show him in the midst of a roiling sea of uncertainty, anger, despair, and bewilderment. Out of these weltering moods come the challenges, the demands, the questionings of fate, the gods, the self, which constitute so much of the actual texture of the poem. Responses come from the gods, from nature, from the saints; but these responses—explanations and utterances meant to quiet and reassure— are not only often shown to be unhelpful but are actually ignored by the questioner. He seems to be neither informed nor reassured, but merely determined to go on with his frustrating pursuit of resolution.

However one views what once were called "digressions" in the poem, explanations of its structure and of the thematic interrelations of its parts lead inevitably to the idea of a poem based on a dynamic of conflict—sometimes between classical and Christian myth, sometimes between innocence and experience, but always between major principles of poetic allegiance which Milton is striving to reconcile. An important consequence for *Lycidas* of its pattern of successive impact and recoil is that it allows Milton to render the experience of the poem's speaker as one of active struggle. The pastoral *persona* is not swept up in the poem's large movements of debate and abortive harmonies; typically, he fights *against* the knowledge that floods the serene "high Lawns" of his mental landscape in the hortatory voices of Phoebus and St. Peter. The struggle is not carried on forensically; the inspired arguments are not refuted; the lamenting shepherd simply sweeps, or tries to sweep, them away, urging himself on through the disordered countries of his mind, while demanding all the time an explanation that never comes. The further reach of Milton's skill, in this portrait of a consciousness defending itself against the knowledge it knows to be necessary and saving, is his ability to show us the gradual, very gradual, growth of understanding that accompanies and emerges from the tides of conflict which shape the surface and structure of the elegy. The final consoling vision is neither conceived nor spoken from a predetermined position of revealed or human wisdom; it does not follow from the elegist's understanding or from his role at the beginning of the poem; nor is it a knowledge held in suspense, a potentiality implicit in the pastoral and in the mind of the shepherd *persona.* Rather, it is a knowledge whose realization depends from moment to moment on his ability to grasp and accept what the experience of the poem is teaching him.

At each stage of this development in the *persona,* changes in consciousness are reflected in the speaker's language as he challenges the fate that governs the pastoral elegy, and as he reacts to the literary and religious doctrines that are given voice in the poem to meet his challenges. Lowry Nelson, Jr., has described this process as "a kind of self-education";[2] it is not presented, however, as a slow and unperturbed ascent of that "hill side" Milton speaks of in *Of Education,* than which "the harp of *Orpheus* was not more charming."[3] *Lycidas* is a dramatization of the first steps in the ascent of that hill, which Milton calls "laborious indeed." Knowing that as fallen creatures our element is "the perpetuall stumble of conjecture and disturbance in this our darke voyage," Milton insists also that "the darknes and the crookednesse is our own," that "our *understanding* [has] a film of *ignorance* over it," is "blear with gazing on . . . false glisterings." "The very essence of Truth is plainnesse, and brightnes";[4] that men cannot perceive that essence is not the result of mere inability, but of their active struggle not to accept truth, a struggle carried on by human energies perverted in the service of self-deception, egotism, sloth, and the "frail thoughts" that would "dally with false surmise."

In *The Reason of Church-Government* Milton sketched the endless battle between the perspicuous power of truth and the labyrinthine evasions of the human psyche in a curiously Spenserian fashion:

For Truth, I know not how, hath this unhappinesse fatall to her, ere she can come to the triall and inspection of the Understanding, being to passe through many little wards and limits of the severall Affections and Desires, she cannot shift it, but must put on such colours and attire, as those Pathetick handmaids of the soul to lead her in to their Queen. And if she find so much favour with them, they let her passe in her own likenesse; if not, they bring her into the presence habited and colour'd like a notorious Falshood. And contrary when any Falshood come that way, if they like the errand she brings, they are so artfull to counterfeit the very shape and visage of Truth, that the Understanding not being able to discern the fucus which these enchantresses with such cunning have laid upon the feature sometimes of Truth, sometimes of Falshood interchangeably, sentences for the most part one for the other at the first blush, according to the suttle imposture of these sensual mistresses that keep the ports and passages between her and the object.[5]

Milton has found in faculty psychology an explanation of the paradoxical status of the lesser mental powers, which both inform and deceive the rational understanding. And the situation he describes in this miniature fable is analogous to the relations between man's understanding and his soul; the understanding, which, "if we will but purge with sovrain eyesalve that intellectual ray which *God* hath planted in us,"[6] will serve as the proper channel of plain truth, is also, in its present state of corruption, the prime enemy and obstructor of that truth. The ray may be purged by grace; but it must also be purged by effort. That effort takes the form of self-education, whose purpose in Milton's view, we know, is "to repair the ruins of our first parents by regaining to know God aright, and out of that knowledge to love him, to imitate him, to be like him, as we may the neerest by possessing our souls of true vertue, which being united to the heavenly grace of faith makes up the highest perfection."[7] Those are also the goals of the true Christian poet, and the education that leads to them is the subject of *Lycidas*.

At the very beginning of the poem we are troubled by allusions to a past we know nothing of. "Yet once more," says the voice we do not yet know as the swain's. The events he recalls are never specified; they exist in the poem as symbolic gestures invoking, perhaps, previous exercises in the same formal genre, or simply other poems, or even other moments of crisis and loss in the putative history of the mourning shepherd. His address to the emblematic, honorific plants combines reverent apology and a grinding, reluctant distaste for his enforced task. We cannot help noting that the thoroughly conventional disclaimer of the traditional elegist—the pretense that he is unqualified to praise the subject of his elegy adequately—is here transformed into a trope that is both wider in reference and more intensely—almost crudely—personal than the tradition would seem to allow. This poet is unready, not because King's virtues are beyond his powers to celebrate (the phrase, "hath not left his peer," is strangely ambiguous in context), but because he has not yet arrived at a desired state of "ripeness." We are made to feel the force of his desire for that ripeness without being told in what it consists or how it will be recognized. With the pervasive obliquity of the opening part of the poem, the ideal state is defined for us largely by images of negation and qualification. Although the berries the swain comes to pluck are "harsh and crude," emblematic both of his unpreparedness and of the act he is forced to perform, the stressed rhymes also draw our attention to "never sere" and "the mellowing year," sounds that contradict the violence of the action in the foreground of the poem and set up a standard of permanence and serenity by which to judge what follows. In this way Milton begins to shape one of the fundamental patterns of the poem: the dramatic *events* we witness and hear described are rendered in a language that simultaneously suggests a reinterpretation of those events; the meanings the swain attaches to them are subsumed in larger and truer meanings that reveal themselves to him only as he submits to the apparently random course of his experience.

Another way to make much the same point is to observe that the voice we hear in the *ottava rima* coda, the voice that guides us to look back at the swain and to consider what he has said and learned during the recitation of *Lycidas*, is in control of the poem's diction from the beginning. He allows us and helps us to see more than the swain does, at the same time that we listen to the swain's speech. Thus, while we translate "forc'd fingers rude" and "Shatter" into perceptions of the speaker's pain and dissatisfaction, we also become aware that "the mellowing year" represents a reality that comprehends, and promises ultimately to justify, the particular "perturbations of the mind" that are being displayed. The symbolic plants that receive the swain's first address have their "season due"; and that prophetic concept governs the development of the poem as it moves through many misapprehensions and false versions of that promised ripeness. Similarly, the first ten lines or so of the poem, as they insist on the idea of death and disruption that come too early, also create the necessary notion of "due season," the stable, knowable criterion by which maturity is judged. Thus the swain, in his very first words, speaks truer than he knows, and the language of pastoral begins to generate the terms of a redefinition of the pastoral mode.

If the pastoral key signature tells us immediately that the poem will have something to say about poetry itself, it is typical of Milton to embody that familiar idea in a sequence of passages ordered by the importance of *sound*. Thus, the "logic" of the opening fourteen lines of the poem says that the "bitter constraint" of Lycidas' death forces the swain to disturb the laurels of poetry prematurely *because* Lycidas was a singer and must not be left to the winds and waters without the "meed" of a mournful song. In the fictive world of Milton's swain, silence is a threat, an unspeaking sign of death, disorder, unnaturalness. So, when the muses are implored to "sweep the string," one strenuous activity of the poem is begun, the act of filling the silence wrought by too early fatality with the music of the "Sphere-born harmonious Sisters, Voice and Verse"; and the necessary continuity of sound is established as the swain looks forward to the silence of his "destin'd Urn," hoping for the propriety of "lucky words" spoken for *him* by another poet.

Miss Tuve made much the same point, by her italics, when she remarked that "decay and disease . . . are 'such' as was the news of . . . loss, *to Shepherd's ear*."[8] But this ellipsis needs to be expanded; and the task is made light and easy by Milton's scrupulous insistence, in the early stages of the poem, on the figural importance of natural and artificial sound in the composition of the pastoral world. As the "eyelids" of the morn open to perceive the two shepherd-figures making their way onto the serene and fertile plains of youth and early, carefree song, the swain testifies to the quality of their common experience by remembering the sultry horn of the Gray-fly, and by showing us the power of their "Rural ditties" to stir the fauns and satyrs to dance, the excellence of the "glad sound" that could please those presumably sterner and better-trained sensibilities of "old *Damaetas*."

The momentary vision of delight that has passed, then, is sketched so that our familiar image of the pastoral landscape is suffused with minor harmonies and lively tunes, appropriate both to innocent immaturity and to its dawning and uncomplicated ambitions. We are then returned to a present transformed by a "heavy change," and denied the comfort, not of a promised future glory, but of the simplicities and satisfactions of a ravaged past. The bereaved shepherd is circumscribed both by events and by the limits of his understanding of them. One way in which the limits of that understanding are made clear is the variation Milton works on the conventional "pathetic fallacy"; the natural scene described by the swain does not mourn actively. The trees do not cast down their fruit, the ewes' udders do not wither, cattle do not refuse to drink, nor do any Libyan lions roar with grief, fountains do not dry up, nor does the earth give forth only darnels;[9] the "heavy change" is defined for us, rather, as the *absence* of a musical sound which once gave order, dancelike pattern, and pleasure to the natural world. The willows fan their leaves "no more" to Lycidas' songs, and the woods and caves mourn the dead shepherd with their "echoes" that can now only reverberate silence. Milton drives the point home unmistakably by having the lines rise in a rhythmic climax to the definition of all disruption and sorrow as a loss to the ear. And as a yet more refined intensification of his dominant idea, that loss is compared to the effect of *premature* death, the cutting-off of "weanling" herds, the "blasting" of flowers which put on their "gay wardrobe" in the earliest days of spring.

The lament thus takes us back to the tonality of the poem's opening lines, the bewildered and dismayed contemplation of an unexpected fate that has overtaken a poet whose youthful harmonies had given life and beauty to an appreciative world. At this point "denial vain and coy excuse" have been swept away not only by the necessary proprieties of elegizing a fellow poet but also by the "sight" of the scars his death has left on the charming and comfortable world sketched for us in lines 25–36. The movement of the entire elegy is rehearsed in the confrontation between the memory of that world and the undeniable present reality. The transformation has been worked and the swain is trying to accommodate himself to its meaning. He defines what is by referring it to what has been, and can go no further than to realize that death has shown itself to be inimical not only to beauty and simplicity but to the potentiality of creation implicit in the figural poet. Still, it is the *shepherd's ear* that has been deprived, just as it had been the swain who was forced to shatter the laurel's leaves too soon.

And it is still that swain who is unable to grapple his mind to that reality for very long. His next thought, sanctioned by pastoral elegiac tradition, is to question the gods, to try to discover a complicity that will explain the death of Lycidas. He chooses the indigenous legendary figures, supposed to stand in a tutelary relation to bardic, prophetic poetry. But the attempt is abandoned as soon as it begins, not because the swain is too clear-sighted to place any faith in such Celtic nonsense, but because he knows that the great Muse, the mother of the true poet's guardian and genius—Orpheus—could do nothing to save her precious charge. Thus he exchanges one myth for another; but in that exchange he has moved toward the acceptance of an emblematic meaning larger than any he has yet acknowledged. "Universal nature did lament" Orpheus' death, and the contemplation of "his gory visage" effectively bars the reentrance to the world of "high Lawns" and "Rural ditties." Nor was it simply a silent and inexplicable act of fate that destroyed *this* myth; Orpheus' "enchanting" powers were drowned by the "hideous roar" of that "rout" whose type was the mad Bacchants but whose embodiments recur throughout human history. They are the forces that crush poetry and the sympathetic alliance with nature that generates it.

Having gone this far toward the recognition of a universal predicament, the swain cannot retreat unthinkingly into the reassuring formulas that had served him. Milton signals this by bringing his mind once again back to the present; but, as before, it is a present transformed by what he has learned in the lines that precede it. What was a memory of two brother poets "nurst upon the self-same hill" becomes an inquiry into the justification of the métier of poetry itself. Once the swain had recalled the pleasure and approval of the fauns and Damaetas; now he speaks of the "homely slighted Shepherd's trade." It is important to realize that nothing has been said in the poem to change our knowledge or opinions of the poet's calling; what the new characterization of poetry reflects is the swain's changing awareness. The atmosphere of pastoral ease and delight which surrounded the image of those glad sounds and carefree dances has been darkened by the memory of Orpheus' fate, and as a consequence the calling of poetry, which then seemed natural and unbidden, is now seen as burdensome and problematical. Furthermore, the swain's questioning of his own relation to his calling is not phrased in nostalgic terms, but clearly alludes to actual contemporary poets, fashionable styles, and immediate rewards. In short, the pastoral pretense begins to dissolve into a discussion of what it means to be a poet in England in 1637. The alternatives are set up in terms of effort and ease. The vision of *otium* usually associated with the pastoral tradition out of which Milton had fashioned the first picture of his youth at Cambridge is now transferred to the naturalists, the erotic poets who "sport with *Amaryllis* in the shade"; and so the expressive figure of pastoral poetry no longer remains unitary, but divides into true and false, or at least worthy and slothful, song. And the former is attributed to those who pursue their calling with "uncessant care," who "meditate" the muse "strictly." These are not the concepts of an untroubled shepherd piping "unpremeditated" tunes to an audience of pagan hedonists; they reveal the grave dedication to a holy and demanding art that has been observed in Milton's own youthful writings. And as the concepts change, so does the audience he conceives as "fit," for the argument taking place within the swain's mind, although it presents us with contrasting images of self-indulgent and self-sacrificing poetic vocations, is addressed to the question of reward, the recognition that is to be the "meed" of the serious poet. The question he asks himself is not simply whether one kind of poetry is better than another, but whether the kind of poetry he knows to be better is worth pursuing if his labors and his achieved excellence are never to be given due praise.

However noble the Renaissance concept of fame may have been, however different from its usual connotations of reputation and public applause, Milton is at pains to show here that it is inadequate to the reassurance the swain is seeking. If it is the "last infirmity of Noble mind," it is nevertheless an infirmity. And the point is underlined by the swain's hoping to "find" it, thinking to "burst out into sudden blaze," thinking, in other words, of a spectacular, unexpected, almost unearned reward of glory and admiration. The very terms belie the characterization of the poetic calling as a strict, thankless, uncessant devotion to the highest standards of personal and artistic integrity. The lines ring with ambition, and their passion is rendered even more compelling by the tight-lipped contempt poured upon the "blind

Fury" in the phrase, "slits the thin-spun life." But this complex burst of energy is checked by the voice of Phoebus, who replied to the swain's question by telling him that he should expect fame only in heaven, that its plant, unlike the laurels and myrtles, does not grow in mortal soil. The change of tense breaks the time sequence that has been established in the poem thus far, and begins to suggest a mental past in which this examination has been carried on previously. It both clarifies some of the implications hinted at by "Yet once more" and looks forward to the coda in which Milton subsumes the entire experience of the swain in his closing comment. But at this point it also creates a momentary confusion about the nature of the utterance we are listening to; if the elegy is being sung *now,* under the pressure of grief and circumstance, then when did Phoebus speak? If the memory of Phoebus' words is reported by the swain as part of the elegy, then what has happened to the pretense of spontaneity and present creation?

The deliberate blurring of the narrative line is Milton's way of creating a fictive time in which the elegy exists, and it functions in much the same way as the suggestive backward glance of the opening words of the poem. The discomfort we feel as a result of such disorientation is a vital part of the experience of the poem, for it reminds us in subtle ways that both the occasion and the statement of *this* pastoral elegy vibrate between the poles of particularity and universal meaning. The strained speculation through which the swain forces himself enacts, but also reenacts, a mental history through which Milton himself, and any serious poet, has lived many times. And so he can immediately return to the waiting current of pastoral imagery, as his "Oat proceeds" in the present time of the poem; the "higher mood" of Phoebus' speech, although it necessitates a decorous invocation of the appropriately legendary Arethusa and Mincius, does not disturb the flow of pastoral conventions in the swain's repertory. The procession of mourners, which Milton might have found in elegies by Moschus, Castiglione, Sannazaro, and others, and in Virgil's Tenth Eclogue, carries us back not only to the familiar traditions of the elegy, but also to the questioning mood of the address to the nymphs in lines 50–55. It is as if the swain has forgotten that both the inquiry into causes and the notion of the protective muses have been discovered to be fond dreams. But these figures—"the Herald of the

Sea" and Hippotades—come unbidden; the sea and the winds send their answer to questions unasked by the swain, as the classical deities of nature exculpate themselves. The important point here is that what they have to say is no answer to the underlying question about Lycidas' death. Even Camus, the simply allegorical figure who recalls for the last time in the poem the fading pastoral emblem of early life at Cambridge, brings only another empty question; his venerable age and his aura of semimystical wisdom cannot offer knowledge or resolution.

At this stage in the poem it seems as if the machinery of conventional pastoral has seized the initiative from the swain. With the exception of the lines on the "perfidious Bark," which seem an explanation *faute de mieux*,[10] he merely reports and describes; the personal tones of anguish and bitterness diminish, and are powerfully subdued by the angry, craggy denunciation voiced by St. Peter.

The conventional procession of mourners, then, erupts from within, as the swain reports an incursion more violent and unassimilable than any that have occurred thus far. The speech of Phoebus might have been a version of any young poet's concerned musings; but this diatribe, if only because of the many ways in which it violates the rhetorical manners of the elegy, is meant to make us feel that a power hitherto unacknowledged and untapped by the swain's mind has now thrust into the fragile framework in order to speak a truth that cannot be softened or distanced by literary technique. The point is made to the ear by a new vocabulary, which includes the sounds and judgmental images of "flashy songs," "scrannel Pipes," and the "hungry Sheep" rotting "inwardly." This is a language that has been only tentatively drawn upon in the lines that spoke of the "homely slighted Shepherd's trade"; but it achieves its full impact now, not simply by sound, but by the way it converts the swain's defensive pastoral mode into a way of revelation. Peter speaks of the same contemporary conditions the swain had deplored in lines 64–69; but in his mouth the figure of the shepherd is no longer an airy and elegant allusion to the life of art. The common pastoral figures are driven back to their root meanings, in which "shepherd" means "pastor" in the ultimately important sense. Theocritus initiated the habit of using shepherds and rural settings as perspicuous disguises for poets and poetry; Virgil followed him and extended the possibilities of such open and understood allegory. But the Gospels, and the many antitypical instances found in the Old Testament, sanctified the use of pastoral as a parabolic way of discussing the cure of souls. The interplay between these two traditions, Peter's speech suggests, is fortuitous and temptingly deceptive. While the swain has been attempting to understand and control the implications of Lycidas' death for his own commitment to poetry, he has been ignoring the significance of the young cleric's death for the health of the English pastorate. Peter's speech reminds him of what he has forgotten, but not in the solicitous manner of Phoebus. Indeed, Peter does not even speak *to* the swain; he simply defines what has been lost by describing the "corrupted clergy" that remain, and foretells retribution. As at every marked turning point in *Lycidas* the bearing of the passage, its relation to the developing elegiac pattern, is left unspecified. Milton provides no easy or obvious way to decide what we or the swain are to understand from Peter's speech; what is to be *done* is even more problematical.

This troubled indecision is underlined by the swain's response. Peter's clarification of the true meaning of "shepherd" is referred to as "the dread voice"; the swain acknowledges only a *sound* whose harsh veracity has disrupted the orderly, plaintive, nostalgic gestures to which he is trying to attune his own thoughts. And so the return to convention, as Peter's words have been more difficult to accommodate than Phoebus', is here more poignant, more detailed; we may even say more desperate. The flower catalogue was as clearly a standard part of the archetypal pastoral elegy as the mourning procession; and we know from the Trinity manuscript that Milton labored carefully over it, meaning it to stand for all similar attempts to find respite from grief and bewilderment in the passive and numerable beauties of a sympathetic nature. Alpheus and the Sicilian Muse are called once again into their mild and uncomplicated relationship with the swain; they are asked to "call the Vales" and ask them to cast their flowers on the imaginary "Laureate Hearse" of the dead shepherd. This request, at least, is answered; for immediately the swain turns to address the "valleys low" himself, and his imagination responds to the comforting "mild whispers" that issue from the gushing brooks of this newly surmised landscape. The flower catalogue sketches for us a *locus amoenus* quite different from the remembered, autobiographical setting the swain described initially. Here there are no "high Lawns," no gaily piped tunes, no dancing pagan deities. Rather, in the extremity of shock wrought by Peter's tirade, the swain conjures the healing and restorative landscape of the literary pastoral, as if the convention itself of the flower catalogue had the power to wipe out the memory of what he has just heard. No longer is he in full command of his chosen poetic mode; no longer does he speak of King and himself as shepherds, assured of the stable meaning of that usage. Peter has bereft him of that simple and complacent equation, and he is driven back to its elemental, underlying pretense of an animate and empathetic nature. The swain tries, by exercising his command of an artificial literary mode, to grasp the consolation that may be distilled from it.

But the grasp is loosening even as it is attempted, for the very beauty of the things described is tempered and shadowed. The elaborate pastoral panoply that Milton draws, we must notice, is at the same time an indirect witness of its helplessness to stave off the effects of Peter's speech, if we conceive that as a new kind of statement, bringing with it a new kind of knowledge. The ambition and confidence adumbrated in the vision of shepherds' life on those high lawns of youth surrender to the mood of the flower catalogue. And that mood is attuned to the "valleys low" and their "mild whispers"; these lines are a demonstration of the pastoral's commitment to a life of ease, disengagement, even immaturity and a denial of responsibility. The flowers belong to the spring season, appropriate still to the theme of Lycidas' early death, but also to the stage of personal development in which the mind and spirit are shielded from the fierce, inevitable onslaught of destructive experience. The "swart Star sparely looks" on *this* pastoral scene; but it is impossible for the shepherd-poet who has faced the apparently random and indifferent harshness of life in the world to avoid emerging into the full blaze of that sun of maturity. The "wanton winds" may blow softly and playfully through these imagined dales, but the heights of poetic achievement that tempt the swain's "clear spirit" are buffeted by "every gust of rugged wings / That blows from off each beaked Promontory." The swain, the poet, the man can wander contentedly in the landscape of *otium* only so long as his mind can accept the literary mode as a real and satisfying substitute for the mode of active responsibility, in whose nature he has been instructed both by the death of Lycidas and by the words of St.

Peter. Once the meaning of the true pastorate is understood, or even recognized, the low valleys must become an eternally desirable but finally uninhabitable region of the mind.

And so the magnificence, the brilliant detail, the lovingly fashioned colors and sounds of the flower passage must ultimately be dismissed as a "false surmise," and the swain must show, to himself as to us, that he understands the intrinsic meaning of the temptation he has overcome by exposing his motives with frank but tender honesty: "For so to interpose a little ease, / Let our frail thoughts dally with false surmise" (152–53). The sting is removed from the charge implicit in "false" by the conscious admission of the frailty of all human thoughts, among which the imagination of pastoral is one of the most beautiful and most fragile. Milton does not mute the notes of lingering nostalgia in these lines, but neither does he allow them to sound with transparent simplicity. The little ease supplied by this dimming glimpse of honied showers and vernal flowers is merely interposed between the acts of unillusioned contemplation that confront the truths of Peter's attack and the facts of King's death. The dalliance is interrupted brutally by the self-aware and resigned expletive, "Ay me!"; and with the utterance of that brief appeal the swain is swept forward finally into the great concluding movements of the poem. Even syntax contributes to our sense of rising and climactic rhythm; we do not grasp the scope of "whilst" until nine lines later, when Michael is asked to "look homeward" while the body of Lycidas follows its uncouth path through the unfathomable waters. But "whilst" also looks backward to the flower passage, as the swain opens himself to the realization that the artistry he has devoted to the invocation of an "enamell'd" and animate nature has neither appeased his grief or confusion, nor stayed the flow of intractable experience, imaged here as the hurling of Lycidas' bones among the monsters of the unimaginable ocean depths. At this point the poetic imagination, in its role as a shaper of forms of language intended to soften, reinterpret, and give pattern to the formless succession of events we call experience, falters and proves to be inadequate. Milton tells us this, in one way, by juxtaposing the "fable" of Bellerus with the "great vision" of the guardian archangel; and the swain's response to his own discovery of the limits of his poetic power is to turn from lamentation and self-recrimination to prayer. He asks for no aid from the muses nor from symbolic rivers and fountains, for to do that would be to maintain the empty fiction of the centrality of the elegiac poet, to insist on the importance of the interpreting voice. Rather, he surrenders those illusory notions of competency, and in doing so surrenders as well the theme of the dead shepherd to the tutelary powers of St. Michael and the legendary dolphins. And that surrender is not entirely an act of conscious choice; he has been led to the discovery of Michael's guardianship by the current of imagination which, as it follows the dreadful vision of Lycidas' body lost beneath the sea, is brought back to the actual place at which knowledge stops, the Irish Channel, and to the actual presence of the "guarded Mount." Once again a question is answered, but not in an expected way. At the moment when the swain's consciousness of inability and ignorance is most profound, both ability and insight are *provided;* not because he has asked for them, but because he has admitted his lack.

The same pattern, the answer that comes unexpectedly and in terms that seem incomprehensible to the questioner, seems to me to govern the speech of consolation that follows the appeal to Michael. The swain has given up the apparently fruitless task of demanding explanations from nature and the gods; his rending doubts about the worth and purpose of poetry have been stilled, if not satisfied. His ambitious sallies into the world of confusion and disappointment that surrounds the various pastoral attempts at order and intelligibility have been reduced to a single, painful speculation on the true whereabouts of the body of his dead friend. And that speculation is resolved, not by yet another voice from outside the frame of the elegy, but by the creation of a new voice for the swain. The first clear demarcation of that new voice is the fact that for the first time in the poem the swain addresses himself to a human audience.[11] He casts aside the obliquity inherent in speaking to muses, nymphs, laurels, and myrtles and turns to a silent group of fellow mourners whose presence we have not been allowed to suspect. And for the first time in the poem he neither questions, nor challenges, nor debates with himself, but simply *tells* what he knows to be true. It is crucial that we realize that Milton forbids us to feel that we understand how the swain has come to this knowledge of truth. The transformation he undergoes has nothing to do, in the poem, with a logical or sequential argument or demonstration; nothing he is told, nothing he hears, can account for his grasp of the new truth he promulgates to the listening shepherds.

The transformation lies in the speech itself that we hear; and the effect of that speech depends as heavily on its function as on its content. The swain's consoling vision of Lycidas comforted in "other groves" is the only passage in the elegy which is directed to the enlightenment of men other than himself. It is neither a private revelation, as is Phoebus' lesson, nor a scarifying indictment of historical reality, as is Peter's; it is, precisely, an example of the service poetry performs which Milton described in *The Reason of Church-Government,* "to allay the perturbations of the mind, and set the affections in right tune, to celebrate in glorious and lofty Hymns the throne and equipage of Gods Almightinesse." It fulfills these tasks by embodying the obligations of the true pastor in poetry divinely inspired. It communicates saving truth in lines whose music is a reflection of the bright vision which is not the reward of study and preparation but of the proper rectification of the will. The swain's ability to speak the lines of consolation is Milton's dramatization of the infusion of grace.[12]

It is not an accident that these lines occur immediately after the swain has reached the deepest levels of sorrow, self-abnegation, and self-knowledge. Not until he has admitted to himself that the noblest ideas of poetry he has held are but false surmises can he receive the gift of true poetry which, as other critics have observed, does not abandon the pastoral mode as a pagan fiction, but transmutes it into a Christian mode of apprehending reality.[13] The classical idea of pastoral is not wrong, but incomplete; and in the poem it serves not only as a conventional allegorical frame, but also as a way of representing the incompleteness of mind and spirit that handicaps all human endeavors that grow from an unexamined assumption of the self-sufficiency of the imagination. The power of this assumption has been demonstrated to us in *Lycidas* in many ways: the serene complacency of the memories of the youthful "high Lawns" of Cambridge; the bitter musings over the comparative rewards of Amaryllis and the "thankless Muse"; the strivings to blot out the "higher mood" of Phoebus and the "dread voice" of Peter by calling up the liquid sounds of Mincius and the Sicilian Muses; the tapestry-work of the flower passage; and the last, despairing clutching at the little ease that all such surmises promise. In each case the inability, or the refusal, to face and accept the inexplicable fact of death, the unbearable fact that dedication and talent are not guaranteed recognition—in each case the swain's struggle against the knowledge that will force him into maturity is cast in the form of an attempt to maintain the flow of the pastoral elegy. The conventions of the genre are used as examples of the mind's defensive impulses; and while they reveal the swain's artistry they also show the hollowness of that artistry when it is used to falsify the reality that true poetry should embody.

Some years ago Michael Lloyd wrote a short piece to show that the position of *Lycidas* in the volume known as *Justa Edouardo King* was not without significance.[14] He pointed out a number of instances in which Milton's poem alludes to themes and phrases that occur in other, earlier elegies in the book; and he even made the case that Milton had incorporated into Peter's speech a defense of dissenting religious views against the High Church attacks on puritanism in the elegy by the Chancellor of Lichfield. It is clear that several of the contributors to the collection had read the poems by some of their colleagues; some of them respond to ideas in the opening poem by Henry King, the dead youth's brother, and Henry More includes an obvious retort to some lines by John Cleveland. And it seems equally clear that, whatever the reason for Milton's elegy being placed last, it allowed him to survey and consider the content of the entire collection and to shape his own work accordingly. Strangely enough, Lloyd does not comment on the fact that, of all the poems in *Justa Edouardo King, Lycidas* is the only pastoral elegy. Milton's choice of the genre must have appeared to his contemporaries an act of conscious archaism, or an instance of his scholarly traditionalism, or even a kind of homage to his "teacher," Spenser. We are, perhaps, in a better position than they to understand that Milton's mind moved almost instinctively toward the pastoral, not simply because it offered a graceful and well-sanctioned mode for elegiac verse, but because its various tropes and symbolic accouterments offered also a rich language to deepen and expand his meditation on the necessary pains of the death of innocence. The death of a young shepherd serves as the formal occasion and frame for the poem; but the death of a way of conceiving the roles of poet and priest is the action that *Lycidas* truly imitates.

As in so many places in Milton's work, the death of an immature or inadequate idea is wrought by the incursion of a new kind of knowledge into a consciousness that wants to preserve its familiar sense of security, but cannot deny the power of truth to change its way of seeing the world. And in all those places Milton does not tell us *how* that change is accomplished; he shows us the results of the change. Adam never speaks about the *experience* of disobedience; what Milton shows us is the change in Adam's speech and behavior after he has eaten of the apple. Samson may speak of "some rousing motions" stirring within him, but the moment of regeneration occurs offstage, away from our view, and in silence. We are not privy to Christ's inner debates in *Paradise Regained;* we listen to the results of that debate as he turns Satan's questions and offers back against him, and we watch Christ's actions. Milton asks always that we learn from the contemplation of his heroes' deeds; and the implicit command is that we try to understand their inward spiritual progress by testing our responses to their situations against theirs. It is in this sense that Milton's major poems are didactic, as well as in the more limited sense of conveying knowledge or doctrine to his audience. The epics and the closet drama teach by submitting us to the experience of trial; they guide our rational understanding by the example of dramatic figures who undergo trial and are moved to act on what they learn in consequence.

Lycidas may, I think, be compared in some degree to these greater poems because the major instrument of its consolation is not the mere recounting of the swain's climactic vision of Lycidas' "large recompense," but the entire, complex process through which he both raises himself and is raised to the vantage point which grants him that vision. I have said that he delivers the consoling speech to the shepherds only after his imagination has surrendered its stiff self-will and allowed itself to follow the idea of Lycidas' corpse to the bottom of the sea. That surrender of the will elicits immediately the assurance of a corrective vision, which sees that Lycidas, "Sunk though he be beneath the wat'ry floor," is not dead because,

> So sinks the day-star in the Ocean bed,
> And yet anon repairs his drooping head,
> And tricks his beams, and with new-spangled Ore,
> Flames in the forehead of the morning sky.

Analogy as a means of discovering truth had been discredited in the progressive disarming of pastoral symbols and language; the equation of shepherd and poet, the swain had realized, does not suffice to explain or justify the true relationships between the poet and his world, or between the poet and the art to which he is called. What is at fault is not the idea of such relationships, but the misrepresentation of that idea inherent in the use of metaphor. Metaphor makes it seem that different realities can be fused by language; the swain realizes, however, that such fusion is brought about by the enlightened understanding, which uses language to reveal both differences and likenesses. And so in these lines the swain comes upon an analogy that brings into consonance the meaning of Lycidas' mortal tragedy, the psychic experience the swain himself is undergoing, and the traditional emblem of that power which guarantees the truth of the analogy and yokes all spiritual histories with their archetype, the "dear might of him that walk'd the waves." The elements of pastoral metaphor, which have been shown to be an incomplete picture of reality, are unfolded and exposed in a simile: "So sinks the day-star . . . So Lycidas." The swain now sees, controls, and explains an identity that exists in natural and supernatural phenomena, rather than in the literary language he has inherited.

Thus it is important to notice that, as a part of the elegy, the description of heaven's "other groves," "the blest Kingdoms meek of joy and love," is no less an imaginative fiction than the fields that first appeared "under the opening eyelids of the morn." Here, as there, are companionship, music, sunlight and soothing liquids. The difference in our response to this setting is not accountable simply by the deliberately muted presence of Christ, but by the tone of the swain's speech. He speaks in a timeless present, describing firmly and clearly what is, not what once was or what is gone. And, finally, he takes upon himself the cloak of prophecy and tells Lycidas what is to come out of the grief and loss with which the poem began. Nor is the prophecy complete without a gesture toward the swain's newly found responsibility to all shepherds, to "all that wander in that perilous flood." The dead shepherd will receive the meed of creation as a tutelary "Genius," but the living poet is granted, and assumes, the charge of explaining the meaning of that uncertain journey to all men who will embark upon it.

To assume such a charge requires both humility and confidence, and the tone of the speech displays both. The confidence radiates through the direct and exalted language that describes for the shepherds a scene they cannot see through their bleared, grieving eyes. And the humility is felt in the swain's reference to the "unexpressive nuptial song." The interwoven pattern of sounds and their significances that we have traced throughout the elegy reaches the point of ultimate clarification here; but the harmony that generates and underlies all music and all poetry is, to the enlightened shepherd, inexpressible. He knows that the "solemn troops, and sweet Societies" to which Lycidas has been assimilated "sing, and singing in their glory move," but the song itself is beyond his powers to imitate. Nevertheless, he accepts the burden, which must have been deeply vexing for Milton, of sustaining both the memory and the prophetic vision of that song, in poetry which he knows to be only a shadow of its harmonious source. The combination of confidence and humility in his speech is exactly parallel to the ambiguous gifts of knowledge the swain accepts as he assumes the obligations of the true shepherd. The calling of priestly poetry confers special powers and special responsibilities. The swain as the grieving pastoral elegist had been conscious only of the talents that separated him from other men, even from other poets. Peter's speech had reminded him of the more important burdens of the pastorate; but his response was a retreat, even if momentarily, into the fictive world of beauty and *otium*. But now, with the acknowledgment of both his ability and his duty to speak of true Christian consolation to "woeful Shepherds" whose salvation lies partially in the power of his inspired voice, he is given a language adequate to the task he agrees to perform, a language both "answerable" and "in strictest measure ev'n" to the "lot" toward which time and the course of the elegy have led him.

The course of impact and recoil, the psychological movement of retreat and reluctant acknowledgment, which I have been trying to elucidate in *Lycidas*, is prefigured in the letter "to a friend" that most scholars agree was written about 1633. The poet is wrestling with the same problems that give poignance to Sonnet VII; he is trying to account for his disinclination to enter the ministry, but the thrust of his argument carries him toward the admission that he hopes to accomplish the proper work of a cleric through the means of learned poetry. And yet, he knows, the "desire of honour & repute, & immortall fame seated in the brest of every true scholar which all make hast to by the readiest way of publishing & divulging conceived merits as well those that shall as those that never shall obtaine it," should impel him more vigorously toward "the fair Guerdon" than has been the case. For answer, in this extremely tortuous and knotty debate that he is holding with himself, Milton resorts once more to the parable of the talents:

Lastly this Love of Learning as it is the pursuit of somthing good, it would sooner follow the more excellent & supreme good knowne & praesented and so be quickly diverted from the emptie & fantastick chase of shadows & notions to the solid good flowing from due & tymely obedience to that command in the gospell set out by the terrible seasing of him that hid the talent. it is more probable therfore that not the endlesse delight of specula-tion but this very consideration of that great commandment does not presse forward as soone as may be to underg[o] but keeps off with a sacred reverence & religious advisement how best to undergoe[,] not taking thought of beeing late so it give advantage to be more fit.[15]

The reasoning might be thought disingenuous, but Milton raised this notion of "a sacred reverence" into a paradigm for his poetic ca-reer. Rectification of the will depended for all men on their ability to submit their wills to God's; but for the poet who felt himself called to, and empowered to perform, a great work of instruction, the command to use God's gifts in God's time was even more pressing.

Despite the variety of forms it took, we can recognize in Mil-ton's works throughout his life—from Sonnet VII to *Samson Agonis-tes*—a grating tension between his will to create the proof of his singular powers, and his will to believe that acts of poetic creation should be and would be prompted by "some strong motion" instilled in him by "Time . . . and the will of Heav'n." This tension is ex-hibited most clearly in Sonnet VII and in the figure of Samson; it is exposed and resolved in the invocations in *Paradise Lost*. But *Lycidas* is Milton's one attempt to dramatize the experience of that tension, and to show how transcending it leads to the attainment of the poetic voice which alone can sustain the continuing act of creation which is the epic poem. It may shed light on Milton's idea of the relation be-tween the poet and his recognition of God's will to consider something he wrote about the priesthood, four years after the completion of *Lycidas*, in the pamphlet *Animadversions upon the Remonstrants De-fence against Smectymnuus*. He is arguing against the notion that the ministry must offer material rewards if it is to attract learned and able clergymen. Milton turns scornfully from this picture of a "hireling clergy" and says in rebuttal:

A true Pastor of Christs sending hath this especiall mark, that for greatest labours, and greatest merits in the Church, he requires either nothing, if he could so subsist, or a very common and reasonable supply of humane necessaries: Wee cannot therefore doe better then to leave this care of ours to God, he can easily send labourers into his Harvest, that shall not cry, Give, give, but be contented with a moderate and beseeming allowance; nor will he suffer true learning to be wanting, where true grace, and our obedience to him abounds: for if he give us to know him aright, and to practice this our knowledge in right establisht discipline, how much more will hee replenish us with all abilities in tongues and arts, that may conduce to his glory, and our good? . . . For certainely there is no imployment more honourable, more worthy to take up a great spirit, more requiring a generous and free nurture, then to be the messenger, and Herald of heavenly truth from God to man, and by the faithfull worke of holy doctrine, to procreate a number of faithfull men, making a kind of creation like to Gods, by infusing his spirit and likenesse into them, to their salvation, as God did into him; arising to what climat so ever he turne him, like that Sun of righteousnesse that sent him, with healing in his wings, and new light to break in upon the chill and gloomy hearts of his hearers, raising out of darksome barrennesse a delicious, and fragrant Spring of saving knowledge, and good workes.[16]

Milton is not reluctant in the least to suggest that the "messenger" works as Christ does, for "in all wise apprehensions the perswasive power in man to win others to goodnesse by instruction is greater, and more divine, then the compulsive power to restraine men from being evill by terrour of the Law; and therefore Christ left *Moses* to be the Law-giver, but himselfe came downe amongst us to bee a teacher."[17]

It is as a teacher, of course, that the swain speaks finally, and he teaches a truth that has not been uncovered by his reason in the course of the poem, but that has been borne in upon him by the action of the poem, as it responds to the guiding pressure of divine will. Milton is certainly playing on the word *uncouth* in the coda, for while the swain had been both uninstructed and unknown as he first laid his hands unwillingly upon the evergreen laurels, he is no longer ignorant. Nor, we are made to feel, will he be long unknown; the address we have just heard does not fit the characterization of a "*Doric* lay," and its majestic rhythms can be described as "warbling" only by the poet who knows fully how far his *persona* has travelled and what heights of wisdom and poetic brilliance he has attained. I find as much humor as serenity in the coda, because Milton is relying on our shocked rediscovery of the pastoral setting to remind us of the scope of the journey we have just undergone. We now find that the swain has been singing for the length of the imagined day, but that we have been raised out of the cycle of time in which we began; the magnificent, telling symbol of the "day-star" flaming "in the forehead of the morning sky" is once again simply the sun, now "dropt into the Western bay." The sensation is that of returning to a familiar, natural, real world; and we can appreciate the flourish of Milton's delighted skill when we remember that the reality to which we have been restored is the world of the literary pastoral, completely mastered and controlled by the poet whose voice we hear for the first time. This fiction has opened the way to a truth that can be expressed only in fictions; and yet the discovery of that truth renders us, and the swain, forever unable to mistake fiction for what it is intended to represent.

That same discovery, the result of the process of self-education at the center of *Lycidas*, is, I think, the key to Milton's renovation of the conventional epic beginning, and to his successive re-creations of himself in the speakers of the several invocations in *Paradise Lost*. A brief examination of the first of these invocations will show the extent to which they depend upon and develop from perceptions Milton first brought to poetic fruition in *Lycidas;* it will show, too, the way in which we may understand the consolation passage in the elegy as the first full-scale sketch for Milton's epic voice.

The opening lines of *Paradise Lost,* after they have outlined the scope of the action the poem will rehearse, are shaped by two requests. As the poet asks for the assistance he will need to fulfill his task, he differentiates precisely between these requests; and the differences between them help to define both the poem's links to earlier epic traditions and its intent to transcend them. The muse Milton invokes, for example, is "Heav'nly," and we are told that it was she who "inspired" Moses, the first of a long line of shepherd-prophets elected to remind the "chosen Seed" in successive ages of their origins and of the original creative act that raised the universe out of darkness and disorder. The implication is unavoidable, in Milton's emphatic signalling of *"That* Shepherd, who *first* taught,"[18] that he is to be included in the prophetic line. But it is equally important to note that the muse is asked specifically only to sing, to "aid" this poet's "advent'rous Song"; even in sketching for us the muse's exalted powers, Milton limits himself to an oblique reference to her ability to "inspire," literally to infuse with life or breath, to play on the poet as on a pastoral pipe. All of these phrases assume the integrity and the suitability of the instrument itself, and the muse is asked to help that instrument play its sacred song better than it would unaided.

In like manner Homer urges the muse to begin the tale of Achilles' wrath, or asks her help in recounting Odysseus' return; both the subject of the poem and the poet's abilities are *données*. What is at issue is the need for the muse's collaborative power to sustain the immense effort of the epic poem, and to reinforce the poet's skill and vision if they flag or prove inadequate. By a similar token, Ariosto asks only that his "sweet saint" "afford some gracious aid" to his "slender muse," making it clear that in this romantic epic the poet acts as his own muse; he has no doubt that his skill will be equal to the demands of his poem, so long as his love flourishes.[19] Ariosto is not so much demeaning the convention as indicating the level of inspiration required for his idea of the epic. Milton's more grandiose ambitions are closer to those of Tasso and Spenser; yet even they, in the invocations that begin their poems, do not approach the audacities of Milton's subsequent address to the Holy Spirit. Tasso seems to speak to the same heavenly muse in the opening lines of the *Gerusalemme Liberata,* describing her as sitting "crown'd with stars' immortal rays / In heaven, where legions of bright angels sing."[20] But he goes on to ask only that she inspire life in his wit, upraise his thoughts, and ennoble his verse; he asks, in other words, that she enrich and elevate his intelligence and his style, qualities that exist before the poem and which are the necessary instruments that will create the poem. Tasso goes on to apologize to the muse for a breach of decorum he implies he is certain to commit—mixing fictions with divine truths, and offering praise to persons other than the muse. Such indecorousness, he says, is not only unavoidable, but it is also germane to the didactic purpose of the epic; he points out, in fairly shopworn Horatian terms, that the sinful world must be brought to the banquet of Christian truth by the lure of Parnassian sweetness. In fact, the need is more immediate than the formulaic *dulce et utile* argument suggests; Tasso reminds the princes to whom the poem is addressed that the Turks remain to be driven from Greece. Ultimately, then, the muse is called on in these lines to make the texture of Tasso's verse so brilliant and appealing that the worldly powers he flatters as his appropriate audience will be moved to further the work of Christian arms in the world. Even Spenser, as he describes himself "enforst" by the "sacred Muse" to blazon forth the contents of history's "antique rolles," assumes that the nature and purpose of the task are known, and asks only that Clio help his weak wit and sharpen his "dull tong." Cupid, Venus, and Mars are urged to lend their influences, and Elizabeth, finally, is implored to raise the poet's thoughts so that his "afflicted stile" may attempt her portrait.[21]

The convention sketched by even these few examples, then, places the poet as a humble petitioner, but not so humble that he does not feel his distinction from other men. He may need to ask that his native and his acquired poetic skills be assisted by intervention of a divine muse; but the relationship between him and his subject is clear and unproblematic—the subject is the song, he the instrument through which or on which it will be played by whatever supernal force or figure wishes to speak to man in inspired verse. The instrument, it must be pointed out, is shaped peculiarly to its end; the poet is as different from his auditors as he is different from the spirit who inspires him.

So much we can conclude from Milton's initial address to his "Heav'nly Muse," since he defines her part in the process of writing the epic as assisting him to surpass the highest reaches of the classical epic, and to carry him toward the hitherto unattained excellences of Christian epic. I take that assistance to be conceived, at least in the first fifteen lines of the poem, as primarily stylistic. Milton asks the heavenly muse, in short, for the power to sustain a song that will tell man's history from the creation to the final triumph of Christ; to be more precise, he asks the muse to inspire and sustain a language the poet has already formed, during the patient and devoted years of study and practice.

But when he turns, in line 17, to what we may call the second invocation, we should be warned by his use of "chiefly" that Milton does not mean this to be the lesser request, an afterthought; quite the contrary. His own thinking about the nature of the Holy Spirit, as reflected in Book I, Chapter VI, of *The Christian Doctrine,* was far from conclusive; most of that chapter is devoted to showing that the Holy Spirit is inferior to both the Father and the Son, while it also surveys references in the Old Testament and in the Gospels that allow the Spirit to be understood, at times, as the emissary of either of the first two persons of the Trinity. The burden of Milton's argument is that Scripture is not clear on the point, and that we must be extremely cautious in reaching firm identifications of the Holy Spirit in varying contexts. But the trend of his discussion leads him to see the "virtue and power of God the Father," represented in both testaments by reference to the Holy Spirit, as preeminently displayed in "that impulse or voice of God by which the prophets were inspired," and in "that light of truth, whether ordinary or extraordinary, wherewith God enlightens and leads his people."[22] With that typical softening of focus that overtakes Milton's theological arguments as they move from *The Christian Doctrine* to *Paradise Lost,* the lines we are examining are addressed to a "Spirit" whose nature and rank are unspecified. But his function is clear, and it is entirely consonant with the view of the Holy Spirit as the channel of saving knowledge. He is asked to "instruct"; the emphatic positioning of the word in line 19 is a sign that Milton is not simply appealing for the radical degree of knowledge demanded by *this* epic, but that he has also gone to the root meaning of the word, realizing that any human vessel, in order to contain such knowledge, must be remade. To follow the metaphor, he must be rebuilt, inherently constructed out of the knowledge infused in him by the Spirit. Thus, in another way Milton supports the notion, implicit in the Spirit's preference for the "upright heart and pure" "Before all Temples," that even the sanctity of Zion, the delight of the "Heav'nly Muse" whose aid he has so recently implored, is a less certain guarantee of prophetic truth than the actual regeneration of a soul by the truth conveyed by the Spirit. Jehovah spoke from a burning bush on Horeb, gave the Law on the tablets on Sinai, and rested in the Ark of the Temple on Zion; but as the Christian Gospels have replaced the Law so has the Holy Spirit made irrelevant to man's salvation the sanctified place.[23] God's chosen temple is now the human body, His Ark the soul open to infused grace.

Milton is speaking, however, from within his chosen role as epic poet; and God's mysterious grace is here interpreted with appropriate decorum as that "light of truth" that Milton saw as one kind of emanation of God's power, the kind relevant to the epic's task of making wisdom available to all who will hear. The lines do not point to conversion, or even to revelation, but to the poet's need for knowledge. Nor are we meant to understand that it is information only that he is asking for, the specific knowledge of events before the creation of man, made available through the inspired authorship of Genesis, possessed properly only by the Spirit as God's agent of wisdom; for the Spirit is not said to know things in particular; Milton's phrase is, "Thou know'st"—knows, that is, in the timeless and uncircumscribed fashion in which all history is present and all acts occur in a providential repetition, progressively revealing their single inherent meaning in human time. The Spirit "knows" in a way that the poet can never know; but his knowledge, if not his way of knowing, can be communicated. Nevertheless, Milton's emphasis in the closing lines of the invocation is on the process of communication, rather than on the details of the knowledge he wants. Recalling the description of creation in Genesis the poet combines the dual aspects of God's power and his loving compassion in the image of the Spirit, with "mighty wings," brooding "Dove-like" over the abyss. But the dark, formless Chaos is not simply shaped and made a world by the creative act; it is impregnated. Even here, as he does more obviously in Book VII, Milton casts aside the familiar doctrine of God's creation of the world *ex nihilo* in favor of the belief that the universe is made out of divine stuff, in this case the apparently hostile and intractable material of Chaos, which nevertheless becomes a womb receptive to the Spirit's impregnating power.[24] The matter of the universe thus responds to the force of creativity, however unwittingly or even unwillingly; it cooperates in the production of an intelligible creation, and its true nature is revealed as it rises from formlessness into meaning. Milton makes the point inescapably by a device that is to become familiar as the poem goes on: the heavy full stop marked by a colon, placed so as to juxtapose two instances, superficially dissimilar, whose underlying mutual relevance we are meant to perceive, not as the poet points it out to us, but as we are forced to that perception by the juxtaposition itself.

>   Thou from the first
> Wast present, and with mighty wings outspread
> Dove-like satst brooding on the vast Abyss
> And mad'st it pregnant: What in me is dark
> Illumine, what is low raise and support.   (*PL* I, 19–23)

He turns the image of the abyss into a figure of the poet. It is he who is dark, he who is low. And he now prays that the Spirit may shed light on this as yet uninstructed creature, "raise and support" him in his flight through realms of knowledge where the "Argument," or subject, of the epic poem is not inherited from tradition but is part of the exfoliating process of learning and coming to know.

It hardly needs saying that this is only the first of many instances in the poem where visual light is equated symbolically with knowledge, where measurable, spatial height is made interchangeable with ideas of truth or understanding, where, most importantly, the change from ignorance to wisdom is rendered in terms of growth, a rising from the base and potential to the light-filled and the realized. In a sense, then, the climactic address to the Spirit in these opening lines of the epic alludes to a process of education, a form of teaching in which the student is remade and regenerated, and by which he becomes fitted to teach in his turn. There can be no separation, in Milton's metaphor, between knowledge and its proper vessel; so powerful, so transforming is the effect of the Spirit's knowledge that it creates a new poet out of the rudimentary elements of the old, a poet able not only to form a style adequate to the truths he is chosen to enunciate, but one who can bear the immense weight of that transforming knowledge.

The "great Argument" of *Paradise Lost*, of course, is truth—the truth of man's condition seen under the aspect of "Eternal Providence." In this opening invocation Milton prays for the kinds of assistance appropriate to the task of asserting that providence *while* revealing its justice to the audience of men. Although he places heavy emphases in the passage on his need for help, on that in him which is "low" and "dark," he speaks as if there is no doubt that, given the power to tell truth, he will inevitably succeed in the conjoint goal of creating assent to that truth. This air of untroubled confidence, which blends so unnoticeably with the suppliant tone of the invocation, may be accounted for, at least in part, by the fact that Milton chooses from the outset to implicate himself in the condition of the audience he is addressing. He speaks immediately of "our woe," looks forward to Christ's coming to "Restore us," and begins the narrative by referring to "our Grand Parents." This is not merely a variation of the familiar Miltonic device of "placing" the narrator and his listeners in the poem; it is also a declaration of Milton's solution to the unique problems facing a poet who chooses to sing to other men of divine and prophetic truths that no man can know simply by taking thought.

There are only the faintest suggestions of the garland and the singing robes in the figure of the poet Milton adumbrates in these lines. The grandeur and power of the epic role, qualities which had obsessed him in his youth, are muted and replaced by the weight of obligation he willingly assumes, his responsibility to "the chosen Seed." Milton's awareness of the change in his idea of the poet's role is shown, I think, in his deliberate identification of himself with Moses. The identity is asserted by the central term, "shepherd," and through that term is extended to all the members of the line whose glory consisted in being burdened with the task of witnessing, explaining, justifying. In the consolation passage in *Lycidas* the swain had assumed a similar burden. But his audience were shepherds only by virtue of literary convention; the swain began as one of them, and ended as a true shepherd, his state defined largely by his differences from them. Milton begins *Paradise Lost* in a voice that combines the hard-earned understanding of the swain and the stable, compassionate wisdom of the coda of *Lycidas*. That meaning of "shepherd" which is created by the long and intricate *agon* of *Lycidas* is the starting point of the epic. And once that meaning has been absorbed into the poet's idea of his relation to his subject, it leads unerringly to the massive, sustained, flexible, infinitely various union of sound and sense that is the music of *Paradise Lost*. Its keynote is the blending of humility and assurance that we hear in the first twenty-six lines, that incredibly exact rendering of the mind and impulses of a man praying to the Holy Spirit for gifts with which to instruct and solace his fellow men. In the climactic speech of consolation in *Lycidas* Milton drew a sketch for the full portrait he achieved in *Paradise Lost*.

University of California
Berkeley

NOTES

1. All quotations of Milton's poetry are drawn from *John Milton: Complete Poems and Major Prose,* ed. Merritt Y. Hughes (New York, 1957). The text of *Lycidas* will be found on pages 120–25 of that edition. All citations of Milton's prose will refer to the *Complete Prose Works of John Milton,* published, in several volumes by various editors, by the Yale University Press (1953–); citations will give volume and page references only. The present passage is from *The Reason of Church-Government, Prose,* I, 816–17.

2. Lowry Nelson, Jr., *Baroque Lyric Poetry* (New Haven, 1961), p. 149.

3. *Of Education, Prose,* II, 376.

4. *Of Reformation, Prose,* I, 566.

5. *Reason of Church-Government, Prose,* I, 830–31.

6. *Of Reformation, Prose,* I, 566.

7. *Of Education, Prose,* II, 366–67.

8. Rosemond Tuve, "Theme, Pattern and Imagery in *Lycidas,*" in *Images and Themes in Five Poems by Milton* (Cambridge, Mass., 1957), p. 89.

9. Cf. Moschus, *The Lament for Bion;* Virgil, *Eclogue V;* Castiglione, *Alcon.* The texts of these poems, with translations, can be found conveniently assembled in *The Pastoral Elegy,* ed. T. P. Harrison, Jr. (Austin, 1939), and in *Milton's "Lycidas,"* ed. Scott Elledge (New York, 1966).

10. See Michael Lloyd, "The Fatal Bark," *MLN,* LXXV (1960), 103–09, for a different reading.

11. Lowry Nelson, Jr., makes much the same point in *Baroque Lyric Poetry,* pp. 149–50.

12. In "The Voice of Michael in *Lycidas,*" *SEL,* III (1963), 1–7, an essay incorporated into his recent book, *From Shadowy Types to Truth: Studies in Milton's Symbolism* (New Haven, 1968), William G. Madsen argues that the consolation speech is delivered by the archangel Michael. For a number of reasons I find Madsen's argument unconvincing; the most obvious ones are: Madsen has difficulty in explaining why the *ottava rima* coda refers to the swain having sung the final verse paragraph, and is forced to divide the paragraph to allow for the swain's sudden reappearance in line 182; nor can he explain why Michael, alone of all the speakers identified quite specifically in the poem, is introduced without comment or identification.

13. See the essay by Rosemond Tuve mentioned in n. 8; and also Isabel MacCaffrey, "*Lycidas:* The Poet in a Landscape," in *The Lyric and Dramatic Milton,* ed. Joseph H. Summers (New York, 1965), pp. 65–92; and Jon S. Lawry, " 'Eager Thought': Dialectic in 'Lycidas'," *PMLA,* LXXVII (1962), 27–32, reprinted in *Milton: Modern Essays in Criticism,* ed. A. E. Barker (New York, 1965), pp. 112–24.

14. Michael Lloyd, "*Justa Eduardo King,*" *N & Q,* N.S. 5 (October 1958), 423–24.

15. [To a Friend], *Prose,* I, 320.

16. *Animadversions, Prose,* I, 721.

17. *Animadversions, Prose,* I, 722.

18. Hughes, *John Milton,* p. 211 (italics mine). Cf. James Holly Hanford, "That Shepherd, Who First Taught the Chosen Seed," *University of Toronto Quarterly,* VIII, no. 4 (1939), 403–19, and the discussion of the passage in Jack-

son I. Cope, *The Metaphoric Structure of "Paradise Lost"* (Baltimore, 1962), pp. 149–64.

19. *Ariosto's "Orlando Furioso": Selections from the Translation of Sir John Harington,* ed. R. Gottfried (Bloomington, Ind., 1963), pp. 25–26.

20. *Jerusalem Delivered,* Edward Fairfax's translation (New York, n.d.), pp. 1–2.

21. *Spenser's "Faerie Queene,"* ed. J. C. Smith, 2 vols. (Oxford, 1909), I, 2–4 (Proem to Book I).

22. *The Christian Doctrine,* in *The Student's Milton,* rev. ed., ed. F. A. Patterson (New York, 1957), p. 967.

23. Cf. David Daiches, "The Opening of *Paradise Lost,*" in *The Living Milton,* ed. Frank Kermode (London, 1960), pp. 55–69.

24. Cf. John T. Shawcross, "The Metaphor of Inspiration in *Paradise Lost,*" in *Th'upright Heart and Pure,* ed. Amadeus Fiore (Pittsburgh, 1967), pp. 75–85.

MILTON'S UNCOUTH SWAIN

Stewart A. Baker

The redemptive vision of *Lycidas* depends upon the imaginative qualities implicit in the pastoral speaker, Milton's "uncouth swain." The swain's youth indicates his ingenuous and reductive point of view. The theme of youthful friendship explores the origins of his Orphic sensibility and prophetic vision. While tracing his growth into the roles of poet and prophet, his style through its range and variety reflects the evolution of pastoral into a comprehensive and encyclopedic form. The swain's voice unifies the diverse modes of pastoral by translating the images of naturalistic and libertine pastoral into the symbols of Christian pastoral, and by employing a principle of inverse reduction, as defined by J. C. Scaliger. The unity of his style expresses itself as an orderly continuum of stylistic levels within a single stylistic mode, as illustrated by Scaliger's analysis of the low, middle, and high styles within the florid mode. This unity of the swain's style, voice, and vision within a comprehensive form of pastoral provides a structural and stylistic model, as well as a thematic paradigm, for the speakers of Milton's epics.

Lycidas CONCLUDES with a surprise. We have relived the speaker's progress from despair to renewed faith, from the contemplation of death in nature to a vision of spiritual rebirth. Then we encounter the speaker himself and find not John Milton but an uncouth swain.

This mannerist readjustment of perspective forces us to reassess the speaker's role. The narrative of this final paragraph—the *commiato* or farewell—recapitulates the themes, imagery, and time span of the elegy. While the elegy traced the cycle of youth, death, and rebirth, the speaker's day, we are told, has moved from sunrise to sunset. The

35

sun, which in the elegy is identified with the dying poet and his rebirth in Christ, describes in the *commiato* the swain's progress from
grief to reaffirmation and confidence in another sunrise in pastures
new. In this way the reductive analogy of the *commiato* restates
the relevance of the elegiac themes in the life of the swain. *Lycidas* is
revealed not as a poem straightforwardly concerned with death,
fame, service, and salvation, but as a poem about an uncouth swain
who achieves in the face of death a vision of redemption. At the same
time it demonstrates the process by which he achieves that vision. The
vision, in which we have to this point participated, is shown to depend upon the visionary medium.

Many aspects of the swain's character have been implicit from
the beginning to a reader familiar with pastoral poetry and theory.
But these implications are not easily validated because of the complexity of pastoral genre conventions and because Renaissance pastoral
theory often seems simplistic, anachronistic, and vague. Nevertheless, genre decorum, which Milton like the Italian critics regarded
as "the great masterpiece to observe,"[1] can guide us to some of these
implicit meanings in *Lycidas*. Conversely, the poem's adaptation of
conventional points of theory contributes to an understanding of Milton's interpretation of genre theory. This mutual interpretation of
poem and theory can thus serve to reveal many of the poet's intrinsic
intentions and at the same time clarify the role of the uncouth swain.

Much of the swain's character is implicit in his youthfulness. He
is therefore uncouth, or unknown, like Lycidas, but his friend's death
compels him to pluck the laurels once more before the mellowing year.
When the swain is confused with Milton, we are told that these first
lines of the poem indicate Milton's self-pity, his "characteristic egotism," or his "reluctance to write a poem before he is mature."[2] But
the swain's youth does not point toward a failure of ability. It refers
instead to the convention that pastoral is the genre for young
poets. This convention implies far more than the poet's age in years.

At the end of the *Georgics* Virgil calls the pastorals the work of
his "bold youth," as though they exceeded the powers of a twenty-
eight-year-old. Donatus and Servius complicate the issue first by insisting that pastoral is for young poets and then by identifying the
young Virgil with Tityrus.[3] Ingenuous yet experienced, at harmony
with nature and society, the meditative Tityrus is the archetypal

speaker for Virgilian pastoral (including *Lycidas*). But Tityrus is not a young man. His beard is growing grey (I, 28) and Meliboeus calls him *senex* (I, 46). Augustus can call Tityrus a boy (I, 45) although Augustus is really the younger of the two (I, 42). Tityrus' youth, then, is a way of describing his rustic ingenuousness, his point of view. It is this point of view that produces the familiar logic of the pastoral metaphor, which sees large issues through small and translates the great affairs of politics, religion, and philosophy into the experience of the shepherd (I, 19–25). Tityrus is growing old but he sees life through the eyes of a young man. He translates the lessons of experience into a poetry of innocence.

The paradox of Tityrus' youth-in-age is made explicit by Mantuan in the preface to his widely read eclogues, appropriately entitled *Adolescentiae*. He addresses the eclogues, most of which he wrote as a young man, to a young friend. But the poet is now a fifty-year-old Carmelite. By adding to and publishing his eclogues, he writes, "In my fifties and already growing grey, I have rediscovered my youth; and so I have youth simultaneously with old age."[4] Thus viewed, pastoral is not a subject matter. It is a habit of double vision, a habit of metaphor which reduces experience to innocence, and it is available to both the aging Carmelite and his young patron.

The youth of the uncouth swain is a way of expressing this double vision. The threatening prospect of Lycidas' swollen corpse, the danger posed to the young poet's fame, the decay of the intellect, poetry, and the church are all controlled by a vision of innocence which perceives nature's sympathy for Lycidas, Apollo's consolation for the short-lived poet, Camus' grief for his scholar, St. Peter's dread prophecy of Armageddon, and finally Lycidas' rebirth in a pastoral paradise. Apparent disorder is thus viewed from a broader perspective of moral order which interposes, corrects, and finally transcends. So much is implied by the pastoral vision of the young poet.[5]

The swain's recollection of his youth with Lycidas is primarily concerned with the young poet's acquisition of this vision:

> Together both, ere the high Lawns appear'd
> Under the opening eye-lids of the morn,
> We drove a field, and both together heard
> What time the Gray-fly winds her sultry horn,
> Batt'ning our flocks with the fresh dews of night. (25–29)

Dr. Johnson's inspired literalism protests that Milton and King "never drove a field, and . . . they had no flocks to batten." Therefore the meaning of the passage, he asserts, "is never sought because it cannot be known when it is found."[6] The sensual mood of the narrative, however, is readily accessible. The young poets experience a newness like birth, awakening, or a new creation, when the mountains, like the high lawns "appear / Emergent, and thir broad bare backs upheave / Into the Clouds, thir tops ascend the Sky" (*PL* VII, 286–88). Although this experience affects the imagination, it is conveyed through deeply sensual ideas such as the aubade suggestions implicit in "the opening eye-lids of the morn." The same is true of the gray-fly, whose buzzing suggests the sultry heat of the afternoon which the young poets contemplate in silence. Their day together finishes with the setting of Hesperus / Venus, the shepherd's star.[7] This reminds us that the chief business of shepherds in libertine pastoral, according to Scaliger and other theorists, is love, here depicted as friendship.[8] This stimulation of the imagination through the senses and through love climaxes in the Dionysiac of satyrs and fauns, danced to the coarse music of the pastoral flute. This scene from libertine pastoral, recalling Virgil's Second and Sixth Eclogues and Tasso's *Aminta,* creates an atmosphere of harmony with nature implied by music and dancing, a youthful spirit of innocent hedonism, and the reconciliation of youth and age in the approval of old Damaetas.

The swain's recollection of his day with Lycidas parallels the day of the poem which is recapitulated in the *commiato.* Implicitly, then, it serves to suggest the origins of the poem's vision. Specifically, it helps to explain some of the natural imagery which, at the beginning of the poem, is associated with the swain's youth. The laurels he comes to pluck of course anticipate Phoebus' promise of the plant of fame. The myrtles and ivy, like the laurel, are evergreen promises of immortality, but they refer more directly to the swain's youth. Since these plants are plucked for Lycidas, they also describe him as well as the swain.[9] Ivy is conventionally associated with the Dionysiac, the satyrs and fauns dancing in the shade, and with the chief priest of Dionysus, Orpheus.[10] Orpheus is the archetype for the young poet whose death nature laments in cosmic sympathy, and for Milton he also serves as the mythological synthesis for the figures of priest and prophet. While embodying the Neoplatonic aspects of poetry and inspiration, Orpheus also suggests the theme of male friendship. Orpheus was killed because the Thracian women were jealous of his intimacy with their men.[11]

The tradition of viewing Orpheus Neoplatonically specifies the friendship of Lycidas and the swain as Platonic in the Renaissance manner. The myrtle also suggests love or friendship. It is associated with Venus in classical literature, and these lines which introduce the swain's tribute of love to a dead friend echo Corydon's sensuous love tribute of laurels and myrtles in Virgil's Second Eclogue: "et vos, o lauri, carpam et te, proxima myrte, / sic positae quoniam suaves miscetis odores."[12] The plucking of the berries in *Lycidas* extends the Dionysiac theme implied by the myrtles and ivy. This is the crushing of berries for wine, accompanied, as was customary in classical rites, by the weaving of chaplets. The weaving of the laureate wreath had also become symbolic of the powers of poetic inspiration and prophecy.[13] The poem itself is a ritual, the crushing of these berries and the weaving of this laureate wreath. In the Dionysiac rites of youthful friendship and its loss, which the poem recaptures and laments, the swain has discovered the origins of the Orphic sensibility which the poem both demonstrates and celebrates.

The swain's sensibility demonstrates itself through the structure of *Lycidas,* which dramatically traces the steps of his meditation on death, his inner vision of the mourners, and his final leap into prophetic vision when he commands the shepherds to weep no more. The very mental or interior quality of the poem is indicated as an intrinsic intention by the retrospective glance we have of the uncouth swain "With eager thought warbling his *Doric* lay." The gray-fly passage has explored the transformation of meditation into sense experience; this passage describes the converse translation of meditation into song and signals the meditative and finally visionary quality that led Northrop Frye to describe *Lycidas* as a poem "contained within the mind of the poet."[14]

The structure of *Lycidas* depends in large part upon the swain's transformation, in the course of his meditation, of the elegiac motifs of naturalistic pastoral into the consolatory vision of Christian pastoral. Our understanding of this process is clarified by the boundaries created within the poem between different concepts of pastoral, boundaries which depend upon the variation and contrast of different

pastoral motifs. Critics have noted the complexity of the poem's dramatic and tonal structure and its exploitation of the general principle
of variety and contrast expounded by late Renaissance aesthetics.[15]
But this principle of variety and contrast was also a traditional feature
of pastoral theory, which in the Renaissance was evolving a concept of
pastoral as a genre capable of a comprehensive though reductive
view of the most diverse experiences. This is the comprehensiveness
usually accorded only to epic.[16] But in their discussions of pastoral
variety, many of the theorists are expressing their intuition that
Virgil's bucolics create a thematic and structural paradigm for the
Aeneid.[17] A similar intention at least is perceivable in *Lycidas*.

Servius is the authority for regarding pastoral as a mixed genre
with a variety of voices, styles, and motifs. Virgil's eclogues, he writes,
include all three voices: the narrative, the dramatic, and the mixed,
which includes both.[18] Although he would prefer the pastoral to remain in the low style, he discovers in Virgil's eclogues a mixture of
styles which complements this mixture of voices. Three of the
eclogues, he remarks, employ a higher style "either so that he might
succeed in pleasing by introducing more elevated subjects, or because he could not [otherwise] create so much variety."[19] Thus in
spite of the one genre–one style demands of the *rota Vergilii*, the
very example of Virgil implied a variety of voices, styles, and subjects
in the pastoral.[20]

The most radical expression of this principle of variety comes
from the early Christian mythographer Fulgentius, who adheres to
the medieval view of Virgil as an encyclopedic poet, philosopher,
mystic, and magician. Fulgentius implies that the meaning of the bucolics is too arcane to be revealed, but he cryptically notes that in the
first three eclogues he finds the pattern for the active, contemplative,
and epicurean life. The Fourth is prophetic, the Fifth describes the
priesthood, while the Sixth deals with music and physics, the Seventh
with botany, and the Eighth with music and magic.[21]

The habit of dark allegory which Fulgentius finds in Virgil was
employed by Petrarch and Boccaccio, but with the Renaissance there
was a tendency toward clarification and finally elimination of allegory.[22] This sense of the variety and range of pastoral, however, remained in spite of attempts to reduce the subjects of pastoral to love
alone. Sébillet writes that pastoral deals with "the death of princes,

historical disasters, revolutions of states, happy events and accidents of fortune, poetic panegyrics, and such things or similar things. . . ."[23] Spenser's scheme to make a "Calender for euery yeare" likewise assumes a broad comprehensiveness of subject which even E. K. seems to recognize in his summary of the eclogues as plaintive, erotic, and moral.[24] Like the epic itself, pastoral had come to be regarded as an encyclopedic form capable of embracing the most diverse subjects under its comprehensive point of view.

This variety and comprehensiveness is indicated as an implicit intention when Milton remarks that the uncouth swain "touch't the tender stops of various Quills." This intention is also suggested at the beginning of the poem, where the three plants with their distinct symbolic meanings promise some degree of variety. Moreover, the swain promises "Yet once more . . . and once more." This is often taken to mean that "Evidently this is not the first time he has come forward with an immature performance."[25] But its primary meaning, surely, must be "Just one more time," as in the first line of Virgil's Tenth: "Extremum hunc, Arethusa, mihi concede laborem." This is to be the last pastoral elegy, the swain hopes, and the last death of a close friend.

The finality and comprehensiveness of this pastoral (in spite of the unforeseen fact that the *Epitaphium Damonis* was to be written two years later) is again indicated by "To morrow to fresh Woods, and Pastures new," which recalls Colin Clout's farewell at the end of Spenser's December eclogue. *Lycidas* traces the swain's progress from despair over the poet's lot to confidence in a new beginning—presumably, as Milton promises in the *Epitaphium Damonis*, a new beginning as an epic poet. Thus *Lycidas* implies an intention to be the last, and the omnium-gatherum, of Milton's pastoral interests.

John Crowe Ransom condemns this variety and comprehensiveness when he remarks that "in the pastoral elegy at large, one of my friends distinguishes eleven different topics of discourse, and points out that Milton, for doubtless the first time in this literature, manages to 'drag them all into one poem': a distinction for him, though perhaps a doubtful one. But in doing so he simply fills up the poem; there are no other topics in it."[26] Perverse as it may seem to condemn a poem first for having too many topics, and then "no other topics in it," Ransom points to the important fact of Milton's attempted synthesis of the major forms of pastoral. Given the variety of pastoral, it would be easy to label eleven topics, or twenty. It would be more useful, from the viewpoint of pastoral theory, to note how Milton employs and often redefines many of the topics which Fulgentius discovers in Virgil.

Clearly, Fulgentius' terms of contemplative, active, and epicurean define the conflicts in the swain's mind in the first section of the poem. The epicurean life with Amaryllis and Neaera is rejected, but its role has been filled before by the friendship of Lycidas and the swain. The loss of this epicurean friendship is to be compensated by Lycidas' genius-ship and his enjoyment of the sanctified hedonism of heaven. The relationship of the contemplative to the active life is clearly at issue in the swain's attempt to evaluate the years of contemplative preparation for the poet-priesthood and in St. Peter's condemnation of those who have exploited their vocations. The priesthood, which Fulgentius discovers in Virgil's Fifth Eclogue, is the business of St. Peter's speech. It is interesting that Fulgentius should have emphasized Caesar's priesthood in Virgil's elegy, since Caesar's dual role as politician and priest anticipates the evils of prelacy which St. Peter condemns and on the positive side looks forward to St. Peter's cryptic prophecy of the political power of the Church Militant wielding its "two-handed engine."

Fulgentius' other topics are botany and physics (which might vaguely be subsumed in any pastoral landscape), magic, music, and prophecy. The last three are related in an important way. Magic in Theocritus and Virgil is associated with love potions and the incantations of disappointed mistresses. In *Lycidas* it is magic which rigged the ship with curses dark. This is usually regarded as obscure, but it seems to me to point to some malevolence, to a failure of love. It stands, certainly, in deliberate contrast to the love of Lycidas and the swain and their resulting harmony with nature. Thus magical curses, which manipulate nature through perverted forms of music and poetry, stand in opposition to the music and poetry of natural and celestial harmony. The swains, satyrs, and fauns provide the music and dance of natural harmony; the saints, that in their singing move, enact the music of consolation and redemption.

Prophecy, which Fulgentius and many other Christian commentators found in Virgil's Messianic Eclogue, is often viewed by Renaissance pastoral as a higher form of poetry. This derives in part from the ancient and Platonic view of poetry as inspired and from the close association of poetry and prophecy in the Old Testament. The pastoral landscape, moreover, because of its interior and mental quality, had become a medium for exploring the relationship of poetry and inspiration. The association of meditation with the pastoral landscape is assumed in the image of Tityrus meditating the muse. In the Renaissance pastoral, especially in Sannazaro, pastoral meditation becomes a direct means toward interior revelation and prophecy.[27] In *Lycidas*, St. Peter's declamation swells into the deliberately enigmatic prophecy of Armageddon in the "two-handed engine." More importantly, the swain moves from his meditations on death and fame to interior visions of the mourners and the bier, to a prophetic vision of Lycidas in Elysium. Only when he has recognized the full meaning of Lycidas' death and the role of the poet-prophet-priest can he pass from the role of poet to prophet in his abrupt command to the shepherds, "Weep no more."[28] In this transfiguration of the swain and in the process from meditation to prophecy lies the antidote to the magic curses that sank Lycidas' ship.

The comprehensive variety of *Lycidas*, then, is not a tour de force. It is a means of tracing the swain's growth into the roles of poet and prophet. It is, finally, his near heroic act of intellectual and imaginative synthesis. In his elegy the swain attempts in one poem what Virgil achieves in ten and Spenser in twelve. In the wholeness of a single controlling vision he brings into focus the various but related points of view on man's place in nature and society that pastoral makes possible.

The comprehensive variety of pastoral also makes possible the processes of reduction and transvaluation from one pastoral mode to another which characterizes *Lycidas*. In employing motifs from the distinct subgenres of pastoral (naturalistic, allegorical, libertine, Christian), Milton's speaker establishes a thematic conflict between them. The poem traces the speaker's meditative progress from a vision of Lycidas' death in the naturalistic mode, to a recollection of their youth in the libertine mode, to a procession of allegorical figures who comment on the poet's significance, and finally to a reconciliation of these modes in the vision of a Christian pastoral. In this process the motifs of the naturalistic or libertine modes are regularly transvalued into the motifs of the allegorical or Christian pastoral.

J. C. Scaliger provides the theoretical background for this process of transvaluation. He sees that pastoral is not so much a matter of subjects or milieu, but rather of a clearly defined point of view—a habit of double vision—through which many subjects may be examined. Within the sphere of pastoral he includes all rustic activities and regards the resulting subgenres as innovative and expandable. Sannazaro has added the piscatorial pastoral; he himself has contributed the *pastoralia villica*. "But this one thing all have in common: they all transform any matter of whatsoever kind to rustic terms."[29]

The most frequent kind of transformation is the reduction from large to small, city to country, heroic to unheroic. The greater the subject, Scaliger asserts, the more it should be reduced. "Thus if one speaks of kings or gods, the more humble their activities and deeds, the more suitable they are to this genre. And so always when Tityrus speaks of his god, he does not attribute to him the thunderbolt or military prowess but 'Ille meas errare boues, vt cernis, et ipsum / Ludere quae vellem, calamo permisit agresti.' "[30]

In *Lycidas* the uncouth swain's point of view is regularly tested against the more elevated perspectives of Phoebus, the mourners, and St. Peter. The decorum of the poem is further complicated by the interpretation of the other modes of pastoral through the piscatorial mode appropriate to Lycidas' death by water. But Scaliger's dynamic principle of inverse reduction seems to hold. Lycidas, the peer of the uncouth swain, is raised to an object of cosmic sympathy, the special care of nature's gods, Camus' dearest pledge, the sacred head of the Orphic poet-priest, an emblem of salvation, and finally the genius of the shore. St. Peter, by inversion, is reduced to "The Pilot of the *Galilean* lake," and Christ to "him that walk'd the waves." Both descriptions seem to me to be modelled on Scaliger's example from Virgil. The point of view of the uncouth swain is thus expressed in a variety of ways, but this variety is consistently controlled by Scaliger's flexible and dynamic concept.

The speaker's meditative process of transvaluation of one pastoral motif into another is also apparent in his translation of the symbolic plants of the first lines, which represent fame, love, and Orphic inspiration, into the plant of heavenly fame promised by Phoebus. Similarly, the willows, hazel copses, rose, white thorn, and other flowers that respond in Orphic sympathy to the death of Lycidas are translated into the symbolic flowers that deck his imagined bier. The pathetic fallacy, assumed ingenuously earlier in the poem and self-consciously in the flower passage, is then exploded by the speaker's return from the deliberate fantasy of the bier to the vision of Lycidas' corpse washed under the sea. This loss of faith in nature's sympathy then requires a further transformation of the motifs and vision of naturalistic pastoral into the consolatory mode of Christian pastoral. The naturalistic plants are replaced by the groves of a Christian paradise, the water of the Irish Sea and the speaker's tears by purifying streams of nectar. Similarly, the Dionysiac of youthful friendship drawn from libertine pastoral, which has been reexpressed through the sympathy of the allegorical procession of mourners, is replaced by the society of the saints.

The success of the poem's structure, then, consists in organizing its different pastoral modes under the flexible but controlling perspective of the speaker, which assimilates and transvalues this variety into a pattern, and finally a vision, of unity. The poem's diverse mannerist perspectives are being reorganized by a baroque sense of unified perspective. The same problem of diversity and contrast affects the style of *Lycidas*. Although the swain is not introduced until the end, he must make us sense that it is his voice, like his vision, which has controlled the poem's variety of voices and visions. His problem (or Milton's), in effect, is to prevent the comprehensive pastoral from becoming a "collection of magnificent fragments."[31] Again it can be seen, I think, that the solution derives from a major tradition of pastoral and stylistic theory.

Scaliger's relevance to the structural problems of *Lycidas* makes him a useful commentator on the much thornier subject of style. Renaissance theorists, following Servius, agree that pastoral uses low characters and should employ the low style.[32] But most of the definitions we have of the three styles—high, middle, and low—are hopelessly abstract. Even Virgil's poetry, upon which the *rota Vergilii* is based, violates the assumption that each genre should be limited to one style (epic:high, georgic:middle, eclogue:low). It is Scaliger, in good pedagogical fashion, who makes some sense out of the *rota*

Vergilii by providing analytical models for each of the three styles from Virgil's poetry.

Scaliger attempts to salvage the one style–one genre principle by admitting to each style a number of "manners" or degrees of elevation. "For neither is the high style always elevated; indeed it is forced to descend to those which in the measure of things are lower. Neither does the low style always either lie low or creep; but from time to time it is raised up."[33] The low style differs from the high style by kind. But the low manner in the low style differs from the high manner in the low style not by kind but by manner or degree of elevation.[34]

Obviously this theoretical distinction of style and its subsumed manners is impractical. We may describe the changes in tone in *Lycidas* in terms either of kind *or* manner with similar results. The important thing is that Scaliger recognizes that any poem may be a continuum of high, middle, and low (styles *or* manners). This opens the door of theory to the stylistic variety and contrast of *Lycidas* and both of Milton's epics.

Moreover, in his analyses of Virgil, Scaliger provides models for this kind of stylistic continuum. These analyses are organized in terms of the modes which each of the three styles may assume. The modes he designates as *cultus, proprietas, venustas, numerositas, plenitudo, floridum, molle, suavitas, incitatio, puritas, acumen, acre,* and so forth. Scaliger defines the qualities of each mode and then gives examples, in most cases, from each of the three stylistic levels. Thus within each mode we are given a ladder or continuum of styles. Any of these modes may be found in a poet like Milton. The utility of Scaliger's analyses is that they provide models for understanding Milton's modulation from one stylistic level to another within the same mode. Eventually one might want to say, in Scaliger's terms, that a pastoral (or low) style controls all of *Lycidas* and that each of these stylistic levels should be treated as "manners." But at this point such a distinction would only further complicate the process of analysis.[35]

Scaliger's chapter on the mode *floridum* is especially useful for a discussion of the stylistic variety of *Lycidas*. The florid mode is like *plenitudo,* the full mode, "to which it adds something, which might be deleted without loss. But let this thing which it adds be pleasant and contribute toward our pleasure in reading." His model for the florid mode in the low style is Meliboeus' speech to Tityrus:

Fortunate senex, ergo tua rura manebunt:
Et tibi magna satis: quanuis lapis omnia nudus,
Limosoque palus obducat pascua iunco.
Non insueta graueis tentabunt pabula foetas:
Nec mala vicini pecoris contagia laedent.
Fortunate senex, hinc inter flumina nota
Et fontes sacros frigus captabis opacum.[36]

The redundancy, parallelism, and loose connectives here are characteristic of Virgil's pastoral style and frequently signal a pastoral
style both in *Lycidas* and in Milton's epics.[37] There is only one major
statement: "Happy old man, so your land still will be yours." But
Meliboeus, with the loquacity of a man who would prefer to linger,
fills in the descriptive details through parallel statements: "Fortunate
senex . . . Fortunate senex." These are joined by a series of loose
connectives for parallel, balancing, or antithetical phrases: "ergo . . .
Et . . . quanuis . . . -que . . . Non . . . Nec . . . Et . . . ." The
same rhetoric continues in the rest of the passage, which I have not
quoted, setting together the disadvantages of Tityrus' situation and
balancing them, through rhetorical antithesis, against the advantages,
weighing in Virgilian fashion disorder against order.

Milton announces his stylistic intentions with an emphatic use
of this florid rhetoric in the first paragraph of *Lycidas*. Through parallelism he is able to build up a sense of the repetitiveness of the experience of death and mourning: "Yet once more . . . and once more."
The parallels work at long range, too, however, and serve to relate
the rhetoric of the low style here to the biblical low style of St. Peter's
speech, which foresees an end to the process introduced by "Yet once
more" in the two-handed engine which "Stands ready to smite once,
and smite no more." Then St. Peter's vision of judgment yields to the
swain's consolatory "Weep no more, woful Shepherds weep no more,"
and the final vision of the saints who "wipe the tears for ever from his
eyes." Many of these parallel sequences in *Lycidas* conclude as here
with an anomalous element ("for ever") which provides the emotional,
as well as the rhetorical, climax.

A more complex use of the rhetoric of the florid mode is apparent
in the chiasmic pattern (ABBX) of "For *Lycidas* is dead, dead ere his
prime," where "dead, dead" provides the chiasmic center. This leads
to the fuller chiasmus (ABBA) in "For *Lycidas* is dead [A], dead ere

his prime [B], Young *Lycidas* [B], and hath not left his peer [A]."
The point is that some other young poet, although not his peer, must
sing. This point is continued by the further parallels of "Who would
not sing . . . ? he knew / Himself to sing, and build the lofty rhyme."
Song is the means of redemption, and these rhetorical parallels contrast with the juxtaposed parallels of "He must not flote upon his
watry bear / Unwept, and welter to the parching wind." Order is,
as in Virgil, opposed rhetorically to disorder. The resolution is in the
rhetorically anomalous element: "Without the meed of som melodious
tear." But this anomaly will find its parallels in the judgment of Phoebus, "Of so much fame in Heav'n expect thy meed," in "Look homeward Angel now, and melt with ruth," and in the singing angels who
"wipe the tears for ever from his eyes."

This rhetoric of the florid mode in a recognizably low style controls the first section of the poem until Phoebus appears. The swain's
tone has been rising in the meditation on death and fame ("Comes
the blind *Fury*") and modulates upward to the "higher mood" of Phoebus' consolation. Phoebus continues to employ the rhetoric of the
florid mode, but his parallels and their connectives are more emphatic:
"*Fame* is no plant . . . Nor in the glistering foil . . . Nor in broad
rumour lies . . . But lives and spreds . . . by those pure eyes, / And
perfet witnes. . . ." The anomalous element in this sequence is the
climactic judgment, "As he pronounces lastly on each deed / Of so
much fame in Heav'n expect thy meed." By modulating from one level
of the florid style to another, Milton has created an emotional intensity
and elevation in the resolution of the swain's meditations. At the same
time he has stylistically stressed the continuity of the swain's thoughts
with the interior voice of the god.

The second section of the poem, which describes the mourners,
returns to a lower style ("But now my Oat proceeds"). The stylistic
key to this passage is Scaliger's principle of inverse reduction. The
allegorical figures—Triton, Hippotades, Camus—are reduced to a
pastoral context and an ingenuous pastoral style ("What hard mishap
hath doom'd this gentle swain? . . . Ah; Who hath reft (quoth he) my
dearest pledge?"). Similarly, St. Peter, in his reduction to "The Pilot
of the *Galilean* lake," employs a biblical style which achieves a certain
elevation through the use of "low" language for a "high" subject, ac-

cording to the principle of stylistic *mimesis* that Auerbach has described so fully.[38]

St. Peter's tone ranges from indignation to denunciation to apocalyptic prophecy, but its rhetoric is generally that of the florid mode in the middle style, for which Scaliger gives this example: "Thus he [Virgil] depicts ambition and avarice and the vain striving of men in the Second Georgic:

> Solicitant alii remis freta caeca, ruûntque
> In ferrum: penetrant aulas, et limina regum.
> Hic petit excidijs vrbem, miserosque penates:
> Vt gemmâ bibat, et Serrano dormiat ostro.
> Condit opes alius, defossóque incubat auro."[39]

This piling up of immoral actions in parallel phrases builds up both a sense of moral outrage in the speaker and of accelerating moral disorder in the world. St. Peter's use of this rhetoric emphasizes his indignation, while the pastoral context and his contemptuous irony reduce evildoing to such a level that the reader is assured of ultimate order:

> How well could I have spar'd for thee, young swain
> Anow of such as for their bellies sake,
> Creep and intrude, and climb into the fold?
> Of other care they little reck'ning make,
> Then how to scramble at the shearers feast,
> And shove away the worthy bidden guest.

The deliberate harshness of St. Peter's "low" diction also resembles Scaliger's mode *acre:* "The bitter style is like the sharp. But it not only pricks, like the sharp, but it even jabs, as in the Bucolics:

> Cantando tu illum? aut vnquam tibi fistula cera
> Iuncta fuit? non tu in triuijs indocte solebas
> Stridenti miserum stipula disperdere carmen?"[40]

St. Peter approximates this rhetoric in: "What recks it them? What need they? They are sped; / And when they list, their lean and flashy songs / Grate on their scrannel Pipes of wretched straw. . . ." Using the homely low diction of Spenser's eclogues and the biblical pastoral, the passage progresses through an accumulation of parallel phrases and ideas, continuing with "The hungry Sheep . . . are not fed . . .

swoln with wind, and the rank mist . . . Rot inwardly, and foul
contagion spread." In this sequence building toward its apocalyptic
climax, the anomalous member is the enigmatic "two-handed engine,"
which leads to the emphatic parallels of "Stands ready to smite once,
and smite no more."

St. Peter's "dread voice" threatens the unity of the poem and
requires the reinvocation of Alpheus and the Sicilian Muse. But
though its tone acquires elevation and violence, its rhetoric remains
within the limits of the florid mode. The swain then interposes the
easiness of the catalogue of flowers; it is his voice attempting to reas-
sert control. But St. Peter's message has demanded transcendence, and
his style has demanded elevation. The swain loses control, not of the
poem, but of his voice; at the moment of prophecy we hear a greater
voice speaking—not to him, as Phoebus and St. Peter have done, but
through him.

This greater voice assumes a high style in the florid mode which
retains the parallelisms of the lower styles while adding a profusion of
alliteration and assonance. In Scaliger's example from the *Aeneid*, this
use of sound values is meant to suggest tranquillity and the harmony
of nature:

> Nox erat, et placidum carpebant fessa soporem
> Corpora per terras: sylvaeque et saeua quierant
> Aequora, cùm medio voluuntur sidera lapsu.
> Cùm tacet omnis ager, pecudes, pictaeque volucres:
> Quaeque lacus latè liquidos, quaeque horrida dumis
> Rura tenent, somno positae sub nocte silenti
> Lenibant curas, et corda oblita laborum.[41]

Milton's swain reaches toward this sense of completion and harmony
in the accumulated parallelisms of the last section, which are now
underlined by heavy alliteration: "Weep no more, woful Shepherds
weep no more . . . your sorrow is not dead . . . Sunk though he
be . . . So sinks the day-star . . . So *Lycidas* sunk low, but mounted
high." The emphatic alliteration of *s*'s climaxes in the swain's vision of
the "Kingdoms meek of joy and love" which have replaced the joy
and love of the shepherds:

> There entertain him all the Saints above,
> In solemn troops, and sweet Societies
> That sing, and singing in their glory move.

The formal qualities of this florid rhetoric thus become a way of expressing the harmony of song, dance, and the society of the saints. The fullest possible use of the florid mode signals the climax of the swain's vision.

Lycidas' oneness with the music and society of heaven is then recapitulated in a lower style in the reductive parallel of the uncouth swain peacefully warbling his Doric lay. The *commiato* completes the parallel structures of the poem. Its anomalous element is the swain's farewell to pastoral: "To morrow to fresh Woods, and Pastures new." It is important, though, that this new beginning is described through pastoral images—woods and pastures. Milton seems to be conscious of the close tie between Virgil's pastorals and the *Aeneid* and to foresee a similar progress for himself. *Lycidas* has provided an opportunity for experimenting—within the framework of pastoral theory—with generic concepts, motifs, implicit generic metaphors, and parallel structures. It has been a proving ground for stylistic modulation and variety controlled by the style and voice of the swain. And through the themes of loss and redemption, death and creation, *Lycidas* has with its meditative discoveries and interior visions provided a thematic paradigm, as well as a structural and stylistic model, for the innovations of Milton's epics.

Rice University

NOTES

1. *Of Education, The Works of John Milton,* ed. F. A. Patterson et al. (New York, 1931–42), IV, 286. (All quotations from Milton in this essay are taken from this edition.) Cf. Bernard Weinberg, *A History of Literary Criticism in the Italian Renaissance* (Chicago, 1961), 2 vols., passim; J. E. Congleton, *Theories of Pastoral Poetry in England 1684–1798* (Gainesville, Fla., 1952), pp. 17–19; J. C. Scaliger, *Poetices libri septem* (Lyons, 1561; reprint, Stuttgart, 1964), Book I. For Milton's interest in Scaliger's genre theory, see *An Apology, Works,* III, 293.

2. E. M. W. Tillyard, *Milton,* rev. ed. (London, 1966), p. 72.

3. *Servii Grammatici qui feruntur in Vergilii carmina commentarii,* ed. Georg Thilo and Hermann Hagen (Hildesheim, 1961), vol. III, p. 3. Cf. E. K.'s "Epistle" to *The Shepheardes Calender,* in *Spenser's Minor Poems,* ed. Ernest de Sélincourt (Oxford, 1910), p. 7.

4. Baptista Spagnuolo Mantuanus, *Opera,* ed. J. B. Ascensius et al., 3 vols. (Paris, 1513), II, fol. CVII^r.

5. Cf. J. A. Wittreich's discussion of the theme of orderly creation which is

discovered through the apparent disorder caused by Lycidas' death. "Milton's 'Destin'd Urn': The Art of *Lycidas*," *PMLA*, LXXXIV (1969), 60–70.

6. *Life of Milton, Lives of the English Poets*, ed. G. B. Hill, 3 vols. (Oxford, 1905), I, 163.

7. Cf. *Comus*, l. 93.

8. Scaliger, *Poetices*, I, iv, p. 7.

9. Rosemond Tuve, "Theme, Pattern and Imagery in *Lycidas*," from *Images and Themes in Five Poems by Milton* (Cambridge, Mass., 1957), p. 88.

10. Cf. "L'Allegro," 16; "Sixth Elegy," 13–18; *PL* VII, 32–38; Scaliger, *Poetices*, I, xviii, p. 28.

11. Caroline W. Mayerson, "The Orpheus Image in *Lycidas*," *PMLA*, LXIV (1949), 189–207; Edgar Wind, "Orpheus in Praise of Blind Love," in *Pagan Mysteries in the Renaissance* (London, 1958), pp. 57–77; W. K. C. Guthrie, *Orpheus and Greek Religion* (London, 1935), pp. 32–33.

12. "And I'll take toll of you as well, you laurels, and your friends the myrtles. Set side by side you blend your perfumes very sweetly." Ecl. II, ll. 54–55, *Virgil: the Pastoral Poems*, trans. E. V. Rieu (London, 1961), p. 35. Cf. *Epitaphium Damonis*, 308–09.

13. E.g., Jacopo Sannazaro, *De partu virginis*, ed. Antonio Altamura (Naples, 1948), I, 236–44.

14. "Literature as Context: Milton's *Lycidas*," *North Carolina Studies in Comparative Literature*, XXIII (1959), 47.

15. H. V. S. Ogden, "The Principles of Variety and Contrast in Seventeenth Century Aesthetics, and Milton's Poetry," *JHI*, X (1949), 159–82; Lowry Nelson, Jr., *Baroque Lyric Poetry* (New Haven, 1961), pp. 138–52; M. H. Abrams, "Five Types of *Lycidas*," in *Milton's "Lycidas*," ed. C. A. Patrides (New York, 1961), pp. 212–31, esp. pp. 224–30.

16. Scaliger, *Poetices*, I, iii; Girolamo Muzio, *Arte Poetica*, in *Rime Diverse* (Venice, 1551), fol. 78ʳ.

17. Brooks Otis, *Virgil: A Study in Civilized Poetry* (Oxford, 1964), p. 97.

18. Servius, *Servii Grammatici*, pp. 30–31. Cf. the scholiast of Theocritus in *Codex Ambrosianus* 222, quoted by Herbert Kynaston, "Preliminary Remarks on the Life and Writings of Theocritus," in *Idylls and Epigrams Commonly Attributed to Theocritus* (Oxford, 1892), p. xv.

19. Servius, *Servii Grammatici*, p. 3.

20. Christophori Landini, *P. Virgilii Maronis opera cum Seruii Donati Christophori Landini Comitii Calderini commentariis* (Nuremberg, 1492), vol. IIIʳ.

21. Fabius Planciades Fulgentius, *Liber de expositione Virgilianae continentiae*, in *Auctores mythographi latini*, ed. Augustinus van Staveren (Lyons, 1742), p. 738. The *editio princeps* is Heidelberg, 1589. See Congleton, *Theories of Pastoral Poetry*, pp. 13–14.

22. W. Leonard Grant, *Neo-Latin Literature and the Pastoral* (Chapel Hill, N. C., 1965), pp. 86–110.

23. Thomas Sébillet, *L'Art poétique francoys* (1548), ed. Félix Gaiffe (Paris, 1932), pp. 159–61.

24. "Epistle" to *The Shepheardes Calender*, p. 11.

25. Cleanth Brooks and John Edward Hardy, *Poems of Mr. John Milton* (New York, 1951), p. 170.

26. "A Poem Nearly Anonymous," in *The World's Body* (New York, 1938), pp. 16–17. Cf. W. W. Greg, *Pastoral Poetry and Pastoral Drama* (London, 1906), p. 132.

27. See my article, "Sannazaro and Milton's Brief Epic," *CL*, XX (1968), 116–32.

28. William G. Madsen ascribes this speech to St. Michael, whom the swain has just addressed. But an unannounced change of speakers would violate pastoral decorum. See *From Shadowy Types to Truth: Studies in Milton's Symbolism* (New Haven, 1968), pp. 11–16.

29. Scaliger, *Poetices*, III, xcix, p. 150.

30. Ibid., IV, xix, p. 193. Ecl. I, ll. 9–11. "He gave the word—and my cattle browse at large, while I myself can play the tunes I fancy on my rustic flute." Rieu, *The Pastoral Poems*, p. 21.

31. G. Wilson Knight, "The Frozen Labyrinth: An Essay on Milton," in *The Burning Oracle* (London, 1939), p. 70.

32. E.g., Scaliger, *Poetices*, IV, xix, p. 193.

33. Ibid., IV, xxiii, p. 194.

34. Ibid., IV, i, p. 175.

35. I have translated Scaliger's *genus dicendi* as "style," *modus* and *gradus* as "manner," and *stilus* as "mode."

36. Ibid., IV, ix, p. 185. "Happy old man! So your land will still be yours. And it's enough for you, even though the bare rock and the marshland with its mud and reeds encroach on all your pastures. Your pregnant ewes will never be upset by unaccustomed fodder; no harm will come to them through meeting other people's flocks. Happy old man! You will stay here, between the rivers that you know so well, by springs that have their Nymphs, and find some cool spot underneath the trees." Ecl. I, ll. 46–52. Rieu, *The Pastoral Poems*, p. 25.

37. E.g., *PR* I, 321–34.

38. Erich Auerbach, *Literary Language and Its Public in Late Latin Antiquity and in the Middle Ages*, trans. Ralph Manheim (Princeton, 1965).

39. Scaliger, *Poetices*, IV, ix, p. 185. "Others seek the blind shallows with oars, and they rush upon swords; they intrude upon the courts and the thresholds of kings. This man seeks the destruction of his city and his wretched homeland. Another finds riches and jealously guards his unearthed gold so that he might drink gems and sleep on Tyrian robes." *Georgics*, II, 504–07. (My translation.)

40. Scaliger IV. ix, p. 185. "You beat him in a match! I don't believe you ever owned a set of reed-pipes joined with wax. All you were good for was to stand at the crossroads and scrape a miserable tune out of one squeaking straw." *Ecl.* III, ll. 25–27. (Rieu, *The Pastoral Poems*, p. 43).

41. Scaliger, *Poetices*, IV, ix, p. 185. "It was night, and throughout the earth weary bodies were enjoying a peaceful sleep. And the woods and savage seas lay silent, while the heavens turned in the middle of their course. While every field lies silent, the herds and dappled birds, and whatever inhabits far and wide the limpid lakes and the fields bristling with brambles, drenched in sleep throughout the noiseless night they assuage their cares and their minds forgetful of suffering" (*Aeneid*, IV, 522–27). (My translation.)

MILTON'S USE
OF COLOR AND LIGHT

G. Stanley Koehler

In the use of color Milton's poetry shows the workings of two influences other than the purposes of description and the dictates of personal taste. One is the influence of emblematic tradition in the meaning of individual colors; the other is the practice of classical literatures. Many of Milton's terms are derived from the color usage of Homer or Virgil rather than from the direct observation of nature. Where emblematic meanings enter, the interpretation is at times complicated by the ambivalence of color symbolism, which shifts meanings with variations of hue and context. It would appear, however, that both in using and in avoiding certain colors, especially in the areas of red and yellow, Milton is affected by emblematic connotations which such colors have had, in both the secular and the religious spheres of meaning. Where Milton's own taste may be thought to govern, there is a marked preference for richness of texture rather than brightness of hue, a preference that is seen in his tendency to favor colors from the midspectrum. As Milton grew older, he inclined toward the use of light and dark rather than effects of color, a development which should be attributed to his own increasingly baroque temper rather than to any physical limitations in vision.

I

IT IS hard to tell how much of the medieval and Renaissance iconography of color is still present in Milton. No doubt any color that is not merely descriptive conveys some conventional or symbolic meaning, but the highly specialized system of religious and secular color usage must have grown somewhat dim by Milton's time. In any case, as W. Flemming suggests, "the symbolic content of a color is rarely tangible like the meaning of a riddle." It is more likely some "vague resonance . . . which gives the description a note of mysterious depth, but defies definition."[1] At other moments, the meanings may be only too obvious. For example, red, the most vivid of colors to the normal eye, goes naturally with the stronger emotions and more important ideas, however these may be opposed, like love and anger, or the Holy Spirit and the Devil. It is identified too with systems and processes, like royalty, purgatory, and the church. Where the literal and emblematic meanings go together—white things standing for purity and green for life and growth—the conventional symbolic meanings will register along with the descriptive effect. But when symbolic color of a less self-evident kind is applied where it happens also to be appropriate, or at least not grossly inappropriate to the purely literal side, we may very well overlook the emblematic part. For example, the "azure wings" and "purple beams" representing the good works of Mrs. Catherine Thomason in Sonnet XIV are apt enough as description; but azure is also the emblem of Heaven and hope, as purple is of penitence, faith, wisdom and love.[2] Purple is in fact an especially good example of the problem of meaning in color terms, for it has two distinct kinds of meaning apart from color itself. It is used in Homer and Virgil largely for effects of light and dark, a practice which Milton follows at times, using purple for suggestions of transparency and brilliance, in things like sunsets and Cupid wings. On the other hand, as the most effective of ancient dyes, it could be inconographic for military and political power.[3] In this sense Milton applies it appropriately to the dress of the angel Michael as God's emissary to Adam, in a passage which spells out the emblematic meaning:

> over his lucid Arms
> A military Vest of purple flow'd
> Livelier than Melibaean, or the grain
> Of Sarra, worn by Kings and Heroes old
> In time of Truce; Iris had dipt the woof. (PL XI, 240–44)[4]

Not only does the costume fit Michael's role as emissary of God; it fits with equal exactness the timing and occasion of his visit to Adam, in the "truce" between the fall and the expulsion. There are times however when the literal and the figurative meanings do not agree at all, as when lightning is seen as red rather than a natural blue-white in PL I, 175, or more markedly in the oxymoron of Moloch's "black fire," an image that combines emblems for Hell that are visually complete opposites (II, 67). For a fine distinction, note that while the "ruddy flames" of Hell are accurate as description, the "red fire" which Moses sees on Mt. Sinai may—since fire is not actually red—be taken as an emblem of divine power (*Nativity Hymn*, l. 159).[5] A similar case occurs when the heavenly angels turn "fiery red" confronting Satan (*PL* IV, 978).[6]

Along with this problem of seeing the emblematic side of a color that may seem purely descriptive, is the problem of interpreting such additional meanings when they are thought to be present, as in the case of the "mantle blue" of the swain in *Lycidas*. If we take the detail literally, there is still the possibility that the blue in question may be one of those classical blues we shall be considering below. If it is emblematic, we must decide then what system of meanings, moral-religious, or social-secular, to consult. In the religious frame, blue suggests resurrection, in key with the closing mood of the elegy. In the secular context, it suggests the humbler station of the swain, blue being the color for servants and apprentices, in Shakespeare's England or classical Rome.[7] Most likely, however, the term reflects a classical convention for expressing grief. In Homer and Virgil, terms for blue like κυάνεος and *caeruleus* mean dark rather than blue especially when they refer to cloth.[8]

The complications of color symbolism increase when variations of light and dark are taken into account. Emblematically, the brighter shades are quite different in meaning from the darker ones. If light blue means truth or heaven, dark blue may mean error, evil, the lower regions.[9] The reason for this may have to do with the place of blue in the spectrum. If red, the upper band of the rainbow, was associated with light, heaven, and truth, then blue, indigo, violet, the lower band tending toward darkness, came to suggest the interior of the earth, the realms of evil and terror.[10] So images like that of Charon's barge, a dark blue, or the "cerulean" snake-hair of Allecto in Virgil may be emblems respectively for death and frenzy, rather than merely visual details (*Aeneid*, VI, 410; VII, 346). Something of this traditional association of blue with evil and ghosts and a hint of its old symbolic relation to the infernal may be heard perhaps in the "blue meager hag" of *Comus*, l. 434. But beyond these matters of distinguishing the descriptive from the symbolic, determining the sphere of reference, or allowing for differences in hue there is the further problem that a given color or given hue can have both favorable and unfavorable implications. Green, for example, which because of the pastoral nature of Milton's subjects occurs more often than any other color term, has figurative meanings of regeneration, youth, life, and so on which operate strongly in the setting of *Paradise Lost,* of course, but which are heard also in things like the "green shops" of the silkworms that serve to image nature's infinite creativity in *Comus,* or in the green laurel shading the tomb of Samson.[11] Yet the sense of approval accompanying the word must be resisted at times. In Sonnet IX, for instance, where the unknown addressee is praised for choosing the difficult Hill of Truth over "the broad way and the green," we are reminded that the term can mean not only such good things as joy and love and life, but jealousy, unripeness or, as in this sonnet, worldly follies and pleasures. This reversal of color symbolism is more strikingly illustrated by the use of red to represent on the one hand such things as love, courage, zeal, or modesty, and on the other such opposite values as anger, adultery, anarchy, or shame. It explains how it is that the black view of Melancholy taken by *L'Allegro* as the personification of midnight, Stygian darkness, Ebon shades, and Cimmerian deserts can yield so readily to *Il Penseroso's* sable-stoled nun, emblem of divinity, wisdom and ideal beauty. One thinks of Cesare Ripa's Memory and Silence in their decent black garb, reflecting the stability of memory, the inviolability of silence.

Such inversions of meaning should be allowed for in dealing with the curious phenomenon in Milton, that while his taste shows a preference for tones of amber and gold, he seems to play down the term *yellow* itself and avoids completely such colors as orange and scarlet in which yellow is present. Perhaps Milton's usage reflects the stigma of jealousy and betrayal which seems to have been associated with yellow at certain periods.[12] The prejudice may also enter into Milton's treatment of the forbidden fruit, as we shall see. Note that a term like *vermilion,* which Milton may associate with widows, brides, and falsehood, occurs only twice, both times with strong cosmetic and sensuous implications. In "Death of a Fair Infant," winter is amorous of the "lovely Dye" that "envermeils" the child's face. In the *Mask,* Comus speaks of the "vermeil-tinctured lip" and love-darting eyes of the Lady. Where yellow is not mixed with red, we begin to get a more favorable sort of impression. In the saffron robe of Hymen in *L'Allegro* we may see the emblem of yellow for initiation and marriage, appropriate to bridal veils[13] for its conventional association with warmth and the fruitfulness of the sun.[14] In the case of cowslips and yellow-skirted fays, we need not expect such meanings, though here too the traditions of the masque may have had an influence.

When it comes to yellow in the form of gold, Milton's practice shows again the typical ambivalence of color symbolism. On one hand it suggests a range of worldly splendor: "barbaric gold of Eastern kings," "pagan religions full of pomp and Gold," Satan's royal seat of gold, contexts where the link between yellow and heresy, treason, arrogance, inconstancy, jealousy, and deceit are relevant, whether or not intended. Since gold shares the ambivalence of other colors, changing suggestion with a change of context, Milton is able to give God too his share of gold, as the standard and almost universal symbol of spiritual as well as material worth. In Egypt and India, it stood for regeneration through the divine spirit. The Greeks saw in the yellow Xanthus a river descending from the throne of Zeus, and for Christians gold, the sunlike metal, meant in the same way goodness, the Creator, and the saints in Paradise.[15] In Ripa, the authority in such matters, a gold crown or robe is worn by such abstractions as Intelligence, Perfection, Benignity, Valor, and Hope. For these reasons, as well as more personal ones we may go into later, Milton gilded rather heavily his images of perfection and power. Hence the golden scales of judgment, gates of Heaven, compasses, crowns, rivers, censers, sceptres, chains, clouds, cups, hinges, harps, and ladders. Not only these, but abstract things are treated the same way, from the slumber of Orpheus to the days and deeds of the new heaven and earth (*PL* III, 337). Where two or more colors or materials combine, it is always gold that ends the sequence: "purple and gold"; "cedar, marble, ivory and gold"; "Plant, Fruit, Flow'r Ambrosial, Gems and Gold." In suggesting why gold, like white with its associations of light, was equated with deity, we return again to the fact that the so-called interior colors of the rainbow (violet, indigo and blue) made a series generalized as dark blue or black, symbolizing the inner regions of earth, while the exterior colors extending on the other side of green through yellow, orange, and red, a series generalized as yellow or white, stood for the firmament above, the abode of deity.[16] Thus there was a precedent for the

link between yellow and white as divine attributes. Since white contained, no doubt, the purer associations of light theoretically, Milton's
preference for gold is especially interesting. Though we may trace it
in large degree to epic decorum, a Christian subject, and the example
of iconography, there is also a large element of personal taste implicit
in these choices, as we shall see below.[17]

A word should be said here on the color of Milton's forbidden
fruit, a detail which gets involved with ancient ideas of the ideal and
the illusory, from the Age of Gold to the Golden Apples. One must
see, first, that Milton did not mean any particular fruit for his Tree of
Knowledge. He uses *apple* as the Greeks used μῆλον, for fruit in general. It could mean quince, peach, apricot, or orange (lemon) de-
pending on whether the epithet was "Cydonian," "Persian," "Arme-
nian," "Median." As for the golden apple (χρυσόμηλον), this would
not be the orange or lemon hardly known to ancient Greece, but
possibly quince.[18] Note that in Milton it is only Satan who calls the
fruit an apple, always in an effort to deprecate it ("Worth your laughter," *PL* X, 488).[19] In all other instances it is simply "the Fruit," with
"fair" as its fixed epithet, and any more specific image of it is contrary
to Milton's intent. As to color, the use of "fair" suggests yellow, the
golden hue always associated with such fruit. In fact, yellow is the
one color constant for all the fruits mentioned, and unfavorable meanings may be implied. In Henry Peacham's *Minerva Britanna* (1612),
"Deceit" wears a golden coat.[20] One thinks too of the gilded cloaks of
the hypocrites in Dante's *Inferno*. The notorious ambiguity of color
symbolism serves well in this instance, the suggestions of "fair," "gold,"
"yellow" suiting equally the idyllic mood before the fall and the dis-
illusion afterward, when "fair" is replaced by "false." Note that though
yellow is the color Milton emphasizes for the fruit, some red is also
present, as in peaches, apricots, and oranges. If Milton has reservations about yellow, he may have even more about yellow mixed with
red. Indeed, the one description he gives speaks of "fairest colors
mixt, Ruddy and gold" (*PL* IX, 577–78). It is the color, not the fruit
that is mixed, a reddish gold (cf. *lutea mala* in "Mansus," l. 39). The
element of red distinguishes this fruit from that of the Tree of Life
alongside it, more simply colored as "vegetable Gold"—distinguishes
it indeed from all other fruit in the Garden, golden and innocuous,
free from the suspicious complexity of color of the forbidden fruit.[21]

We shall see below that Milton shows a preference for effects of light and dark rather than of color. As with the older English religious poets with whom he shares this tendency, there is an emblematic equation of light and dark with good and evil which makes Milton's use of black and white especially interesting.[22] In Milton the proportion of literal to emblematic use is fairly equal. (Of twenty-three occurrences of the color black, roughly half refer to such concrete things as gunpowder and asphalt.) Elsewhere, as the visual element yields to psychological suggestion, there is a tendency toward the figurative: Comus embowered in black shades extends darkness into the moral sphere; the gloomy consistory of Satan's peers (*PR* I, 42) reflects their separation from truth as well as their meeting in a dense cloud. So Milton speaks, after the fall, of "black" air and "usurping" mists. As the substantives become abstract, the metaphorical sense takes over: enchantment, insurrection, perdition, destruction are termed *dark* because of their connection with evil, in symbolism that seems an extension of literal meanings. This association of white with order and creation, of black with disorder and destruction, touches the imagery of the poem at almost every point. There is, of course, more than a slight risk of the obvious in all this. J. Huizinga suggests how the deeper implications of symbol may be lost in the more superficial mode of allegory, which puts a stereotyped figure in place of a living idea.[23] Milton, however, is willing to take the risk. He treats such details with a seriousness that redeems them from convention, investing them with suggestions deeper than mere metaphor. A notable case is his description of creation, where God infused a vital warmth, "but downward purg'd / The black tartareous cold Infernal dregs / Adverse to life" (*PL* VII, 237–39). In the context, "black" itself does not get much attention, yet nothing sums up better the imagery of darkness, formlessness, coldness, downwardness, and death, or prepares so effectively for the symbolic contrast, four lines later, of "let there be light."

The symbolism of white in Milton is equally obvious, and just as important. Here again, if one needed precedent, there was the *Iconologie* of Ripa with its endless whites for Modesty, Pity, Courtesy, or Fidelity. In the form of the Lily, it is Beauty in women, but is bestowed also on such diverse things as Invention, Logic, Praise, Divinity. In Milton, snow is the saintly veil of earth in the *Nativity*

Hymn, his souls in heaven wear white robes and fillets (Elegy III), and so on.[24] The note of purity which invests the figure of Milton's late wife in Sonnet XXIII is rendered more touching by the connection of white with hope—the "white-handed Hope" of the *Mask*—which increases the emblematic despair of the last line, "and day brought back my night." Here again the effect can be mechanical, as in the wings of Fame, one black, one white, in *Samson Agonistes.* One prefers the fusion of the literal and the emblematic seen in an obvious, not to say dazzling, equation of whiteness and light with truth and revelation, when Michael appears to Adam after the fall:

> Why in the East
> Darkness ere Day's mid-course, and Morning Light
> More orient in yon Western Cloud that draws
> O'er the blue Firmament a radiant white.   (*PL* XI, 203–06)

In this connection, the term *gray* offers some ambiguity. Its physical equivalent would be the mingling of air and substance, of light and shadow, represented by mists. Though black mists are associated with Satan and Comus, the white mists of Eden rising to heaven with the prayers of Adam and Eve are described as dusky or gray, and here it is the favorable suggestion of whiteness that comes out. The same is true of Milton's twilight, whether it be the gray-hooded evening of the *Mask,* or the gray-sandalled dawn of *Lycidas.*[25]

One of Milton's more interesting epithets, with overtones that may be richly emblematic, is applied to the river of Eden, in the "milky stream" from which Eve draws nectarous draughts in Book V, l. 306. This may be a classical touch. Virgil describes foaming water in this way in *Aeneid* VIII, 672,[26] and the current that passes beneath the mount of Paradise is indeed rapid (IV, 227). But a boiling stream is not in keeping with so idyllic a scene, and one discolored by minerals like the sulphurous Nar of the *Aeneid* (VII, 516–17) is hardly more so. Perhaps since it is food that is in question, not a description of water primarily, "milky" is meant to suggest the wholesome nourishment of unfallen man. Other explanations have been given. Miss Bodkin, noting a similar phrase in *Samson Agonistes* (ll. 547–51), points out the incongruity of the term *milky* applied to clear water in a rosy light, and suspects archetypal overtones, as in Thompson's appeal to Nature to show him "the breasts of her tenderness."[27] Whatever explanation we choose, it is possible that for Milton's time a suggestion of life, purity, and innocence attends the image of white water.

It is in the flower passage of *Lycidas,* however, that the suggestive, emblematic qualities of whiteness itself are most effectively used. For the middle ages, white was seen as a veiling rather than a union of colors, and was thus an appropriate medium for the expression of grief. D. C. Allen notes the absence of color at the beginning of *Lycidas:* "Alone in this autumnal garden the white thorn blooms unseasonably, showing the mourning color, or rather absence of color, for those who die too young."[28] Wayne Shumaker also remarks upon the dullness of the imagery here.[29] For Allen, there is a heightening of color in the flower passage, marking a recovery of confidence in the brightness of the flowers and the energy of the sea: "All is color and motion as the brooding melancholy of the poet is swept away."[30] But this may not be the case. Milton makes a false start toward such an effect, but from the tendency of his rather painful revisions it would seem that grief, not confidence, is the final mood of the flower passage, just as terror and violence, not redeeming energy, are meant by the sounding seas. If this is so, the mood of joy is reserved for the concluding section, which comes then as a revelation, quite without preparation. Since Milton's revisions of the flower passage seem involved mainly with questions of color, we should look more closely at those changes, with a view to their motive.

At the beginning of the passage, concerned to restore the pastoral vein after the attack upon the church, Milton thinks first of flowers in full color: "Bells and Flowrets of a thousand hues," the very ground impurpled. Yet how little of this potential is realized in the flowers Milton finally uses, or the way he describes them. Aside from the glowing violet (Shakespeare's in *The Winter's Tale* was "dim"),[31] color ebbs rapidly out of the list, the effect becoming more and more subdued as Milton works on it. "Sorrow's livery" is changed to "sad escutcheon" in the second draft, but the heraldic touch of "escutcheon," evoking a brighter color than "livery," gives way in turn to the "sad embroidery" which is more in keeping with mourning, and which gets back in effect to "sorrow's livery." The shift from "escutcheon" to "embroidery" involves a change in verb from "bear" to "wear." At the same time there is a change from the indicative mood in "beares" to the subjunctive: "and every flower that sad escutcheon *weare.*" In the indicative ("beares") the reference was backward to colors in the preceding lines, "that" being a relative pronoun. In the subjunctive to which Milton momentarily shifts, "that" is a demonstrative pronoun in a clause with a hortatory verb: that is, "let every flower wear that sad escutcheon." The return, then, to the indicative "weares" gives us back also "that" as a relative pronoun, which is to say that the flowers wearing sad embroidery are those already mentioned, not the two about to be mentioned, the amaranth and the daffodil, whose colors are bright and joyful.[32] Thus what Milton does here is to add, to flowers that are naturally quiet in color, those that are by nature and definition bright, and bid them join the others in a show of grief. Amaranthus, whose name means "unfading," is told to shed its beauty; the yellow daffodil fills its bright cups with tears, calling our attention from visible beauty to emblematic sorrow. That the daffodil was mentioned at all may be due to Spenser, whose lines in the April eclogue are as lively as Milton's are restrained: "Strowe me the ground with Daffadowndillies, / And Cowslips, and Kingcups, and loved Lillies" (40–41). Another point of interest is Milton's change from woodbine to columbine and back. At first thought, the woodbine was given no modifier. It became, perhaps after a glance at Spenser, the columbine, presumably purple as in Spenser. But since "purple" stood already as a verb to introduce the whole passage, it was called simply "garish." Seeing how Spenser was leading him astray into a vividness at odds with his purpose, Milton returned to the woodbine, now more modestly described as "well-attired."

All of Milton's revisions seem to look in this direction. As the soft-hued woodbine wins out over the purple columbine, so the primrose, also a light yellow, is described as "forsaken" rather than merely "unwedded"; the reference to its "coloring the pale cheeke of unenjoyed Love" is taken out; and, perhaps to the same end of playing down the color, the hyacinth which Milton had alluded to earlier in the Camus passage as "that sanguine flower" is also dropped. It may have seemed, finally, too vivid for his ends, with its reference to "woes" written "on the vermeil grain." (Note again, in the elimination of *vermeil*, the tendency to avoid the vermilion reds.) The narcissus is also sacrificed, for what purpose is not clear, unless Milton was ruling out the chance of a bright yellow at this point. It would seem then that Milton worked over the passage very carefully to strengthen its emblematic content, the theme of grief conveyed by the palest of nature's flowers. It is an unusual study of a poet trying to keep his composition in line with a purpose that was changing as he wrote.

Another place where emblematic meanings may be missed or misunderstood is found in Book VIII of *Paradise Lost,* in the conversation between Adam and the angel Raphael. We have seen red as a sign of violence and the wrath of God; but "rosy," red softened by white, is used by Milton as by Virgil to express milder aspects of divinity. The most celebrated instance is that where Raphael responds to Adam's questions about love "with a smile that glow'd / Celestial rosy red, *Love's proper hue*" (VIII, 618–19). To take this reaction as a blush of embarrassment, as is usually done, is mistaken, but it is almost as bad to see a suggestion of hearts or roses or any of our human metaphors for love, since this only produces another sort of bathos. What we are dealing with is not a metaphor but a simple case of color symbolism. In the angelic hierarchy, Raphael is a seraph, a member of that order of angels who stand nearest to God's throne worshipping him through love while the cherubim, who stand next, worship him through knowledge. The cherubim are conventionally represented by blue as the color of truth, the seraphim by red, the color of love.[33] Most of the discourse of Raphael in the central books of the epic is involved with knowledge—the account of Satan's revolt, the creation, and the constitution of the heavens. But it is when Adam brings up his feeling for Eve that Raphael comes to his true purpose, to instruct Adam in the nature of love. Even Raphael's name ("God hath healed," "medicine of God") suggests in Hebrew his connection with that aspect of God's power which shows itself as healing love. Note that Raphael's relation to God through love is matched by his relation to Adam through friendship: he is a "sociable spirit," conversing as "friend with friend." For the Renaissance, love and friendship stood in a peculiarly close relationship, as common manifestations of divine affinity between souls equally bent on union with God.[34] The relation of angel to man thus sets the stage for the more essential one of man to God, which may, though it need not, conflict with his relation to woman. Adam's account in Book VIII of his feeling for Eve reveals the possibility, noted with some concern by Raphael, that human love will not reflect the affinity with God that was intended at creation, but will become instead a simply amorous attachment between two of God's creatures. In that rosy and celestial smile, glowing with "love's proper hue," we have a sign of the love intended by God as the means of man's rise. It should not be confused with the more sentimental earthly love that is to be the cause of his fall.

One other color may be mentioned as having possible emblematic meanings. Milton had a special fondness for both the color and the substance of amber, the yellow-brown resin. Because of its luster, or the mysterious attractive property it has when rubbed, it seemed endowed with supernatural qualities to the Greeks, who took the phenomenon of static electricity as a link between the physical and the spiritual. The evidence for this was found in the presence, supposedly, of amber in the waters of the Eridanus, the river into which Phaethon plunged, infusing it with properties of the sun of which amber was the visible sign.[35] This is why Milton refers to the Choaspes as an "amber stream," "the drink of none but kings," why the River of Bliss in Heaven "Rolls o'er the Elysian Flow'rs her Amber stream." At other times it is light that Milton speaks of as "amber," as when the pale moon passes through an amber cloud in the *Mask* (l. 333). The moon is usually silver, argent, or pale for Diana, silver being the emblem of virginity. Perhaps Milton is thinking here of the "pale" amber which Pliny distinguishes from the tawny in his *Natural History* (XXXVII, xii). When he speaks of Sabrina's "amber-dropping hair," however, he may be thinking of the resin, or of liquid amber, the yellow balsam of the sweet gum, in which case the image is literal, not emblematic; but the vagaries of our topic are such that he may have in mind still a third possibility, namely amber as metal, the alloy of silver and gold which the Greeks called electrum. Such an image would suit the waters of the Severn, with its molten crystal, beryl, and golden ore. One instance of emblematic use may be the throne of sapphire which is inlaid with amber in the chariot of the Son in Book VI of *Paradise Lost*. Milton may have recalled some account like Pliny's of the magic properties of electrum which can, for instance, show the presence of poison by iridescence, or he may have been thinking of Iris, the messenger of the gods, as the daughter of Electra, who symbolized a universal cosmic attraction.[36] In any case, the rainbow itself forms a climax to a description in which the colors of the spectrum join over the paternal chariot, "inlaid with pure / Amber, and colors of the show'ry Arch."[37] Over the whole scene looms the figure of the Son, wearing the stone of Aaron's breastplate, "radiant Urim, work divinely wrought," a mysterious sort of stone which, whatever its nature, was a symbol of truth for the Hebrews.

II

With this we have looked at virtually all of the instances of color symbolism in Milton. Seldom does this symbolism operate like a code on which meanings not otherwise apparent depend. To the implications of red or blue, or white or black, we respond in ways that are primitive, ageless, and universal. The foregoing discussion has been meant to suggest something of the sort, and also to clarify some places where the premises of Milton's time may have differed from our own or those of classical times. There is another virtue in the discussion, perhaps. Having seen the part that convention played in Milton's choice of colors, we are in a better position to judge the role of his own taste, and thus venture some elementary generalizations on style. Before doing so, however, we must make some allowance for still another influence than iconography. Looking at studies of the use of color by one literary period or another, studies that were fashionable in another day,[38] one is reminded that the usages of classical writers or of literary groups or movements like the *Pléiade* or the English Romantic poets reflect in a very visible form their own peculiar practice and sensibility, and may in themselves become an influence on later poets. There is the further question of a physical as opposed to psychological difference in color perception from one era to another. It was thought at one time that the color usage of primitive times shows an earlier stage of physical development in the ability to distinguish hues. The impression may have been based on the fact that distinctions of any degree of fineness are not represented in the vocabulary of primitive peoples. More recent research shows the difference to be more mental than physical in nature, reflecting interest rather than capacity. Savage tribes have been observed to match colors more for vividness than for hue. In such cultures, a term like yellow might be used for colors of a similar degree of saturation, and for tones of orange and green, as against red and blue, colors from the extremes of the spectrum where yellow is not present. Since our concern is with literature, not physiology, we shall limit our discussion to the practices of classical literature as these may have influenced Milton, with occasional instances from other languages.

Greek literature in its earlier stages does not appear to have distinguished blue from green very clearly. In fact, the more one contemplates the colors of Homer and Virgil, the more it seems that we are dealing with the sort of distinction spoken of above, between conditions of light rather than between differing hues. In Homer, for example, blood is not red but black (μέλαν, κελάινον), a practice that Milton imitates in *"sanguine nigro"* (Elegy VI, l. 75). Milton never does give any other color to blood, though once, in a sharp contrast that suggests the difference between earthly and heavenly blood, he speaks of a nectarous humor issuing from the wound of Satan. The same tendency toward nonchromatic color terminology is seen in the case of purple, referring not to color but to effects of lightness, darkness, or iridescence. If the image of the river Adonis running purple to the sea is not a literal reference (blue water plus red blood?) or a borrowing from a source like the *Dictionarium Historicum, Geographicum et Poeticum* of Charles Stephanus, it must mean simply an effect of shading, light or dark. Such a nonchromatic or generalized purple occurs in Homer in the dark snakes writhing like rainbows on the breastplate of Agamemnon (*Iliad* XI, 26–27). Note the additional effect of iridescence here, as perhaps in Milton's description of the wings of Cupid (*PL* IV, 764). The difficulty of registering color references is increased by the tendency to use the same term for light effects of either sort, bright as well as dark. Milton's dawn "purples" the East; his sunset is also "purple and gold" (*PL* VII, 30). In the flowers that "purple all the ground" in *Lycidas*, purple is not, as we have seen, the dominant color in the flowers given. Since Milton was bent on subduing the color effects in the passage, we may take this particular purple as a classical note, suggesting Virgil, for whom the purple narcissus was gleaming rather than purple, and who emphasized in the same way the lustrous qualities of violets.[39] Note in Milton the concentration on sheer intensity in the "glowing violet" of *Lycidas* and in the purple light suffusing the face of Mansus in heaven ("Mansus," 99).

The same problem arises in the handling of blue. More often than not, blue is used by Milton for effects of light and dark, rather than as a color. What is more, both in Milton and in Virgil a term like *caeruleus* covers both the lighter hues of sky and water on one hand and the darker tones of grapes, the leaden hues of turbid water and storm clouds on the other.[40] Such doubleness of usage is complicated further by a tendency in both poets to favor streams like the Tiber and the Thames with terms that are more flattering than descriptive. It may be doubted that either of these muddy bodies was ever as green or blue or silvery as terms like *caeruleus, glaucus* or *argenteus* would suggest, if we took the words as having specific color values. It may be of course that terms like this, referring to water and other shining surfaces, convey an effect not of color but of luster, combined with some implication of light and dark, as Homer uses γλαυκός. At other times we may be misled by the device of the transferred epithet, by which a term that does have chromatic value is applied to things that do not. Thus Proteus is called "cerulean" not because he is green or blue but because he lives in an element that is.[41] Milton's description of the chariot of the river goddess Sabrina as "Thick set with Agate and the azurn sheen / Of Turquoise blue and Emerald green" is probably an elaborate version of the device. The blue-haired deities of *Comus,* indirectly connected with the ocean through their relation to Neptune, are another matter. Hanford explains the detail as a touch from the contemporary masque. But if there was such a connection to explain so picturesque an item, it was probably because someone misread an epithet like κυάνεος, used for the kind of dead-black hair that was characteristic of the Mediterranean. The association of these gods with Neptune shows that Milton's term is a rendering of κυανο-χαίτης, used to describe the hair of Poseidon in Homer, a term given in poetry and in painting as sable, or blue-black.[42]

Milton's blues reflect other usages as well. There is a sense of blue that comes not from the Middle English *blew* but from the Germanic *bla* meaning leaden blue in color: "And from the Boughs brush off the evil dew, / And heal the harms of thwarting thunder blue" (*Arcades,* ll. 50–51). Such a blue gives the effect of lightning, a pale light without the red glare of flame.[43] The usage here suggests, again, that the "red" lightning of *PL* I, 175, mentioned earlier, is to be taken as emblematic, not descriptive. The light of Hell is the same, "pale and dreadful," cast by "livid" flames: again, the colorless quality of "pale," the leaden blue of "livid" (*PL* I, 181–83). In the same way Milton refers to the "furnace blue" around which the infernal dance of Moloch goes on (*Nativity Hymn*, l. 210).

In his occasional use of brown, Milton may be reflecting native English usage. There is no instance in Milton of brown as a color in the real sense. The term almost always means simply "dark," as it does in *Beowulf*. In Old English, the term was used more widely than in modern English for shades of darkness approaching red or black. This use is typical also of Greek and Latin, which, having no special term for brown, combined browns with grays as ὀρφναῖος or *fuscus*. Both sides of this combination would seem to be covered by the "russet lawns" and "fallows gray" of *L'Allegro*, so unrealistic if taken literally. Quite a different sense of brown as "burnished" or "darkly shining" occurs when it refers to metal, as in the field of war "all iron," casting a "gleaming brown" (*PR* III, 326). An Italian usage is felt in phrases like the "shadows brown that Sylvan loves" (*Pens*, l. 134), the "umbrage . . . brown as evening" (*PL* IX, 1088), the "myrtles brown" of *Lycidas*. In this sense the term is a favorite with Milton, from the third Italian sonnet (*al imbrunir di sera*) to the shade that "imbrowns" the noontide bowers of Adam, or the "alleys brown" that offer refuge for meditation—a typically Renaissance thought—to the Savior in *Paradise Regained* (II, 293).

Considering the influence we have seen of emblematic and linguistic convention, it is clear that a poet's handling of color is not an entirely private process. Having made allowance for precedents of this sort, we may proceed to the colors Milton used for their own sake, and to his own ends.

III

We have seen that Milton's taste in color as revealed in the language of the poems is more subdued than splendid, more rich than bright. So much is clear from the present discussion, even without the support of such figures as are given below. Where red does occur (visual, not emblematic), it is usually softened by white or muted toward brown, russet, amber, and the like. D. C. Allen notes that Milton's description of Heaven (*PL* III, 344–71), which seems to contain so many color terms, is actually almost without color: "Those that are here . . . belong to almost the same grade in the spectrum. Gold, the . . . symbol of 'Holy Light,' suffuses the whole scene with shadow variants of amber, jasper yellow or brown. . . ."[44] Miss Pratt likewise mentions a tendency to work with "glooms and glories," ranging from dark to radiant white rather than through specific colors. She finds this true especially of the later poems, the use of color being four times as lavish before 1654, a difference she lays to the exuberance of youth and the pastoral nature of Milton's early subjects.[45] Considering the pastoral nature of *Paradise Lost,* it would seem that the difference must be laid not to a change in subject but to a development of taste, as Milton's style moved in the direction of the baroque.[46]

At this point we might look at the statistics of Milton's color terminology. Table 1 indicates color words as they occur in the poetry, with equivalent terms listed under each in the order of descending frequency.

TABLE 1

MILTON'S COLOR USAGE

White	48	Black	48	Yellow	39	Green	38	Red	28
pale	17	*black*	23	gold(en)	29	*green*	31	rosy, roseate	7
white	12	dusky	10	amber	4	verdant	7	(en)sanguine(d)	3
silver	7	sable	5	*yellow*	3			*red*	3
hoar	5	dun	2	tawny	2			ruby, rubied	3
wan	4	ebon	2	sallow	1			blushing	2
argent	1	sooty	2					carnation	2
blanc	1	swart	2					(en)vermeil(ed)	2
pearl	1	jet	1					ruddy	2
		smutty	1					carbuncle	1
								cloudy red	1
								fiery red	1
								rosy red	1

Blue	16	Purple	14	Gray	14	Brown	11	Orange	1
blue	8	*purple*	12	*gray*	14	*brown*	6	saffron	1
azure	5	grain	1			brinded	2	(*orange*)	0
sapphire	2	impurpled	1			imbrowned	1		
sky-tinctured	1					russet	1		
						tanned	1		

Even so simple a tabulation presents its difficulties.[47] In these figures, no allowance is made for usage that is emblematic rather than literal, nor for the classical blues and purples that stand for conditions of light and dark rather than color—adjustments which would reduce further the concentrations under red, blue, and purple. Again, the larger groupings given here are at best rough. Tawny and sallow, which are included under yellows, might be thought closer to brown and gray. Even single terms can present so many problems that it is all but impossible to arrive at a true count. For example, twenty-nine "golds" are listed. The real total is an even hundred, yet only about one-fourth of these are actually involved with color, the others referring to money or to metal. The same situation obtains for green, though here the use of the word as a noun for "lawn" has not been discounted, since the difference is one of syntax rather than meaning. Even where figures can be arrived at there is the matter of interpreting them, and of deciding then how far they can be trusted as an index of the use or avoidance of a color for discernible reasons. What is normal frequency of use for any color, granting the variables of subject matter and setting? In Herrick, for instance, the classic tone and urban setting give occasions which scarcely occur in Milton's more pastoral atmosphere for the use of red for costume and complexion. The frequencies for red (six in Milton, seventeen in Herrick) would be meaningful only in relation to a norm, lacking which one wonders whether Milton simply had less occasion for the color, or whether he avoided it for certain emblematic associations with monarchy and Catholicism, or perhaps on grounds of taste. We have noted that scarlet, a color used as a badge of office in church and court, does not occur in Milton, although *Paradise Lost* is full of symbols for royalty. Other objections to scarlet could be found besides its connection with Rome. We have seen that as a color combining red and yellow, it takes on unfavorable meanings, as mixed colors are likely to do.[48] Since the only visible evidence is statistical and negative, we will not argue whether one with less bias against Rome or the Stuarts than Milton had would have used scarlet or red more often. We may settle for two generalizations of a larger sort which table 1 substantiates rather clearly: not only do the more vivid colors, the reds, blues, and purples occur less often than the colors of the middle spectrum—the yellows (or golds, rather) and the greens; but even more significantly the spectrum colors themselves yield to whites and blacks, which stand in even balance well at the top of the list. The simple fact of this subordination of chromatic effect to effects of light and shade is striking enough on the face of it; but it is even more extreme than the figures themselves suggest. Elimination from the table of emblematic or achromatic use of color words would take away more cases from the ends of the spectrum and shift the weight even more heavily toward the middle—would, in fact, take these instances out of the color range entirely into effects of light and shade. In this connection, note the relatively large number of grays and browns, colors that are largely or wholly achromatic, as opposed to the one case of saffron under orange.[49] Note too that the whites and blacks listed do not include the large number of terms primarily concerned not with hue but with the presence or absence of light. *Dark,* for instance, occurs over sixty times, forms of *shade* another hundred or so. On the other side, *light* and *bright,* not to count their endless variants, are even more numerous. Finally, the balance we have noted between effects of light and dark, as between tones of white and black, is still further supported by a balancing out of terms for texture and mood: words like *dim, sober, lowering, gloomy, dismal, sullen,* as opposed to *snowy, milky, alabaster,* and the like. Having noted this equilibrium, and the moral equation it represents, and emphasizing again how heavily Milton's interest in light outweighs his interest in color, let us go on to see what this may tell us about Milton as man and artist, rather than as moral agent and handler of emblems.

There is also, of course, a physical side to Milton's treatment of light and dark. Although opinion differs on the relation of Milton's color usage to his blindness, and although we are concerned here with stylistic preferences rather than physical limitations, one must still see the subjective implications of a blind poet handling the ancient associations of darkness with ignorance and evil, so that something of Milton's own personal darkness is felt in things like the "dark and dreary vales of Hell," the sun "in dim Eclipse" shedding disastrous twilight. On the other side is the paradox of physical blindness as the inverse of spiritual illumination: "So much the rather thou Celestial light / Shine inward." Even in the earlier verse there is this equation of darkness and insight in the poet who, as much from a meditative bent perhaps as from photophobia, felt the lack of shade at Cambridge, or shrank from the light of a spring morning (Elegies I and VII), or equated a "dim" with a "religious" light in *Il Penseroso.* Although the physiological aspects of Milton's vision are not in question, there are things about his handling of color that might prompt the suspicion, at least, that he may have been color blind. If there is actually in Milton the limitation in response to red which we have suggested above, it could be attributed as well to a deficiency in color perception as to factors of taste and emblematic meaning—as could the peculiar sensitivity to the middle frequencies which accompanies color blindness at either end of the spectrum. Note too that although Milton brought home boxes of Italian music from the Continent, there is no evidence of any such response to Renaissance painters, who made such brilliant use of color. Perhaps he was simply more musician than artist, but a deficiency of the kind in question, or simple nearsightedness, would have impaired his appreciation of the stanzas of Raphael or the ceiling paintings of Michelangelo. One thinks, at this point, how much of the resonance of the poetry depends on the music of language, the rich auditory quality of words for colors that are generally subdued in themselves, like gold,[50] tawny, amber, alabaster, *smaragdis*. In giving an image of the waters about Heaven's gates, Milton calls them first a "bright Sea of Jasper" (*PL* III, 518–19). The detail may be realistic, since jasper is green in the Bible; yet in classical terms it might be yellow, brown, or red. Perhaps it is the sound and texture of jasper as word and substance that appealed to him. In any case, he changes the image in the same line, perhaps to avoid conflicting suggestions of color, perhaps to idealize the setting even further: "or of liquid Pearl." Later, the heavenly waters become still more translucent in the "clear Hyaline" or "glassy sea" of *PL* VII, 619. One suspects that Milton is enjoying this inventory of possible materials. In his preference finally for clarity and translucence over color we see a note more and more characteristic of Milton's poetry. When tied to its complement, a preoccupation with shadow, it strongly suggests an aspect of the baroque style or, to use Wölfflin's term, "painterly."

It is a common error to confuse "painterly" and "colourful." Our analysis of the painterly style shows that variety of colour was quite unnecessary to it. Indeed Rembrandt, the greatest master of the painterly, preferred the medium of the etching, a technique that works only with variations of light and dark. If colour, therefore, was a useful additional element to increase the atmospheric quality, it was not an essential component of the painterly style.[51]

The relevance of this is obvious. Milton showed his temperament as an artist as clearly in matters of texture and light as in managing the elements of mass, space, or movement usually emphasized in discussions of the baroque style.

Milton's choice of a subject in his epic clearly supports the tendencies we are speaking of, if indeed the choice was not to some degree conditioned by them. He is least at home in Heaven where all is light; much more in hell where it is mostly dark, and most of all in Eden with its evenly apportioned light and dark. It may not be the doctrine that puts us off in Book III so much as our impression that poetically Milton responds so little to the celestial scene. Such details as are given are seen in a monotony of light relieved by periods of arbitrary darkness. Milton's art expands in the more congenial atmosphere of Hell. He is fascinated, for example, by the flames that, as Satan rises from the burning lake, "Driv'n backward slope thir pointing spires, and roll'd / In Billows, leave i'th' midst a horrid Vale" (*PL* I, 223–24). The light is put in a form that Milton can feel. Tangible things like the lake and the burning plain assail one so sharply through the other senses that one begins to wonder if noise, heat, and odor are being used as a substitute for seeing, as in the simile of Aetna

> whose combustible
> And fuell'd entrails thence conceiving Fire,
> Sublim'd with Mineral fury, aid the Winds,
> And leave a singed bottom all involv'd
> With stench and smoke.   (*PL* I, 233–37)

It is in Eden, of course, that these opposite effects of light unexpectedly set off with shadow and dark fitfully relieved with light are held in balance. There is not only the succession of day and night in natural cycle, but a simultaneous juxtaposition of sun and shade:

> Another side, umbrageous Grots and Caves
> Of cool recess, o'er which the mantling Vine
> Lays forth her purple Grape, and gently creeps
> Luxuriant.   (*PL* IV, 257–60)

As early as the fifth Elegy, Milton could see in a grotto the favored haunt of a poet: "*Perque umbras, perque antra feror, penetralia vatum.*" Yet for all that has been said of Milton's deficiency of visual imagination, and for all his fondness for complex form and dim lighting, specific detail is still visible in his description of the bower, where we can make out every one of the flowers: "Iris, all hues, Roses, Jessamin / Rear'd high thir flourisht heads between." Not only is there a mosaic here of violet, crocus, hyacinth broidering the ground, "more color'd than with stone / Of costliest Emblem," but there is a literal complexity or weaving in of detail that is missing in the flower passage of *Lycidas,* where the flowers were separately laid on, with a reduction of hue ascribed in that instance to symbolic intent rather than to stylistic preference.

As for color in the Eden passage, note that it is given only as a general impression, not at all specialized in effect, "all hues." It is here that we see the difference between Milton's earlier style insofar as it favored color, line, and form, and his later manner involving light and dark, mass and movement. Compare for instance the picture of Sabrina in the *Mask,* with her weightless, smoothly sliding, richly colored vehicle, "Thick set with Agate and the azurn sheen / Of Turquoise blue and Em'rald green" (ll. 893–94), and that of Satan in Book VI of *Paradise Lost,* the huge form "high exalted" in a rushing chariot accompanied by a single visual impression of sunlight, flames, and gold. Though such a picture lacks the relieving shadows Milton normally favors, there is still the painterly obscuring of edges in that "narrow space" in which Satan dismounts, "before a cloudy Van, / *On the rough edge of battle ere it join'd*" (*PL* VI, 107–08). Still more impressive in this genre is the description of the Son's own chariot, with its precious stones inlaid, its whirlwind sound, its involved structure of wheel within wheel and, most characteristic of all at this period, the interplay of light and dark in rapid motion, "Flashing thick flames . . . careering Fires between" (*PL* VI, 751 ff.). We become aware in such an image how much of Milton's symbolism depends on a richness of context that loses much of its validity in analysis. We can see that it is not simply the "red" of fire that represented God's power to Moses on Mt. Sinai in the instance noted earlier from the *Nativity Hymn.* Really to get Milton's emblem we must add the "horrid clang" and "smold'ring clouds" that accompany that red fire in Milton's full and richly sensuous image. Inevitably, then, when Milton is being most himself, the simple polarities of the emblematic method dissolve in the complexities of a more painterly aesthetic, in which events of Heaven or Hell can be portrayed with a common means. The first blast of Satan's artillery, for instance, is thus described: "Immediate in a flame, / But soon obscur'd with smoke, all Heav'n appear'd" (VI,

584–85). The same details served earlier to convey the anger of God, at the beginning of the war in Heaven:

> So spake the Sovran voice, and Clouds began
> To darken all the Hill, and smoke to roll
> In dusky wreaths, reluctant flames, the sign
> Of wrath awak't.   (*PL* VI, 56–59)

Leaving iconography to one side, what unites effects of such differing contexts is the underlying consistency of taste. It would appear that — light confounded in this way with darkness is virtually an emblem for Milton's mature style.

University of Massachusetts

NOTES

1. W. Flemming, *Der Wandel des deutschen Naturgefühls vom 15 bis zum 18 Jahrhundert* (Halle, 1931), VIII, in S. Skard, "The Use of Color in Literature: A Survey of Research," *Proceedings of the American Philosophical Society,* XC, no. 3 (July 1946), 178.

2. D. C. Allen, "Symbolic Color in the Literature of the English Renaissance," *PQ,* XV, no. 1 (Jan. 1936), 89.

3. F. Edward Hulme, *Symbolism in Christian Art* (London, 1891), p. 27.

4. The text of Milton's poetry cited throughout is *John Milton: Complete Poems and Major Prose,* ed. Merritt Y. Hughes (New York, 1957).

5. Especially since the image of power is masculine here. Cf. Herbert A. Kenyon, "Color in Talisman and Charm," *Papers of the Michigan Academy of Science, Arts and Letters,* XVI (1931), 70. See also Kenyon's "The Protective Power of Red," ibid., V (1925), 34–35.

6. Cf. Nahum ii, 3: "The shield of his mighty men is made red, the valiant men are in scarlet." In Isaiah lxiii, 2, red symbolizes divine anger: "Wherefore art thou red in thy apparel, and thy garments like him that treadeth in the winefat?" This use is echoed perhaps in *PL* II, 172–74, in the reference to God's "red right hand" as an instrument of vengeance.

7. For the conventional meanings of color in liturgy and in social custom, see M. Channing Linthicum, *Costume in the Drama of Shakespeare and His Contemporaries* (Oxford, 1936), p. 25.

8. Since neither blue nor black was very effective as a dye in ancient times, mourning garments were actually more apt to be described as dark than black. Thus the blue mantle may be simply a version of the *toga pulla,* or dark gray mourning robe of the Romans. Homer uses κυάνεος (dark or dark blue) just once for a garment, in describing the mourning veil of Thetis (Florence Elizabeth Wallace, *Color in Homer and in Ancient Art,* Smith College Classical Studies, vol. 9 [Northampton, Dec. 1927], p. 11). Virgil's description of the funeral rites of Polydorus may show a Roman use of blue, tinged perhaps with violet (*Aeneid,* III, 64).

See Georges Lanoë-Villène, *Le Livre des Symboles: Dietionnaire de symbolique et de mythologie,* 2nd ed. (Paris, 1935), II, 133–34.

9. George Ferguson, *Signs and Symbols in Christian Art* (New York, 1954), p. 272.

10. Lanoë-Villène, *Le Livre des Symboles,* I, 127–28.

11. Cf. Cesare Ripa, *Iconologie ou la Science des Emblemes, devises, etc.* (Amsterdam, 1698), p. 76, and Lanoë-Villène, *Le Livre des Symboles,* V, 115 and 130.

12. The odium attached to the yellow-reds is noted by Linthicum, *Costume,* p. 37. Cf. Paull F. Baum, "Judas' Red Hair," *JEGP,* XXI (1922), 524. Yellow itself, however, seems to have been favorably viewed in ancient times. Herman Gauger sees the fondness of Virgil and Horace for yellow as typical of their age (*Optische und akustische Sinnesdaten in den Dichtungen des Vergil und Horaz* [Stuttgart, 1932], p. 20).

13. As in Pliny, *Natural History,* XXI, viii. Cf. Linthicum, *Costume,* p. 42.

14. Linthicum, *Costume,* p. 15. Cf. the "First Fruits, the green Ear, and the yellow Sheaf," *PL* XI, 435. Linthicum notes straw, the harvest color, as the color of abundance (ibid., pp. 20 and 45). In Alciati, *flavus* is given as *color cupidinis* (*Emblematum Flumen Abundans* [London, 1871; facsimile reprint of Lyons ed., 1551], p. 128).

15. Lanoë-Villène, *Le Livre des Symboles,* V, 153–54 and 102.

16. Ibid., I, 128.

17. It is the same taste that in the Renaissance led to the use of gold in place of white in representations of the Father. Note that the gifts offered to Phoebus in "Mansus" were specifically the golden grain, yellow apples, and saffron crocus (ll. 39–40).

18. Lanoë-Villène, *Le Livre des Symboles,* IV, 184–85. As for Milton's fruit, the fact that Eve offers Adam a bough of fairest fruit "that downy smiled" might suggest the peach, as would the color, a mixture of yellow and red. But "downy" may be an echo of Virgil's "fruit with tender down"—*tenera lanugine mala*—and Virgil is referring to the quince. A. von der Heide takes "downy" as a softening epithet for "gold" (*Das Naturgefühl in der englischen Dichtung im Zeitalter Miltons,* Anglistische Forschungen, vol. 45 [Heidelberg, 1915], p. 8).

19. There is an early occurrence of the apple, or some choice fruit, as an instrument of temptation in Milton's early school exercise *Apologus de Rustico et Hero.* It is not described, other than as *sapidissima poma.*

20. Rosemary Freeman, *English Emblem Books* (London, 1948), p. 74.

21. It is possible too that an audience trained in emblem lore might see, in Milton's later description of the serpent's neck as "burnisht, verdant Gold" (*PL* IX, 501), the negative attitude of iconography toward colors that are mixed or shifting, or its prejudice against iridescence. See Ripa, *Iconologie,* the notations for "Flatterie," p. 91; "Inconstance," pp. 115–16; "Rumeur, ou Discorde," p. 222.

22. William E. Mead, "Color in Old English Poetry," *PMLA,* XIV (1899), 174. Mead notes that *beorht* and other terms for light occur over eight hundred times, black and its variants between four and five hundred times. The one instance of "blue" in Old English poetry may, he suggests, mean simply "dark."

23. *The Waning of the Middle Ages* (New York, 1954), p. 205.

24. Just as redeemed souls and Christ after the Resurrection are clothed in white (cf. Hulme, *Symbolism,* p. 16; Linthicum, *Costume,* p. 16).

25. That gray may share some of the favorable associations of white is further suggested by the use of a gray nimbus for Christ in the mosaics in S. Apollinaire Nuovo in Ravenna (ca. A.D. 500) noted by C. R. Morey in *Early Christian Art* (Princeton, 1942), p. 160. Compare the tradition of a black nimbus for Judas (Hulme, *Symbolism*, p. 28).

26. "*Fluctu spumabant caerula cano*," a detail from the shield of Aeneas. "Milky" in *Paradise Lost* may possibly be connected with *niveus*, "snowy," but this term, which Virgil uses to suggest both the coolness and shining clearness of streams, seems not only too cold, but topographically wrong for the center of Eden. "Silver" would be a better choice for swiftness without disturbance. Milton uses it for lakes and rivers (*PL* VII, 437) and to suggest the "glassy cool translucence" of the Severn (*Comus*, l. 865), Sabrina, "virgin pure," being the "goddess of the *silver* lake." For the emblematic meaning of silver as purity, virginity, see Linthicum, *Costume*, p. 17. Cf. also *argenteus Thamesis*, the silver Thames with "pure urns" in "Mansus," l. 32.

27. Maud Bodkin, *Archetypal Patterns in Poetry* (New York, 1958), pp. 105–06.

28. *The Harmonious Vision* (Baltimore, 1954), p. 65.

29. "Flowerets and Sounding Seas: A Study in the Affective Structure of *Lycidas*," *PMLA*, LXVI (1951), 488.

30. Allen, *Harmonious Vision*, p. 68.

31. The subdued quality of Milton's catalogue is best seen by putting it alongside Shakespeare's, whose bolder daffodils "come before the swallow dares," and "take the winds of March with beauty" (*The Winter's Tale*, IV, iv, 118–20). Actually, many of Shakespeare's flowers seem to have been chosen for the potency of their savor rather than for their color. Note the concentration on the mints: "Hot lavender, mints, savory, marjoram" (l. 104).

32. For this reason the use of a colon instead of a period after "wear," as in most texts, seems wrong. Note that in the manuscript the next line began, originally, with a capital.

33. Anna Jameson, *Sacred and Legendary Art* (Boston and New York, 1897), p. 42. Cf. Harold Bayley, *The Lost Language of Symbolism* (London, 1912), p. 151.

34. E. L. Marilla, "Milton on Conjugal Love Among the Angels," *MLN*, LXVIII (1953), 485.

35. The legend is one of those "Greek vanities" that Pliny rejects in *Natural History* XXXVII, xi. Pliny gives all one could wish to know about amber, its varieties, origins, and properties, in this and the following sections of that work.

36. Lanoë-Villène, *Le Livre des Symboles*, I, 87–88.

37. The contrast between this jewelled Chariot of God and Satan's artillery, "Brass, Iron, Stony mould" (*PL* VI, 576), is in itself a significant bit of symbolism.

38. Besides the work of Miss Wallace cited above, see Alice Kober, "The Use of Color Terms in the Greek Poets" (Ph.D. diss., Columbia University, 1932), and "Some Remarks on Color in Greek Poetry," *CW*, XXVII (1934), 189–91; Thomas R. Price, "The Color-System of Vergil," *AJP*, IV (1883), 1–20; S. L. Levengood, *The Use of Color in the Verse of the Pléiade* (Paris, 1927); Alice Edwards Pratt, *The Use of Color in the Verse of the English Romantic Poets* (Chicago, 1898).

39. *Violae sublucet purpura nigrae* (*Georgics*, IV, 275). Thomas Price

translates this in terms that reduce the color value of *sublucet:* "The purple of the black violet *tones down* its color" ("Color-System of Vergil," p. 20). The difference in intensity reflects the variation in the Greek uses of purple, πορφύρεος being used to suggest both high and low brilliance, as well as the color itself. Price thought Virgil's sense of color did not register violet at all, and that in general it worked best in the middle of the spectrum (pp. 17–20), an observation that is interesting in view of a like tendency in Milton to be remarked below.

40. There may be uncertainty on both scores, as to both color and light. We may thus, for instance, see Charon's barge (*caeruleam puppim*) as "pale" (lurid) for the deficiency of color, or "dark" (livid) for the lack of light (*Aeneid,* VI, 410). Compare also the *vada livida* of the Styx (*Aeneid,* VI, 320) and Milton's *liventi morte* ("Mansus," l. 89).

41. Parallels in Milton may be *caeruleam Dorida* and *virides Deos* in Elegy IV, ll. 6–7; the *caerula mater,* or blue mother ocean, of Elegy V, l. 82. Kenyon, in "Color in Talisman and Charm," notes a concentration on blue as a talismanic color in the Mediterranean area, the association of blue with the sea being suggested in the *caeruleae vittae* of sacrifices to the sea deities (pp. 70–71).

42. Wallace, *Color in Homer,* p. 20. On the other hand, while Miss Kober notes πορφύρεος used of hair with this same meaning, she sees κυάνεος as possibly blue in the case of sea deities, as in the Roman use of *viridis.* See "The Use of Color Terms," p. 70, and "Some Remarks on Color," p. 189. Horace has *"viridis nereidum coma."* Poseidon is κυανοχαίτης in Lucian ("On Sacrifices," XI). Arion has a mane of this controversial "blue" in Pausanias (Lanoë-Villène, *Le Livre des Symboles,* II, 134).

43. In Milton's Latin poems *caeruleus* is used of lightning with apparently this meaning: *"caeruleae flammae"* (*In Quintum Novembris,* l. 24); and possibly in *"Naturam non Pati Senum,"* it may be used similarly of the moon, unless it means merely "heavenly" (l. 50).

44. *Harmonious Vision,* p. 98.

45. "The Use of Color Terms," p. 11. Although Eleanor Brown finds the color in *PR* and *PL* tending toward effects of golden and black, she finds no connection with Milton's loss of sight, the limitation in color tones being just as evident for her in the earlier poetry (*Milton's Blindness* [New York, 1934], pp. 134–35).

46. A tendency of maturing taste to shift from red to blue is noted by Gauger, *Optische und akustische Sinnesdaten,* p. 12.

47. These statistics are based on the concordance of Bradshaw, and agree roughly with those offered by Miss Pratt, *The Use of Color,* p. 116. Discrepancies are due to the factors mentioned.

48. As the color of betrayal, for instance, it is linked with Judas (Baum, "Judas' Red Hair," p. 520).

49. Along with the figures for Milton's English poetry, it might be of interest to give a similar listing for the Latin poems, a body of verse almost as substantial as the poems in English in the 1645 volume. The usual difficulties are increased by the problem of equating Latin with English terms, but the following summary is roughly accurate. Of some 80 uses, the reds number 6, purples 8, yellows and golds 29, greens 3, blues 6. In the nonchromatic range: grays 2, blacks 13, whites 12. These figures are much the same as for the English verse, with fewer instances at the ends of the spectrum, a concentration toward the

middle heavily reinforced by gold, and a strong representation of black and whites in even balance.

50. That gold supplies an aural as well as visual richness is clear from the way Milton almost invariably places it at the line ends (33 times) or before a caesura (12 times). In the six cases where Milton does not use gold in this way, he tends to use it with a deprecatory tone as mere money (*PR* II, 422–25).

51. Heinrich Wölfflin, *Renaissance and Baroque,* tr. Kathrin Simon (Ithaca, N.Y., 1967), pp. 34–35.

TASSO'S *IL MONDO CREATO:*
PROVIDENCE AND
THE CREATED UNIVERSE

Albert R. Cirillo

Torquato Tasso's *Il Mondo Creato* is a theological-contemplative poem which attempts to look at the created world as a way of picturing the synthesis of earth and heaven described by Raphael in Milton's *Paradise Lost* (VII, 154–61). It is a meditation on the function of the created universe in the providential scheme. The central character of the poem is the human soul for whom God's creation is the ladder by which it returns to eternity. The light which infuses and illuminates all being—and which attracts the soul—is inherent in creation and leads the soul to God. This view of the world—that light, by infusing creation, leads man to God—is similar to Milton's in *Paradise Lost,* as articulated in Raphael's description of the scale of created nature "whereon / In contemplation of created things / By steps we may ascend to God" (V, 510–12).

I N G E N E R A L , Christian thought of the Renaissance clung to the view, inherited from the Augustinian Middle Ages with Neoplatonic colorings, that the created world was a step on the journey back to the heavenly city; that the world itself, properly viewed, was an object which could help to guide us "home." Man was to carry on his moral pilgrimage to heaven through the created world given him by God. John Milton's view of the final end of creation, revealed in *Paradise Lost* (especially in V, 469–512),[1] conforms to this traditional one which regarded the world as man's means of returning to his creator.[2] As Raphael tells Adam, when he repeats God's words after the fall of Satan, man's final end was to be achieved in terms of a synthesis between the created world in which he was placed and the eternal world from which he came (*PL* VII, 150–61). Raphael is explicit in describing this process as an ascent by which one becomes the other, and his words are the Father's:

> and in a moment will create
> Another World, out of one man a Race
> Of men innumerable, there to dwell,
> Not here, till by degrees of merit rais'd
> They open to themselves at length the way
> Up hither, under long obedience tri'd,
> *And Earth be chang'd to Heav'n, and Heav'n to Earth,*
> *One Kingdom, Joy and Union without end.*
>
> (VII, 154–61; my italics)

When the Fall made it impossible for man to achieve this synthesis or ascent without further divine aid, the Divine descended and became part of creation. In this way God himself bridged the gap, bringing heaven to earth that man might bring earth to heaven.

The poem which, perhaps, best illustrates the kind of contemplative synthesis which Raphael describes is Torquato Tasso's understandably neglected hexaemeral work, *Le Sette Giornate del Mondo Creato,* or *Il Mondo Creato,* a theological-contemplative poem which attempts to look at the created world as a way of picturing the synthesis of earth and heaven, mentioned in Raphael's account above, and of showing man's moral ascent, by means of this synthesis, back to his place with God.[3] In spite of its essential unimportance as literature the poem does deal with certain themes and concepts of significance in *Paradise Lost;* and it deals with them in a way that helps us to understand one of the basic issues in Milton's poem: the ultimate purpose of the created universe in the providential scheme. This essay is not an attempt to demonstrate any possible influence— stylistic or conceptual—of Tasso's poem on Milton's; rather, it is an attempt to understand one aspect of the English poem more fully in the perspective of the Italian work by a poet of considerable reputation in Milton's day, one whom Milton himself placed next to Homer and Virgil in the epic tradition.[4]

One of the foremost Tasso scholars of our day, Giovanni Getto, defines the nature of *Il Mondo Creato* succinctly: "More than the poem of the creation of the world, this is the poem, as the title suggests, of the created world. The ideal and poetic subject is, briefly, not really that religious one of God creator of the world but, on the contrary, that profane one of the world contemplated in its aspects and in its forms."[5] This is the theme which Tasso—in spite of many lengthy involutions—manages with considerable skill; and a good deal of the skill by which he maintains this perspective is due to the infusion of a prophetic tone throughout the poem. Tasso works within the framework of an account that represents the inspired atemporal view of God speaking through the *persona* of a divine writer who exists in time but whose sight and inspiration transcend it. The point of view in the poem is a similitude of God's own omniscient view, a technique which places it clearly in the genre of prophetic poems of which *Paradise Lost* is the greatest exemplar.

The poem follows the biblical account of God's creation of the world in six days followed by a day of rest. According to a long tradition the seventh day is the present, and it will last until Christ ushers in the eighth day with the final judgment at the end of time.[6] We must conceive of Tasso as *persona*, writing from the vantage point of the extended present which is the seventh day. His initial implication of divine inspiration becomes a keynote of this view. The parallel is equally striking from a personal standpoint, for this is a poem written in the twilight of Tasso's years when his thoughts were turning to the illumination of the end of his own spiritual pilgrimage. This, too, is one aspect of the consciousness of light which permeates the poem from the very beginning.

In the long epic and creedlike invocation to the Trinity which opens the First Day, we are in the presence of the essential light that emanates from God and is infused throughout creation. This infusion of light is a parallel to the inspiration of the sacred author who sang of creation:

> Padre del Cielo, e tu del Padre eterno
> Eterno Figlio, e non creata prole,
> De l 'immutabil mente unico parto:
> Divina imago, al tuo divino essempio
> Equale; e lume pur di lume ardente;
> E tu, che d'ambo spiri, e d'ambo splendi,
> O di gemina luce acceso Spirto,
> Che sei pur sacro lume, e sacra fiamma,
> Quasi lucido rivo in chiaro fonte,
> E vera imago ancor di vera imago,

In cui se stessa il primo essempio agguaglia,
(Se dir conviensi) e triplicato Sole,
Che l'alme accendi, e i puri ingegni illustri;
Santo don, santo messo, e santo nodo,
Che tre Sante Persone in un congiungi,
Dio non solingo, in cui s'aduna il tutto,
Che 'n varie parti poi si scema, e sparge:
Termine d'infinito alto consiglio,
E de l'ordine suo Divino Amore;
Tu dal Padre, e dal Figlio in me discendi,
E nel mio core alberga, e quinci e quindi
Porta la grazie, e inspira i sensi e i carmi.   (I, 1–22)

[Father of Heaven, and you, of the eternal Father, Eternal Son, and un-created offspring; sole fruit of the immutable mind; divine image like unto your divine model; light also of burning light; and you, who breathe and shine from both, enflamed Spirit of the double splendor, who are also a sacred light and a holy flame, like a shining stream in a clear fountain; true image of true image with which the first pattern compares (if it must be said), and triple Sun who enflames souls and illuminates the simple abilities; holy gift, holy messenger, and holy knot which joins three Divine Persons in one; unsolitary God in whom is gathered everything which then is diminished and disseminated in various parts; boundary of the infinite high wisdom, and of the order of his Divine Love; from the Father and from the Son descend unto me and lodge in my heart, and from one and from the other bring grace and inspire my senses and my songs.][7]

The invocation of the Holy Spirit to descend and lodge in the breast, in terms of light, keynotes the poem with the concept of a descent which implies an ascent. The Holy Spirit descends and lodges within the poet that it may elevate his spirit to dwell in the divine light.[8] With this, the image of a movement from darkness to light becomes the vehicle for the meaning of the poem. Tasso has provided us with the unitive theme of the poem—the light which, in one manifestation, is the inspirational flame of the Holy Spirit is also the contemplative light by which man returns to God. This theme is underlined by the use of the world *alberga* which recurs, in its various forms, with regularity throughout, and is one of the closing notes of the entire poem. The light that is infused through the Holy Spirit is the interior vision by which the poet sees, the same light which illuminates Chaos.

On the first day the poet sings, in epic fashion, of the eternal mover and of the creation of light. The theme of the entire poem is announced:

> Perch'io canti quel primo alto lavoro,
> Ch'è da voi fatto, e fuor di voi risplende
> Maraviglioso, e 'l magistero adorno
> Di questo allor da voi creato mondo,
> In sei giorni distinto.   (I, 23–27)

[Because I sing that first high work which is done by you and which shines marvelously from you, and the majestic workmanship of this world then created by you in six days.]

Coincident with this light which returns to God is the original cosmic harmony which is expressed in the traditional metaphor of the musical instrument on which God plays His cosmic tune. God is the hand while the poet is the instrument through which He plays His song. The poet is the inspired Moses of the Pentateuch singing of the creation:

> Signor, tu sei la mano, io son la cetra,
> La qual, mossa da te, con dolci tempre
> Di soave armonia, risuona, e molce
> D'adamantino smalto i duri affetti.
> Signor, tu sei lo spirto, io roca tromba
> Son per me stesso a la tua gloria, e langue,
> Se non m'inspiri tu, la voce e 'l suono.   (I, 63–69)

[Lord, you are the hand, I am the lyre which, strummed by you, with mild dispositions of sweet harmony, echoes and soothes of its hard glaze the painful affections. Lord, you are the spirit; by myself I am a hoarse trumpet to your glory and languish if you do not inspire me, my voice, and my music.]

Tasso, the poet, is God's instrument. In his function as divine poet lies his likeness to the creative act which he celebrates; he is the instrument through which God works to write His cosmic theme; but this particular poet-*persona* is, in a sense, Moses, the poet of creation who was for Milton "That Shepherd, who first taught the chosen Seed, / In the Beginning how the Heav'ns and Earth / Rose out of Chaos" (*PL* I, 8–10).

Tasso begins his formal account of the first day with an allusion to the state of things before creation ("Pria che facesse Dio la terra e 'l cielo" [Before God made the earth and heaven]—l. 78), and a digression to defend belief in one God rather than in many gods. This involves an explanation of the Trinity and its operations. Following his Catholic doctrine, Tasso, however, unlike Milton, makes Father, Son, and Holy Spirit coeternal in the internal divine plan for creation:

Nè solitario in un silenzio eterno
In tenebre viveasi il sommo Padre,
Ma col suo Figlio, e col divin suo Spirto
In se medesmo avea la sede, e 'l regno,
De' suoi pensati mondi alto Monarca:
Perch'opra fu il pensier divina, interna.   (I, 81–86)

[Not solitary in an eternal silence in darkness lives the high Father, but
with His Son and with His Holy Spirit in Himself has the seat and the
kingdom of His pure thoughts, the high sovereign: because the divine
work was His thought, internal.]

In a statement of the difficulty of making the human intellect understand the workings of God, the poet uses an argument similar to that
of Milton's Raphael (*PL* VIII, 112–18):

Ma narrar non si può, nè 'n spazio angusto
Cape de l'intelletto umano e tardo,
Come 'n se stesso, e di se stesso il verbo
Generasse ab eterno.   (I, 90–93)

[But it is not possible to relate, nor in narrow space to be contained by
the slow human intellect, how in itself and of itself the Word generated
from eternity.]

For Tasso the purpose of creation is the extension of God's goodness and glory through the Divine Wisdom. Here he again approaches
his unifying poetic theme—the chain of being, the material world
harmony infused with divine light, by which man returns on his
pilgrimage to God.[9] In language poetically concrete and Neoplatonic
in tone, Tasso stresses the theme already prefigured in the invocation:
God is a clear fountain, a sun from which emanate rays of goodness.

È buono Iddio, tranquillo e chiaro fonte,
Anzi mar di bontà profondo e largo,
Che per invidia non si scema, o turba.
Ma quel, ch'è buono, e 'n sè perfetto a pieno,
La sua bontate altrui comparte e versa.
Dunque Ei, di sua bontè fecondo e colmo,
La sparse, quasi un mar, che l'onde sparge;
La spiegò come un sol che spiega i raggi,
E volere e natura in un congiunse.   (I, 161–69)

[God is good, a peaceful and a clear fountain; much more, a deep and
broad sea of goodness which is not diminished or disturbed by envy. But
that which is good and in itself perfect in fullness distributes and pours

out its bountifulness to others. Then He, of His fruitful and full goodness, spread it like a sea that scatters the wave. He unfolded it like a sun that unfolds its rays, and (His) will and nature joined into one.]

In the eternal circle that leads to the seventh day, in the timelessness that is part of God's essence, time and space become fixed points returning to God:

> Così lo stabil punto, onde si volge
> Il tempo in sè, non è il suo spazio, o 'l tempo,
> Che parte dal principio e 'n lui ritorna.   (I, 238–40)

[Thus the stable point, whence time turns into itself, is not his space or his time, which moves from the beginning and into him returns.]

This consciousness of time is of extreme importance in the poem for, as I have said, the whole point of view is from the seventh day in time which is an eternal day with God. The eternal, timeless, limitless God imposes the forms of time and space, the beginning of time and the end of time which comes with the eighth day of final judgment:

> Già di quel, ch'ab eterno in sè prescrisse
> Dio, ch'è senza principio, e senza fine,
> Era giunto il principio, e giunto il tempo
> Co 'l principio del tempo.   (I, 211–14)

[Already from that which had been ordained by the eternal God, who is without beginning and end, was joined the beginning and time with the beginning of time.]

The poetic play on the image of rays of light, circles, and the apparent dimensions of time and space are referents in the poem. As Giovanni Getto suggests, we look at the *created* world along with the poet, rather than at the creation of the world. Situated in time, the poet-*persona* is in the seventh day, the still point of the turning world, between creation and destruction. To this still point the whole poem builds cumulatively as the poet becomes infused with the interior light which he invokes at the beginning. Through this light in creation man transcends time and space in the contemplative pilgrimage to the eternal. Spatially and temporally, then, these six days are also eternal —one perpetual day that returns in a circular motion to and with the seventh day as part of God's eternal present; with God there is no time and all things are coeval.

On the first day, too, according to Tasso, light was created before darkness—in Milton's terms, "first of things, quintessence pure" (*PL* VII, 244)—part of the essential light of God, the eternal light which in an interior manifestation illuminated the senses. Of this light, the sun, created on the fourth day, is a mere ray ("Essempio, da cui lunge il sole è raggio" [I, 496]), a reflection of the light of God. Thus the actual or material sun of the fourth day draws its own light from the essential light of God:

> Or chi presume
> D'annoverar le pure eterne menti?
> Deh non vedete or quanti raggi intorno
> Sparga questo corporeo instabil sole,
> Lo qual del sommo Sole è quasi un raggio?　　(IV, 727–31)

[Now who presumes to number the pure eternal minds? Pray do you not see now how many rays are spread about this corporeal unstable sun which is like a ray of the high Sun?]

With the creation of light comes the creation of the angels:

> Ma quasi eternità (se dir conviensi)
> Precedevano ancora il mondo e 'l tempo,
> Da che furon creati al primo lume
> I secondi splendori Angeli santi.　　(I, 502–05)

[But like eternity (if it must be said) from which they were created at the first light, the secondary bright holy angels also preceded the world and time.]

The same light that makes the angels reflections of God infuses all of nature, irradiating it with divine rays so that it participates in the whole divine plan. For this reason the poet can apostrophize the divine light which has been a dominant theme in the poem and is one aspect of Tasso's "light invisible" as a contemplative focus in created nature. This light disperses darkness from the human mind. As grace, it is that interior light by which man sees and is recalled to his heavenly origin:

> O bellissima luce, o luce amica
> De la natura e de la mente umana,
> De la divinità serena imago,
> Che ne consoli e ne richiami al cielo,
> Potea intorno portar virtuti e doni
> Celesti in terra a' miseri mortali
> Da quei tesori, e da quei regni eterni,
> Ch' a noi dispensa con sì larga mano
> De' lumi il Padre, e 'l donator fecondo?　　(I, 562–70)

[O most beautiful light, O friendly light of nature and of the human mind; serene image of divinity which may console us and recall us to heaven, is it possible to bring virtue and heavenly gifts to wretched mortals on earth from those treasures and from those eternal kingdoms which the Father of lights and fruitful giver dispenses to us with such a generous hand?]

With this light goes the succession of days. Again, we must remember that Tasso is the contemplative onlooker who sees the seventh day as the present, lasting until the final judgment which will usher in the eighth day. Creation was in time; in fact, it marked the beginning of time. With the light of the first day human time began; with the light of Christ's second coming on the eighth day, it is to end. The light motif is thus synthesized in the image of the final judgment which represents, for the just man, the end of the pilgrimage towards which this poem is oriented. For this reason Tasso ends his account of the first day by telling man to look for the light of the eighth day of eternity:

> Ma voi, che del Signor cercate il giorno,
> Deh non sequite i sogni antichi, e l'ombre
> Di questo di ne l'orrida tenebra.
> Seguite omai, ch'a voi riluce e splende,
> La chiara de l'ottava e nova luce;
> La qual non corre faticosa al vespro,
> Non ha sera, o confin di fosco e d'ombra. (I, 637–43)

[But you who look for the day of the Lord, pray do not follow the ancient dreams and shadows of this day into the horrible darkness. Follow henceforth what to you glitters and shines, the brilliance of the eighth and new light which does not hasten toilsomely to evening, does not have evening or a boundary of darkness and of shadow.]

In the Second Day, Tasso continues the hexaemeral-theological procedure of his sacred poem and describes the creation of the firmament, the imposition of form on the matter created on the first day. Throughout the whole account, however, he never loses sight of the light infused through creation, that internal light which illuminates for him the world as the path of human ascent. Thus, the earth is compared to the porch or gateway to the Tabernacle (II, 1–11); and the motifs of light and seven days fuse and center in the image of the seven-pronged candelabra shining in heaven, an image that vividly suggests the end of the ascent from the mist of darkness to the serenity of light:

> Di lui parlando, e di terreni obietti,
> Or da caliginose alte tenebre
> Già traspassati a la serena luce,
> Siam dove in sette lumi appar distinto
> Il candelabro, e 'nestinguibil lampa.   (II, 12–16)

[By speaking of him and of earthly objects now from misty high darkness already passed to serene light, we are where in seven lights clearly appears the candelabra and inextinguishable lamp.]

To the Third Day—again taking his pattern from the brief account in Genesis—Tasso devotes the poetry of the formation of the earth and the seas, with a digression on the cause of the tides (III, 230–90). Significantly, his conclusion to the problem of movement (focused on the tides) is that God is the first mover, the first cause. After the movement of the first cause the operations of nature are allowed to proceed from secondary causes:

> Che la prima cagion fu l'alta voce,
> Movendo il cielo in giro e i mari insieme.
> Da'quai, com'altri disse, in giro parte
> L'onda, ed al suo principio in giro torna.   (III, 302–05)

[That the first cause was the high voice by moving the heaven in a circle and the seas at the same time. From this, as another person said, the wave divides into a circle and returns to its beginning in a circle.]

Giro is the circle of world harmony that accompanies the divine light in its return to its origin. Operation through secondary causes leads the poet back to a consideration of the operation of Nature implied in God's initial actions; the work of Nature is the work of the first mover:

> E 'l magistero di Natura è l'arte
> Del Fattor primo, ond'è fattura e figlia
> La gran Madre Natura; e 'n lei s'onora,
> E 'n lei si riconosce e si contempla
> Il saper e 'l poter che tutto avanza
> De l'alto Re, ch'è suo fattore e Padre.   (III, 590–95)

[And the skill of Nature is the art of the first Maker whose handiwork and daughter is the great Mother, Nature; and in her is honored and acknowledged and contemplated the knowledge and power which proceeds wholly from the high King who is its maker and father.]

God thus "Fermented the great Mother to conceive" (*PL* VII, 281); and the emphasis is quite clearly on the contemplation of *created* things. In the standard representation of a favorite poetic theme by its conventional image—mutability and the fading flower—Tasso emphasizes the existence of created things in time. The greenery of nature will fade *in time,* he tells us in a passage (III, 973–94) reminiscent of his famous panegyric to the rose in the *Gerusalemme Liberata.* As a concomitant of time, mutability is, for the poet-*persona,* one aspect of creation. Creation was in time for man who is in time. Paradoxically, it is only through contemplation of temporal creation, of *natura naturata,* that the poet-*persona* himself transcends time in the poem—by the very *act* of the poem, in fact. And it is only by a similar contemplation that man too transcends temporal and spatial creation.

Contingent with this concept of the created world as the object of contemplation is the treatment of what scholastic philosophy would label ontological goodness. Every plant, every herb, every tree, no matter how noxious, has its use and is therefore good. The divine hand which made the world is not to be accused of creating evil (III, 1042 ff.). In effect, the fruits of nature are writings in God's hand (III, 1163–64), and for this reason the rose, created perfect and without thorns, is now a reminder of our original sin (III, 1165–75). This concept of ontological goodness reminds us that God looked on his creation and saw that it was good.

Physical light is the subject of the Fourth Day as the poet celebrates the creation of the sun, moon, and stars, reflections in nature of the heavenly light—a motif with which the poem began. As a result, the association of light emanating from God with the theme of the contemplation of the world is given some of its clearest expression. Elevation of the pilgrim spirit is through the light that raises the eyes to heaven and the creator's works:

> Piacciati tanto al mio turbato ingegno
> Compartir di quel santo e puro lume,
> Che transfuso da Te, conduca e scorga
> L'alme gentili e i pelligrini spiriti.
> E se giamai gli occhi levaro in alto
> In bel sereno, lucido, notturno
> A l'immortal beltà de l'auree stelle,
> Pensando a l'opre del Fattore eterno.   (IV, 56–63)

[May it so please you to grant to my imperfect intellect (some) of that holy and pure light, which, transfused from you, may lead and guide gentle souls and wandering spirits. And their eyes were ever raised on high into the beautiful, calm, bright night (sky) to the immortal beauty of the golden stars in thinking of the work of the eternal Maker.]

Juxtaposed are allusions to the fall of Satan, the temptation in the garden, and the final judgment (IV, 87–145), as the poet-*persona* sees through the all-encompassing eyes of God to those actions which have not yet occurred in time. Although Satan brought evil to man, human destiny is essentially the same as it was before the Fall. To know oneself as part of creation, frail and earthly, is to know God through the world. Human destiny—man's purpose in the created world as a prelude to the next—is thus phrased in almost catechistical terms:

> E conoscendo se medesmi, alzarsi
> A conoscer Iddio, che fece il tutto,
> Ed adorar il Creator del mondo,
> E servir al Signor, dar gloria al Padre,
> Amar quel che ci nutre e ci conserva,
> Lodar quei ch' i suoi beni a noi comparte,
> Principe a noi de l'una e l'altra vita
> Caduca ed immortale, in terra e 'n cielo.   (IV, 107–14)

[And by knowing themselves, to rise up to know God, who made everything, and to adore the Creator of the world, and to serve the Lord, give glory to the Father, love that which He nourishes and conserves; to praise those of His goods which He bestows upon us; our Prince in the one transitory life and in the other immortal life, on earth and in heaven.]

To the overall discussion of the light of the sun and moon on the fourth day, Tasso brings the tradition that vaguely suggests the "light invisible" and "darkness visible" of Milton's heaven and hell. It must be remembered that light was created on the first day, before the creation of the sun and the moon. Light, then, can be separated from the sun just as fire can be divided into that which burns and that which shines. The ruby is the illustrative example; in this stone God placed the brilliant light of flame with none of its incendiary qualities. God can remove the flame from the fire and, in this way, at the Last Judgment when Christ comes in light and flame, the just will ascend to the light without fire, and the guilty will descend to the fire without light (IV, 225–41).

The image of the moral pilgrimage which man makes through

the contemplation of the light of creation is related to the mysteries of Tasso's faith when, like Dante before him, he celebrates baptism as the means of aspiration to the true fatherland of the soul:

> Benchè d'Adamo i mal concetti figli
> Non sian affatto a l'ampio cielo esterni,
> Perchè celeste è l'alta e bella origo
> De l'alma umana; e lieta al ciel ritorna,
> Sì come a vera patria, e patria antica,
> Da questa de la terra ombrosa chiostra,
> Ove ella visse peregrina errante.
> E se l'uom cinto di corporee membra
> Nacque d'Adam, che di fangosa terra
> Fu generato, ei pur di Dio rinacque
> Rigenerato poi d'acqua e di spirto,
> E come erede de' paterni regni
> Aspira a le celesti alte corone.   (IV, 761–73)

[Although from Adam the evil conceptions (pass down) to the children, they may not be quite outside the spacious heaven because heavenly is the high and beautiful origin of the human soul, and with joy (it) returns to heaven like to a true and ancient fatherland from the shadowy earthly boundary where it lived as a wandering pilgrim. And if man, enclosed in bodily members, is born of Adam who was generated from the slimy earth, he is born again of God, regenerated then by the water and the spirit, and like the heir of his father's kingdom he aspires to the high heavenly crowns.]

Opening the Fifth Day with a long passage which uses this recurrent image of pilgrimage, or the return of man and his soul to true habitation with God (V, 1–28), Tasso continues the central movement of the poem from darkness to light. As he describes the creation and multiplication of fish and birds on the fifth day he conflates this image of the soul's movement from darkness to light with the Gospel metaphor of the fisher of souls: life itself is the great sea which man inhabits, and Peter (or the Church) is the fisherman (V, 616–38). Given Tasso's doctrinal framework, of course, the reader has little difficulty in recognizing the point. The Church is the fisher, the guardian, the saver of souls swimming in the great sea of life. Man is ever to rise out of the dark sea of life and aspire to the light of heaven:

> Ma sorgi omai, sorgi dal mar profondo,
> E 'l nostro ragionar da l'onde emerga.
> Miriamo in alto, alziamo al Cielo i lumi,
> Veggiam mirabilmente il lido adorno.   (V, 652–55)

[But arise at last, arise from the deep sea, and our reason may emerge from the wave. Let us gaze at the heights, let us raise ourselves to the lights of heaven. Let us see the wonderfully glittering shore.]

Here, too, we find the long passage on the Phoenix, *unico augello,* the bird that is its own father and son and the symbol of Christ (V, 1278–591).

The Sixth Day, the last of creation, reaches its climax with the creation of man and his immortal soul. The basic theological orientation of the poem leads to a long discussion of the animal as opposed to the human soul and the divine light of grace that illuminates the latter. All objects are described in terms of a paradise of light and perfection:

> E la progenie, e le diverse stirpi
> Di piante e d'animai perfette usciro
> Nel bel paese de la chiara luce
> A l'alta voce del suo santo impero.   (VI, 1261–64)

[And the offspring and the different races of trees and animals went out perfect into the beautiful country of white light at the high sound of his holy command.]

But the key passage, the passage that sums up the central meaning of the poem within its own terms of light, comes near the end of the sixth day when the creation of man is imminent. The ancient command, "Know thyself," now embraces as its object not only the self, but also creation and created nature (*natura naturata*) as ultimate extensions of the self. In effect, this is a process of contemplation that has God as its object, a God who is read in the book of nature, who is known by his effects. By means of the invisible light that descends from God through creation into the soul as grace, the path of ascent is clear:

> Uom, conosci te stesso! Oh santa scorta
> Che per questo sentiero a Dio conduci,
> Perchè la nostra mente a Dio s'inalza
> Sovra se stessa, e lui conosce e intende
> Nè contemplando i bei stellanti chiostri,
> E 'l gran giro del sol che tutto illustra,
> Così possiam ne l'invisibil luce
> Conoscere il gran Dio che fece il mondo,

> Come dal contemplar la nostra mente
> A conoscer la sua leviamo in alto
> L'ali del pronto e fervido pensiero,
> Che non si ferma ne gli umani obietti. (VI, 1609–20)

[Man, know thyself! O holy guide that through this path leads us to God, and knows and understands him by contemplating the beautiful starry boundaries, and the great circle of the sun that illuminates all. Thus we can, in the invisible light, know the great God who made the world as by our mind's contemplation to know his, we raise on high the wings of swift and ardent thought which is not fixed in human objects.]

This is the path through visible creation. For Tasso, such a view of creation would have even greater validity because of the important doctrine of the Incarnation by which God submitted Himself to time and space in that ultraspiritualization of sense which Counter-Reformation Catholicism found so congenial to the medieval concepts of knowledge and the chain of being.

The invisible light flowing through all creation is part of the onto-logical goodness that every creature and object has. Infused with part of the essential light, the world and its objects are good just as God had seen when He looked at His handiwork. His greatest creation was man, whose invisible eternal light was in the soul, its tripartite division making it the image of the Trinity itself (VI, 1691–708). The creation of man and the description of his primacy over all created things thus comes as the climax and end of the work of creation.

The movement of the poem is now brought to the Seventh Day when God rests and views His labors. With that delight in the occult meaning of numbers which the Middle Ages and the Renaissance enjoyed,[10] Tasso reviews the various significations of the number 7 (VII, 166–248), leading into the full movement of the coming eighth day, the Day of Judgment. In describing this day, Tasso brings the light motif of the poem to its climax; for here the goodness of creation, the light of the created sun, yields to the higher light of the uncreated Son, Christ. For the blessed, this day will mark the culmination of that path of light entered on the first day. Thus Tasso combines this idea of light leading to God with his image of *albergo*, the dwelling, for this pursuit of the contemplative light leads to the end of the pil-grimage through time and creation, and the end is a constant dwelling in light, the invisible light, the unchanging day of eternal peace

(VII, 369–84). The reward for the long victorious war with Satan is thus a reward in terms of light, a *dwelling* in light (VII, 385–93).

Recalling himself out of his digressive reverie about the last day and its eternal reward, Tasso returns to consider man after his creation—that is, in his original state in the earthly paradise when he was not subject to death (VII, 636–46). The earthly paradise, too, is a happy dwelling (*felice albergo*) in which trees are sublime thoughts nurtured in contemplation of the creator spirit (VII, 795–800). With this image of the tree as thought, the poem falls firmly into a meditative pattern; man is the metaphorical tree: "Dio l'uomo in guisa di traslata pianta, / Ché pianta è l'uom" (VII, 807–08).

In this image we have, perhaps, the whole meaning of the poem. Man, as part of creation like the tree, rises in time and space; but, at the same time, like the tree, nourished by the light from above, he rises above time and space. In the spiritual meditation on which the poem is now focused, this represents man's aspiration through his spark of divinity. Like the tree, man has roots in the earth, from which nourishment comes and from which he also was created. When he realizes that earth, as part of the essential goodness of creation, is also filled with the infused light of God (and to show this is the purpose of the hexaemeral poem), man, doubly nourished from above and from below like his counterpart, the tree, can aspire even higher, using his earthbound roots to reach his heaven-fixed destiny. This is the aspiration through the earthly pilgrimage, the glorification of the ambivalence of man who straddles two worlds and must use one as the bridge to the other. All of Tasso's most emphatic images have thus converged in the image of the tree as the aspect of created nature which grows, cultivated by heavenly light on the one hand and pushed upwards by the essential goodness of the created world on the other. Therefore it is fitting that the world itself, the *created* world, ends the whole poem with a prayer to its creator for His divine grace, His light of love and sustenance. It is a deaf soul, Tasso tells us, that does not hear this song, and does not join with its lamentation and prayer.

Tasso's poem, then, can be seen as a long theological meditation on the created world (*natura naturata*). The human soul is the central character here, the human soul created in time but with a destiny in eternity. For this soul, God's creation is a chain, the ladder of return to its eternal heavenly dwelling. The world is the meditative object, the object in time and space which must be used to overcome that time and space; the focal point of this meditation, that which draws the human mind upward, is the light diffused from God which permeates and illuminates all being. Through this illumination man moves from the self-centered to the God-centered world. Light is the symbol of the aspiration upwards.[11]

This context, rather than the hexaemeral tradition as such, provides the common conceptual ground between Tasso's poem and Milton's epic. The hexaemeral tradition was available to both poets from innumerable sources and Milton could not, in any case, accept it with Tasso's Catholic theological ramifications. Nor is the conceptual ground between the two poets provided by the idea of the creation itself, which is less Milton's theme than it is Tasso's. Rather, it is this view of the world—of light in the world—as the initial focus of man's aspiration. Visible creation thus becomes inseparable from God's purpose in creating man. In this context Milton's Raphael turns to the tree as the great image of the chain of created being moving to God's light:

> O *Adam,* one Almighty is, from whom
> All things proceed, and up to him return,
> If not deprav'd from good, created all
> Such to perfection, one first matter all,
> Indu'd with various forms, various degrees
> Of substance, and in things that live, of life;
> But more refin'd, more spiritous, and pure,
> As nearer to him plac't or nearer tending
> Each in thir several active Spheres assign'd,
> Till body up to spirit work, in bounds
> Proportion'd to each kind. So from the root
> Springs lighter the green stalk, from thence the leaves
> More aery, last the bright consummate flow'r
> Spirits odorous breathes. (*PL* V, 469–82)

And by the same token he can promise Adam that man can return to spirit:

> And from these corporal nutriments perhaps
> Your bodies may at last turn all to spirit,
> Improv'd by tract of time, and wing'd ascend
> Ethereal. (*PL* V, 496–99)

We are in Tasso's created world where, in Adam's words, the scale of nature (created nature) is set "whereon / In contemplation of created things / By steps we may ascend to God" (*PL* V, 510–12). In this conception, the world is "but the shadow of Heav'n" (V, 575), and the ontological goodness of every created thing participates in the light of God.

The same light that illuminates Tasso's world radiates through Milton's poem. Milton is illuminated by the interior light and, by reflection in his poem, this becomes the light of creation, the light of the sun which Satan must address in "no friendly voice." After the Fall, in Milton's poem, there is darkness, but there is also the promise of a new light, a new sun (Son). The visible light of creation now becomes invisible. Milton's poem, covering the broader canvas of man's fall from the light of grace, can move through the contemplative light of Tasso's created world to the new pilgrimage out of the garden.

Like the tree, nourished by the light of creation (and, after the Fall, in the Christian scheme, by the light of Christ's redemption), man moves through the time and space of God's created world to the timelessness and spacelessness of his true home in eternity. This is Milton's contemplation "by order dew," the rise planned before the Fall, when out of the evil of the angelic rebellion was to come the good of man's obedience. Out of the evil of man's Fall came the fortune of redemption and the second chance for man to achieve the quest of the pilgrimage begun when God said, "Let us make man to our own image and likeness"; and, from a more distant point, when man was forced to leave the garden—significantly, with the world all before him. For both Tasso and Milton the pilgrimage out of the earthly paradise paradoxically became the pilgrimage through creation, home to the heavenly paradise.

Northwestern University

NOTES

1. For Milton, in *Paradise Lost*, not the creation itself, but the purpose and implications of that creation are what is important; they, as well as man's part in the scheme of creation, are integral to the meaning of the Fall and hence to Milton's poem. See Raphael's account, VII, 150 ff. All Milton citations refer to *John Milton: Complete Poems and Major Prose*, ed. Merritt Y. Hughes (New York, 1957).

2. The background and history of this rather commonplace idea has been rather fully explored and discussed (in a somewhat different context) by Ruth Wallerstein, *Studies in Seventeenth-Century Poetic* (Madison, 1950). For a view of comparable, complementary notions in the thinking of Renaissance Christian Neoplatonists, see my "Giulio Camillo's *Idea of the Theater:* The Enigma of the Renaissance," *Comparative Drama*, I (1967), 19–27.

3. There seems to be little disagreement, however, that Tasso's is a thoroughly unsuccessful poem. It is diffuse and pedantic in its theological conceptions, and unrewarding when viewed as a Christian or Catholic "epic" in any sense. Its 8,816 lines are filled with long, tedious catalogues in the medieval encyclopedic tradition, redactions of Aristotelianism, Thomism, and patristic writings. The whole poem is a compendium of hexaemeral lore used polemically to defend Catholic cosmological and ontological doctrine; it is a learned poem, a preconceived display of erudition on doctrinal-historical Catholicism. Nevertheless, Tasso *is* dealing with the formidable problem of life as he saw it. In terms of his own religious background and environment, he is dealing with man's destiny, perhaps the most formidable problem in life. It was a destiny inextricably centered on the problems of creation and the purposes of that creation. Tasso is not simply saying that this is the *way* God made the world, but that this *is* the world God made. The purpose of this created world as an element in human destiny is to be, in space and time, that man may overcome space and time in his actual spiritual pilgrimage back to his creator.

4. *Reason of Church Government,* p. 668.

5. *Interpretazione del Tasso* (Napoli, 1951), "Il Mondo Creato," pp. 351–78. The passage which I translate is from p. 364. All translations in this essay are mine.

6. This tradition was not without variations, one of which placed the present during the sixth day and the eternal era, ushered in with the final judgment, as the seventh day. Much of this tradition is explored, in its relation to the Christian conception of history, by C. A. Patrides, *Milton and the Christian Tradition* (Oxford, 1966), pp. 231 ff. But the conception of the total history of the world as composed of seven ages or eras of which the last corresponds to the Christian era (or the present) prior to the coming of eternal life, or the eighth day, is basically Augustinian. See J. Daniélou, "La Typologie Millenariste de la Semaine dans le Christianisme Primitif," *Vigiliae Christianae*, II (1948), 1–16, esp. 1. See my subsequent discussion of the Seventh Day in Tasso's poem, below.

7. Although this passage is substantially quoted by F. T. Prince, *The Italian Element in Milton's Verse* (Oxford, 1954)—see pp. 34–57 for discussion of Tasso and Milton, esp. pp. 50–57—I repeat it here for convenience and my emphasis. All quotations from the poem are from the edition of Giorgio Petrocchi (Firenze, 1951).

8. For a discussion of these aspects of light and related themes, see my "'Hail Holy Light' and Divine Time in *Paradise Lost*," *JEGP*, LXVIII (1969), 45–56.

9. On light embodied in nature as part of the "chain of light" by which man returns to God, see Joseph Mazzeo, *Medieval Cultural Tradition in Dante's Comedy* (Ithaca, 1960), ch. II, pp. 56–90, discussed in my "'Hail Holy Light' and Divine Time," pp. 48–50.

10. On this matter see Alastair Fowler's controversial *Spenser and the Numbers of Time* (London, 1964), and Maren-Sofie Röstvig, "The Hidden Sense: Milton and the Neoplatonic Method of Numerical Composition," in *The Hidden*

Sense and Other Essays, Norwegian Studies in English, vol. 9 (Oslo, 1963), 1–112.

11. For a study of light and interior illumination as focal points in meditation, see Louis L. Martz, *The Paradise Within: Studies in Vaughan, Traherne, and Milton* (New Haven, 1964). See esp. pp. 126–27 for an account of Milton's use of the hexaemeral story for a poetic meditation. See also Mazzeo, *Medieval Cultural Tradition,* pp. 76 ff., and my " 'Hail Holy Light' and Divine Time," 48–50.

SELF-KNOWLEDGE
IN *PARADISE LOST:*
CONSCIENCE AND CONTEMPLATION

Lee A. Jacobus

The relationship between self-knowledge and the knowledge of God is very carefully developed in *Paradise Lost*. Milton supports Calvin by treating the two forms of knowledge as wholly reliant on one another and as being forms of conscience and of contemplation. Satan's self-knowledge suffers in direct proportion to his dimming knowledge of God. The war in heaven can be seen as a result of the failure of both these knowledges. Eve's failure of self-knowledge in the pool scene compares with Adam's growth into knowledge. After he is created, he lifts his eyes to heaven for knowledge of who made him; Eve looks down at a liquid plain she thinks is the sky. Unlike Satan, who feels he is self-created, Adam, by knowing God and himself "aright," knows he did not create himself. Eve's pausing at the pool can also be seen as part of a tradition, developed by the Cambridge Platonists, of the soul's contemplation of itself in search of divinity. Eve is entranced by herself because, as Sterry says, she is looking at a beatifical vision.

L IKE MOST of his contemporaries, Milton was well aware of the importance of self-knowledge. Albert Fields, in his recent article, has surveyed in depth both the classical references to self-knowledge and Milton's own relatively infrequent specific references.[1] Fields suggests that Milton's "notion of self-knowledge pervades the thought of much of his prose and perhaps serves as an ordering motif in his longer poetic works." He also says, "Knowledge of self might be achieved by introspection or by one's viewing himself mirrored in the world's stage." These two approaches to self-knowledge—contemplation and the mirroring of conscience—are significant in relation to what is to follow.

In the first books of *Paradise Lost* Satan gives some evidence of the failure of self-knowledge. His understanding of the nature of God's law is, in itself, characteristically distorted by his thought. For example, he blames God for his own condition when he delivers his long soliloquy at the beginning of Book IV (37–61), a soliloquy in which it at first seems that he does indeed understand who he is. He fully understands the nature of God's goodness and the "bright eminence" that had been Satan's own created self. God's service, in all its ease, and the gratitude he should have felt in all its abundance, too, were very plain to him. Satan says that he knows God and that he knows himself, but the fact is that, in blaming God for his fall, he belies his own statements: he does not understand his relationship to God. He tells us one thing but shows us that he in truth understands quite the opposite.

In blaming God for Satan's own failure to be grateful, for his failure to serve, for his inability to afford submission (obedience to God is a most significant expression of love for God), Satan demonstrates clearly his misunderstanding. Satan "sdeind subjection" by the force of his own will, but his own will—though God made it free as He did in all His creatures—is no longer free: it is a will in subjection. Thus, it is ironic when Satan says of hell, "Here at least / We shall be free" (I, 258–59).[2] Satan is not free: Abdiel is right in saying, "Thy self not free, but to thy self enthralld" (VI, 180). He is constantly subject to one or another passion, as for example when he is standing on top of Mount Niphates once he has left Uriel and "Now conscience wakes despair / That slumberd, wakes the bitter memorie / Of what he was" (IV, 23–25). And as "each passion dimmd his face" (IV, 114) his genuine evil character becomes evident beneath the masquerade of the cherub he has put on to deceive Uriel. His passions enchain him, "Disdain" and "necessitie, / The Tyrants plea" drive him relentlessly through the poem. When he melts at Adam's and Eve's "harmless innocence" "yet public reason just, / Honour and Empire with revenge enlarg'd, / By conquering this new World, compells me now / To do what else though damnd I should abhorre" (IV, 388–92). It is necessity, the avowed necessity of revenge, that drives him. Rather than being in command of himself, he is commanded, a slave.

One is tempted to suppose that in those scenes in which Satan seems to soften momentarily, in which he searches for the reasons to do what, except that he were damned, he would not do, his conscience has awakened not only despair, but doubt as well, as when "horror and doubt distract / his troubl'd thoughts, and from the bottom stirr / The Hell within him" (IV, 18–20).

Milton is more overt than this, however, in letting us see that Satan is not always certain exactly who he is. For example, when he meets and fails to recognize his offspring, Sin, at the gates of hell, he says, indignantly, "Retire, or taste thy folly, and learn by proof, / Hell-born, not to contend with Spirits of Heav'n" (II, 686–87). Satan is no longer a spirit of heaven, but is in point of fact the spirit responsible for hell's existence; if one is to be considered hell-born, then it must be Satan, despite his actual origins.

When Zephon and Ithuriel explode Satan "Squat like a Toad, close at the eare of *Eve*," their first question is "Which of those rebel Spirits adjudg'd to Hell / Com'st thou, escap't thy prison; and trans-formd, / Why satst thou like an enemie in waite / Here watching at the head of these that sleep?" (IV, 822–26). Zephon and Ithuriel do not recognize Satan, once their superior in the angelic hierarchy. And in a marvel of ironic misunderstanding, Satan replies, "Know ye not mee? ye knew me once no mate / For you, there sitting ye durst not soare; / Not to know mee argues your selves unknown" (827–29). What Satan does not know, of course, is the extent to which his physical appearance has altered dramatically since his fall; he is no longer the "bright eminence," but is tarnished and dimmed virtually beyond recognition. At first glance this may seem a relatively insignificant detail, however much it may demonstrate Satan's disadvantage when he is confronted by angels of God. But the fact is that Satan's failure to recognize the change which has taken place in his appearance means that he is unaware of the change which has taken place in-wardly. "In Heaven before the rebellion, appearance conforms strictly to reality. The angels are physically beautiful because they are beautiful in essence. After the rebellion, the same direct correspon-dence is seen in Hell. Satan acknowledges the external alteration in his appearance, but is unable to recognize the inward change that it represents. . . . Satan never does accept the fact that appearance is reality, despite being told this directly."[3] Raymond Waddington quotes

IV, 835–40, in which Zephon tells Satan "thou resembl'st now / Thy sin and place of doom obscure and foule." Thus, Satan gives us sufficient evidence that while he is accusing the angels of failing at self-knowledge it is, in fact, he who is most lacking.

Satan does not accept the fact that he is inwardly changed when confronted by Zephon, and he does not accept the fact that his power is limited, as is the power of all creatures, by the will of God. After threatening, with idle bravado, Zephon and Ithuriel with violence, he sees Gabriel, possessing "in Heav'n th'esteem of wise" (886), who tells him his power is limited, that in fact both of them are limited: "Satan, I know thy strength, and thou knowst mine, / Neither our own but giv'n; what follie then / To boast what Arms can doe, since thine no more / Then Heav'n permits, nor mine" (1006–09). Satan does not believe Gabriel, who has already proven his wisdom by blasting Satan's claim that he was loose from hell because he dared "To wing the desolate Abyss" (936). Gabriel expresses angelic disdain, "To say and strait unsay, pretending first / Wise to flie pain, professing next the Spie, / Argues no Leader, but a lyar trac't" (947–49). But Satan, persisting in his course, still unaware of the significance of what has transpired, squares off against Gabriel only to have Gabriel, virtually exasperated, demand that Satan look aloft "And read thy Lot in yon celestial Sign / Where thou art weighd, and shown how light, how weak, / If thou resist. The Fiend lookd up and knew / His mounted scale aloft: nor more; but fled / Murmuring, and with him fled the shades of night" (1011–15). Satan must have outright sensory "proof"— since he will not trust the testimony of the wisest of angels in matters relevant to his own nature any more than he will trust the word of God—and he sees, finally, what for him is proof: the scales of Libra in the Crystalline Sphere palpably demonstrating to him that he is unable to defeat his adversary. This palpable proof, expressive of an almost Hobbesian faith in direct sensory evidence, finally makes the points that the three angels in the Garden had been trying so long to make: Satan is no longer the vast power he once was and still imagines himself to be. No one could expect him to believe, even at this point in the poem, but he most assuredly acts to avoid further pain.

And when we recall Calvin's rather telling comment that self-knowledge implies knowledge of God since none of us can consider ourselves without realizing that we are creatures of God,[4] we recall that long before the action narrated in Book IV, during the very first "consult" in the vast north, Satan gave convincing evidence that he was lacking in self-knowledge. In reply to Abdiel, who challenges Satan by reminding him that "by his Word the mighty Father made / All things, ev'n thee" (V, 836–37), Satan says,

> That we were formd then saist thou? and the work
> Of secondarie hands, by task transferrd
> From Father to his Son? strange point and new!
> Doctrin which we would know whence learnt: who saw
> When this creation was? rememberst thou
> Thy making, while the Maker gave thee being?
> We know no time when we were not as now;
> Know none before us, self-begot, self-rais'd
> By our own quick'ning power.   (V, 853–61)

By Calvin's estimate, then, Satan, in assuming himself self-generated, displays the most thorough form of failure of self-knowledge known to Christianity.

By contrast, Adam, before the fall, gives evidence of possessing a very certain self-knowledge. In his late conversation with Raphael, Adam recounts the story of his creation from his own point of view, demonstrating conclusively that his first impulses toward knowing himself drew him toward heaven. From the first, Adam's self-knowledge is intact and sound:

> Strait toward Heav'n my wondring Eyes I turnd,
> And gaz'd a while the ample Skie,
> . . . .
>   Thou Sun, said I, faire Light,
> . . . .
> Tell, if ye saw, how came I thus, how here?
> Not of my self; by some great Maker then,
> In goodness and in power præeminent;
> Tell me, how may I know him, how adore.   (VIII, 257–80)

Contemplation of himself leads his eyes and his thoughts upward, toward first the sun, in the natural world in which he lives, thence to God, his "Maker," whom he seeks to offer his gratitude for life. God Himself, of course, had earlier explained His purposes in creating man, and He explained, too, that Adam was created "self-knowing" (VII, 510) and Adam himself tells us his first impulses were directed toward giving thanks to heaven.

But the situation with Eve is by no means as clear and by no means as simple. If anything, there is some question as to whether or not she was included in God's description of man, as he is explained to the Son by the Father in the passage above. One would normally expect that Eve, like Adam, would be created fully self-knowing, but this is not unquestionably the case. In the celebrated passage in Book IV in which Eve describes her first waking moments we see that there are some similarities, but some even more crucial dissimilarities between their experiences. Like Adam, when she awakes she wonders who she is and where she is. But instead of looking upward, as Adam had done, she turns her eye downward, looking eventually not at the sun, nor seeking God, but looking at herself and remaining unaware of who she is. As we see, her ear led her to this pass by informing her of the murmuring of the waters:

> Not distant farr from thence a murmuring sound
> Of waters issu'd from a Cave and spred
> Into a liquid Plain, then stood unmov'd
> Pure as th' expanse of Heav'n; I thither went
> With unexperienc't thought, and laid me downe
> On the green bank, to look into the cleer
> Smooth Lake, that to me seemd another Skie.   (453–59)

Thus her ear, Aristotle's principal source of wisdom, leads her to the pool, which deceives her by seeming "another Skie." Whereas Adam looks toward the genuine sky, Eve is led to look toward a surrogate sky, one which returns to her an image which she does not understand. This deception has deep consequences in that Eve's fascination with her own image produces in her a "vain desire" like that of Narcissus' self-worship. Much of this passage is proleptic. Eve's ear leads her to the pool, just as Eve's ear leads her to consider the Serpent's situation and argument in Book IX; Eve is deceived in what she sees just as she is deceived in Book IX in that what she sees is not a mere serpent. And yet this is not a fall or even a "pre-fall." There is no sin involved here, no genuine fault. What the passage demonstrates is that a greater trust of "outsides" can lead to deception—at first perhaps innocent, but eventually of a serious and grave consequence.

Even in this paradisal scene there are implications which should be disturbing. As the passage continues,

As I bent down to look, just opposite,
A Shape within the watry gleam appeerd
Bending to look on me, I started back,
It started back, but pleasd I soon returnd,
Pleasd it returnd as soon with answering looks
Of sympathie and love; there I had fixt
Mine eyes till now, and pin'd with vain desire,
Had not a voice thus warnd me, What thou seest,
What there thou seest fair Creature is thy self,
With thee it came and goes: but follow me,
And I will bring thee where no shadow staies
Thy coming, and thy soft imbraces, hee
Whose image thou art, him thou shalt enjoy
Inseparablie thine.   (IV, 460–73)

What Eve sees in the water is a figure of "sympathie and love," a figure which naturally attracts her. Her reaction demonstrates how "faire" and "winning soft" she is, and it may well be innocent folly that she should be so deeply taken by her own image. If, in fact, she were not deceived to such terrible purpose later this passage would, indeed, be innocuous and amusing—an indication, perhaps, of nothing more than the differences between Adam as a man and Eve as a woman. Yet in the context of the poem's total action the passage takes on much more meaning for us. True, it shows the difference in reaction between man and woman, but it also shows concretely the approaches by which Eve is likely to be tempted. We see, in other words, that she is vulnerable and we see exactly the character of her vulnerability. Further, we see —again proleptically—the weakness that man in general has for beauty. It is for love of Eve that Adam falls, though it must be remembered that his fall is significantly different in character from hers. At any rate, we see in the passage above that it is a voice (and therefore Eve's receptive ear) which finally leads her to the right path and toward knowledge of the nature of man. She is to see herself in relation to Adam, thus gaining self-knowledge. Milton is in agreement with Aristotle in admitting that the senses, while subject to deception, and while surely no reliable ends in themselves, can produce knowledge of a desirable and verifiable kind. However, the uncertainty which this entire passage develops about the trustworthiness of the senses and the conclusions which can be drawn from them ought to serve as a warning for all the poem to come.

The voice of God (Adam's account of this scene in Book VIII, 485 f. identifies it, while giving a substantially different view of Eve's creation and the events which follow) leads Eve to Adam, apparently expecting that the mere sight of Adam will clarify her situation for her. She explains that she saw him, fair and tall, under a platan, but she thought that Adam was "less faire, / Less winning soft, less amiablie milde, / Then that smooth watry image" and when she returns to find that image, Adam calls out, explaining to her that "to give thee being I lent / Out of my side to thee, neerest my heart / Substantial Life. . . . Part of my Soul I seek thee," not expecting gratitude from her (and surely not getting it, either), but expecting only that she would see her true situation as his helpmeet. But seeing Adam is not enough. Hearing him reason with her is not enough. The fact that her life came from his is not enough. It is not until Adam's "gentle hand / Seisd mine" that she "yeilded, and from that time see / How beauty is excelld by manly grace / And wisdom, which alone is truly fair." Force, however gentle, and coercion, keeping her from her desired returning to the pool, are necessary for Eve to begin to come to awareness of herself. This contrasts sharply with Adam's "instinctive" understanding.

The mirror imagery in this passage is, as we have already seen, quite powerful and pronounced. When Eve sees herself the lines themselves echo the mirroring: "As I bent down to look" "A Shape . . . Bending to look on me, I started back, / It started back, but pleasd I soon returnd, / Pleasd it returnd." Nature mirrors itself later in Eve's speech, even after she accepts Adam as her "Author and Disposer" (635), which must be taken to mean that she sees in the law something of her own character: "so God ordains, / God is thy Law, thou mine: to know no more / Is Woman's happiest knowledge and her praise" (636–38). Nature's mirroring is again present in the remarkable passage in which Eve explains what it is that she is willing to give up for Adam (we remember that she already gave up the image in the pool for him, and reluctantly):

> With thee conversing I forget all time,
> All seasons and thir change, all please alike.
> Sweet is the breath of morn, her rising sweet,
> With charm of earliest Birds; pleasant the Sun
> When first on this delightful Land he spreads

His orient Beams, on herb, tree, fruit, and flour,
Glistring with dew; fragrant the fertil earth
After soft showers; and sweet the coming on
Of grateful Eevning milde, then silent Night
With this her solemn Bird and this fair Moon,
And these the Gemms of Heav'n, her starrie train:
But neither breath of Morn when she ascends
With charm of earliest Birds, nor rising Sun
On this delightful land, nor herb, fruit, floure,
Glistring with dew, nor fragrance after showers,
Nor grateful Eevning milde, nor silent Night
With this her solemn Bird, nor walk by Moon,
Or glittering Starr-light without thee is sweet.　　(639–56)

This passage is extraordinarily powerful, if only as a paean to nature
and its beauties, which, of course, should rightfully be appreciated.
But the duplication beginning with line 650 can be interpreted as a
mirroring, and is so pronounced and so reminiscent of (as well as
proximate to) the poolside passage, that we are led to link them and
to conclude that Eve, now fully experienced—as she was, to a lesser
degree, when she saw and rejected Adam—is no longer tempted to
reject him in favor of what else she may see. But in refusing to reject
him, in admitting that truly the world without him would be joyless
and bitter, her language helps us see how really powerful the world
of physical and natural beauty is for her. The higher knowledge of
Adam interests her, too, as her question about the stars which follows
immediately should indicate: she loves to hear him discourse on
nature. But we are sorely tempted to feel that the passages quoted
are suggestive of an instinctive (the word may be too strong) appreciation of nature's surfaces which Eve's experienced mind modifies, but
which it does not entirely renounce.

But of course we know Christian tradition admits that an appreciation of nature can aid in coming closer to God. One of the
reasons for this may well be that if nature is somehow a reflection of
God, then we may, by examining ourselves in its light, come to understand more about God and thereby more about ourselves. This may
or may not be part of the inspiration for a lesser-known, but imagi-
natively vital mirroring tradition which could possibly help us see
Eve's situation at the pool more clearly than we have done. This tradition is represented by William Fenner's *The Souls Looking-Glasse*

(London, 1640). In the light of Fenner and others to be mentioned, however, one begins to wonder if there is more at work in this passage than the comparison with Narcissus.[5]

The problem of the soul's coming to have self-knowledge is a crucial one, despite Augustine's assurance that such self-knowledge is so immediate a perception of the soul by itself that no mirror is necessary. Numerous subsequent commentators, particularly of Milton's time, suggested that a mirror of some kind—most often a natural mirror, as a pool—is of considerable advantage in the soul's coming to know itself. For example, Book III of John Frith's *Vox Piscis: or the Book-Fish* (London, 1626) is titled "A Mirrour or Glasse to know thy selfe," and it begins,

The Philosophers to whom God had inspired certain sparkles of truth, acknowledged that the chiefe point of wisdome and direction of a mans life was to know himselfe, which sentence the Scripture establisheth so cleerely, that no man may dissent from the truth of the same. For *Salomon* saith, that the feare of the Lord is the beginning of wisdom. Now who can feare the Lord, but onely he that knoweth himselfe, as the Scripture teacheth him? (pp. 1–2)

Thus, for Frith, self-knowledge has much the same implication as it has for other contemporary commentators, and he adds that some kind of mirror can be helpful to self-knowledge.

Henry More, one of the Cambridge Platonists, in his poem, *Psychozoia*, has a significantly complex view of the soul examining its reflection in the world at large. He sees the soul as developing a means by which to see through the world of appearances, in a way that Narcissus does not. The conception he offers is particularly interesting in view of the fact that Eve, in contemplating herself, is not quick to develop that greater skill:

11

Like to Narcissus, on the grassie shore,
Viewing his outward face in watery glasse;
Still as he looks, his looks adde evermore
New fire, new light, new love, new comely grace
To's inward form; and it displayes apace
It's hidden rayes, and so new lustre sends
To that vain shadow: but the boy, alas!
Unhappy boy! the inward nought attends,
But in foul filthy mire, love, life and form he blends.

12

And this I wote is the Souls excellence,
That from the hint of every painted glance
Of shadows sensible, it doth from hence
Its radiant life and lovely hue advance
To higher pitch, and by good governance
May wained be from love of fading light
In outward formes, having true cognisance,
That those vain shows are not the beauty bright
That takes men so, but that they cause in humane spright.[6]

These stanzas demonstrate a faith in the power of the soul to do that which Narcissus could not do—to see through the surfaces of reality to what lay beneath. The soul, by its nature, sees something like reality, because its insight penetrates the world of sense. As he says in stanza 28 of the same poem, "But well I wote that nothing's bare to sense; / For sense cannot arrive to th' inwardnesse / Of things, nor penetrate the crusty fence / Of constipated matter close compresse." Whether Eve's insight penetrates sense or not is a most curious question, one which we would be tempted to answer in the negative, particularly if we ask whether she, unaided, would be able to see beneath the surfaces of things. Apparently she would not. She relies, ultimately, upon the ministering voice of God and the greater wisdom—providing she submits—of Adam. Alone, we must assume, she would still, like Narcissus, be worshipping a glimmering surface.[7]

A truly remarkable example of the soul's examining itself in the hope of knowing itself may be seen in Peter Sterry's *A Discourse of the Freedom of the Will* (London, 1675), a fascinating document which has very little to do with free will but a great deal to do with the ways of knowledge in the seventeenth century. The document is in agreement, essentially, with the positions outlined by Ralph Cudworth in his *A Treatise Concerning Eternal and Immutable Morality,*[8] particularly in reference to the nature of universals and their validity: "The eternal truths of things in the Divine *Mind* . . . where they shine *immediately immutably;* These are the Rock."[9] Of self-contemplation, Sterry says:

God then alone most perfectly and substantially enjoyeth Himself in the contemplation of Himself, which is the *Beatifical Vision* of the most beautiful, the most blessed *Essence of Essences.* This *Act* of *Contemplation* is an Intellectual and *Divine Generation,* in which the Divine Essence, with an eternity of most heightened Pleasures, eternally bringeth forth it self, within it self, into an Image of it self.[10]

There is something of the Narcissus myth itself implied in this passage —implied, that is, in a comparison of God's self-contemplation with the self-contemplation of Narcissus. What Sterry is saying is that the kind of contemplation of self which we know in the poolside scene of Eve and in the classical analogue of Narcissus is the prerogative of God.

But Sterry had often warned of the dangers of surface and sense. Like a good Platonist, he devoted himself to seeing, or trying to see, beneath the surfaces of things. To this end he developed his own theory of knowledge based on three principles of truth: sense, reason, and spirit:

Sense, Prov. 20.12. *The seeing eye, and the hearing eare, God hath made them both.* God hath made the Senses, *standards* and *judges* of Truth, within their own *circuit*, in such things, as may be *seen* or *heard*, as appertain to *Sense*.
. . . .
Reason, Prov. 20.26. *The Spirit of man is the candle of the Lord, searching out the hidden parts of the belly.* Though the *candle* of *Reason* excell in light the Glow-wormes of sense; yet is it but a *candle*, not the *Sunne* it self; it makes not day, only shines in the darknesse of the night.
. . . .
The Spirit, I Cor. 2.11. *The things of God knoweth no man, but the Spirit of God.* The Spirit searcheth out the deep things of God. Divine truths are the *depths* of things; the rest are only the *surface*.[11]

The process, then, from sense to reason to spirit, or from perception of surfaces, through judgments, toward real knowledge, is not only possible for Sterry, but tremendously desirable. It becomes, virtually, a Christian's mission. We see, too, that in the case of Eve, her knowledge began with perception, broke down with a failure of judgment to make the sensory perception reveal its proper subject, was revived only with the intervention of the Spirit, and then sustained by her assuming her proper role next to Adam.

His further analysis of the soul—according to the best of the "Philosophers" as he tells us—implies something of the same kind of division of labor. It implies, too, something of the same kind of division of knowledge proper to each aspect of the soul. His fourfold division is: "The Sensitive, Rational, Intellectual, or Angelical, its

Divine Unity."[12] The first of these is the "lowest Orb of the Soul," the part which is "all set and adorned with the sensitive and shadowy forms of things, as a Meadow with the Trees, and Flowers by a River-side, are seen, by their shadowy Figures, playing in the water." The rational orb is "more ample and more Lucid," though the angelic order of things is still seen through an Augustinian mist, a *"cloudy medium."* The third of these orbs reminds us of Marvell's "The Garden":

> The Intellectual part of the Soul, is the Orb or Sphere of Angels. This is the Souls Angelical part. Here the Soul's *abstract*, and separate from the Body, (which is called the *Divine Death* of the Soul) beholds the Intellectual Forms of things, the immortal Essences and Substances, the Angels in their own bright and universal Glories, in their own Intellectual Air and Light, which is the Air and Light of Paradise. As a man sees the pleasant Plants of a flourishing Land, walking upon the Land in the midst of them. At the same time, while the Soul thus walks in this paradisical Land, she enjoyeth the pleasure of seeing the River, as a shady lustre or water cast from her self, within her self, the shadowy figures of this Paradise, with her own reflection playing in these waters, and her self from beneath them, with the same Land of Gardens and of Angels, answering exactly, looking to her self above them.
>
> Give me leave to interpose one word in this place, for the sake of the more learned *Reader;* This is the *Intellectus Agens,* or the Actual, and *Active Understanding* of the Schools. The Soul in its Intellectual part *above* the River. As that above, like the living Face before the Glass, appears at the brink of the waters, upon the shore, with all its Angelical Glories round about it, in their Paradisical Region, which lies within the Soul it self. So the Soul beneath appears, looking up from its *pearly Cave,* at the bottom of the River, like the God of the River, answering and meeting it self above.[13]

This passage is remarkable for numerous reasons. Among them, the treatment of the Aristotelian (scholastic) division of the active mind, that which creates from within, and the passive mind, or that which is impressed from without, is most interesting. The active part is above the river, like Eve, while the passive part is "meeting it self above." Further, the comparison of the soul in Paradise with Eve in Paradise is almost too tempting to resist. And perhaps we should not resist. Sterry would not have read the second edition of *Paradise Lost,* since he died in 1672, but, as a Platonist, Cromwellian, and Puritan, he might easily have been among the early readers of the 1667 edition. The *Dictionary of National Biography* even mentions him as possibly the "Mr. Sterry" assigned to Milton as an assistant in the 1650s, though this is not a certain link.

Sterry's passage may offer us a way of reading the poolside scene with not only a suggestion of innocence but a suggestion of glory attached to it. If Eve in her quest for self-knowledge (she is trying to discover who she is) can be likened to the soul in its quest for self-knowledge as Sterry interprets it, then Eve, in paradise, even though she is not separate from her body, does just what might be expected of her. She enjoys the pleasure of seeing the river and of seeing herself. For Sterry, there is no reason to deny this pleasure to the soul—provided it is a pleasure enjoyed by the intellectual or angelic part of the soul.[14] The imagery and subsequent action in *Paradise Lost* would suggest, however, that Eve's sensitive soul (along with every "orb") is operative on the riverbank, too. What the reader must decide is whether Eve at any point fails to proceed from the sensitive apprehension through the intellectual apprehension. Or, perhaps more relevantly put: would Eve, without guidance from the Holy Spirit (if we can take God at that point for the Holy Spirit), have progressed to the self-knowledge which she feels she has when she is with Adam?

The ambiguity which criticism has discovered and the two basic points which criticism defends, prolepsis and innocence, are unquestionably inevitable. The scene in paradise has all the innocence of paradise, when looked at from the point of view of the soul's discovering itself, the soul's admiring its beauty, Eve questing for self-knowledge. But since innocence gives way to the fall we cannot help but see in the scene something more than (or less than) pure innocence at work. We can, if we choose, see something of an Aristotelian potential present in Eve and in Adam as well, though less markedly, toward resting at the surfaces of apprehension rather than proceeding on to the last orb of the soul, the Plotinian concept of unity with God.

Thus the quest of self-knowledge in *Paradise Lost* is no insignificant one. And the often-quoted scene of Eve examining and admiring herself at the pool may be one of the most crucial of the many examples of the quest. That Eve's quest would resemble the soul's quest appears fairly certain. And if the comparison between Eve and the soul is legitimate, then the complexity which such a comparison develops would seem in harmony with the complexity of the scene as read by critics. It would, even as things stand, seem almost essential to develop a critical view which, while taking the comparison with Narcissus into account, would go far beyond the implications such a direct comparison would imply.

University of Connecticut

NOTES

1. "Milton and Self-Knowledge," *PMLA*, LXXXIII (1968), 392.
2. All Milton citations refer to *The Poetical Works of John Milton*, ed. Helen Darbishire, 2 vols. (Oxford, 1952–1955).
3. Raymond B. Waddington, "Appearance and Reality in Satan's Disguises," *Texas Studies in Languages and Literature*, IV (1962), 390.
4. As Calvin said, "No man can survey himself without forthwith turning his thoughts towards the God in whom he lives and moves; because it is perfectly obvious, that the endowments which we possess cannot possibly be from ourselves; nay, that our very being is nothing else than subsistence in God alone" (*Institutes of the Christian Religion*, I, i; tr. Henry Beveridge, 2 vols. [Grand Rapids, 1962], I, 37).
5. This tradition, of the soul examining itself in a "glass" or mirror, is not mentioned by editors such as John Shawcross, Merritt Y. Hughes, Helen Darbishire, or Douglas Bush. The passage in question (458 ff.) is glossed ordinarily with a reference to Ovid, *Metamorphoses* III, 402 f. Bush's gloss is the latest and most thorough: "Eve's behaving like Narcissus (Ovid, Met. 3.407 f.), while natural and blameless, gives a first faint hint of potential vanity and self-centeredness. Also in Christian tradition, some of the newly created angels looked up to God, others fell in love with themselves; cf. Donne, *Sermons*, ed. Potter and Simpson, 3, 254." This note appears in *John Milton: The Complete Poetical Works*, ed. Douglas Bush (Boston, 1965), p. 286.
6. Henry More, *Psychodia Platonica*, I, i (Cambridge, England, 1642), p. 3. An even more dramatic treatment of the soul and its mirroring is in Joseph Beaumont's *Psyche* (London, 1648). See particularly Canto VI, stanzas 76–78, in the first edition (not Grosart's edition).
7. The most recent works to treat the scene have been Dennis H. Burden's *The Logical Epic* (Cambridge, Mass., 1967), pp. 83 f., which sees the passage as preparation for Adam and Eve's "marriage"; and Stanley Eugene Fish's *Surprised by Sin* (New York, 1967), pp. 216 f., which surveys the older discussions of Millicent Bell, Davis W. Harding, A. J. A. Waldock, Joseph Summers, and Northrop Frye. Fish's discussion is thorough and establishes two basic positions: one, which assumes the incident indicates the vulnerability of Eve by comparison with Narcissus, and the alternative, which sees the incident, in contrast to Narcissus, as innocuous and "childlike."
8. (London, 1731); see pp. 223 and 231.
9. Peter Sterry, *A Discourse of the Freedom of the Will* (London, 1675), p. 15, first of the three parts of wisdom.
10. Ibid., p. 48.

11. Peter Sterry, *The Spirit of Convincing of Sinne* (London, 1646), pp. 9 and 10. This is a sermon preached to the House of Commons, November 26, 1645.

12. *A Discourse of the Freedom of the Will,* p. 107.

13. Ibid.

14. In *The Anatomie of Conscience* (London, 1623), Immanuel Bourne says something quite relevant to this issue: "Even as in a looking-glasse a man seeth his owne face by reflection, and discerneth the beauty or deformity of that, & the eye seeth it selfe, which else it cannot: So, in Conscience, which is the eye and glasse of the Soule, the Soule beholds her selfe, and sees her owne beauty or deformity" (p. 8).

"UNCLOISTER'D VIRTUE":
ADAM AND EVE IN MILTON'S PARADISE

Thomas H. Blackburn

Milton, following Genesis, dates man's Fall from his eating the fruit of the "Tree of the Knowledge of Good and Evil," yet in *Paradise Lost* Adam and Eve know evil before they disobey God's command. Set forth in part in Raphael's instructive discourses and acknowledged in the speeches of Adam and Eve themselves, this prelapsarian knowledge is conceptual. It makes Adam and Eve free and responsible moral agents, but is not therefore incompatible with innocence: they may "see, and know, and yet abstain." The series of choices they survive in innocence proves them "sufficient to have stood," yet also foreshadows their corruption by manifesting potentialities which make them "free to fall." By eating the fruit they for the first time actualize evil in their own existence, and the "event" for which the tree is named is this new and catastrophic knowledge of evil as an experienced actuality. The Fall is neither the inexplicable ruin of an ignorant bliss nor the inevitable result of a flawed creation. Milton's conception of a knowledgeable, yet sinless, innocence not only is congruent with his analysis of virtue in *Areopagitica*, but also makes possible a narrative rendering of the Fall which is coherent, credible, and dramatic.

I F T H E innocence of Adam and Eve in *Paradise Lost* is, or should have been, a condition very like that "cloister'd virtue" which Milton "cannot praise" in *Areopagitica*, then the integrity of the poet and his epic may be seriously questioned. Either Milton has chosen a subject which requires him to present a static and ignorant bliss as the highest human happiness, or to avoid that aesthetic and psychological pitfall, has undercut the dramatic and doctrinal center of his poem by enduing Adam and Eve before the Fall with some of the failings of fallen mankind. Were their innocence truly "cloister'd" Adam and Eve would be not only sinless, but also incapable of sin—moral, as it were, by default. They could neither "see" nor "know" what "vice promises," and thus would not face that choice between vice and virtue which is for Milton the very essence of reason.[1] Possessing no true freedom of the will they could not will their own corruption, nor could they be justly held responsible for so doing. The alternate assumption, that they were created impure from the beginning, is equally as destructive to Milton's argument for the justice of God's ways to men. The punishment of Adam and Eve for a disobedience they could neither will nor avoid in either case would be a monstrous injustice, and the promise of redemption through Christ would become a cynical farce. The literary consequences would be no less drastic: a flawed innocence would destroy the premise of drama in the Fall, and an incorruptible innocence would preclude any credible epic plot.

Of those critics who find the innocence depicted in Genesis incompatible with any credible shift to a fallen state, Millicent Bell's views are typical: "The transition between Man and Woman incorrupt and mankind corrupted is simply to be accepted as having happened. Yet the mind cannot accept the fact that perfection was capable of corruption without denying the absoluteness of perfection."[2] A most cloistered virtue, bearing within itself no potentiality for change and immune to external influence, is suggested by "the absoluteness of perfection." Like E. M. W. Tillyard, Miss Bell sees an Adam and Eve innocent in this definition as impossible characters in a narrative which requires, to use Aristotle's terms, a "probable or necessary" sequence of events. With Tillyard, she suggests that for this reason, "in one way or another it was necessary to create an Eve liable to temptation and so to remove the threshold of her transition to sin to some indefinite moment in the past."[3] Tillyard fixes this point in Eve's dream (V, 28–94), but one can easily enough find traces of what he calls "feelings which though nominally felt in the state of innocence are actually not compatible with it" as early as Eve's first inclination to prefer her own reflected image to Adam, or Adam's initial self-assertion in his petition to his creator for a mate.[4] Once innocence is equated with Miss Bell's "absoluteness of perfection" it becomes impossible to find that Adam and Eve were ever innocent. The corollary is inevitable, and as drawn by A. J. A. Waldock and others it becomes an argument for the view that God's ways to men cannot be defended: if Adam and Eve were never innocent, then God must have created them flawed, and thus punishes their defection under false pretenses.[5]

Bell and Tillyard agree that Milton did not, or could not, portray innocence as they believe Genesis requires, either because no successful epic narrative could incorporate such a state, or because the poet's sympathies were secretly with the "wayfaring Christian" of the fallen world.[6] Basil Willey, however, thinks that Milton did achieve the required portrait of perfection (and here he is in the company of Dr. Johnson), but that to do so involved not only a fault in the poem, but also a paradoxical betrayal of his deep humanist belief in rational freedom:

Genesis, to which Milton must needs adhere, represented the Fall as due to, or consisting of, the acquisition by Man of that very knowledge, the Knowledge of good and evil, by the possession of which alone Milton the humanist believed man could be truly virtuous. Here indeed was a strange situation: Milton, believing, as we have seen, in "Knowledge," and in "Reason" as choice of good by a free agent cognisant of evil, selects as the subject of his greatest poem a fable which represents the acquisition of these very things as the source of all our woe. It may be said that it is only in a fallen state that moral knowledge has become essential . . . ; that, in a word, innocence would have been better than morality. But Milton does not really believe this, as is clearly shown by his failure to convince us that the prelapsarian life of Adam and Eve in the "happy garden" was genuinely happy. "Assuredly we bring not innocence into the world, we bring impurity much rather": this is what Milton knew and believed; yet his adherence to Genesis involved him in the necessity of representing man's true and primal happiness as the innocence of Eden.[7]

The assumption that innocence and morality are not compatible shows Willey to understand "innocence" as "absolute perfection." And, it must be admitted, if Milton either believed in or represented the state of innocence to be so perfect or immutable as Willey and others suppose, the coherence of his narrative, the integrity of his belief in free will, and his "proof" of God's justice would all be suspect.

The possibility of such damaging conclusions arises in part from an ambiguity inherent in our notions of *innocence.* We use the word, on one hand, to characterize the naive purity of an infant, not only untouched by evil, but also ignorant of its very existence and unmoved by the passions which may draw men from righteousness. On the other hand, we also use the word as the antonym of *guilty*, signifying neither ignorance of evil nor the lack of any capability or inclination to indulge in it, but merely that no particular evil or sinful act has at that point been committed. The former idea of innocence is too often that presumed to be implied by Genesis and used by Milton in his epic. The latter idea, however, may well be closer to Milton's conception of man's unfallen state. The *OED* notes that the restriction of the word *innocence* to mean "unacquainted with evil" is essentially a modern usage specialized from the general sense "doing no evil: free from moral wrong, sin or guilt." An innocence fitting the latter sense is suggested, to take a very early example, by the characterization of Adam and Eve in the Caedmonian Genesis: "Young were they both, in beauty fashioned / By God's own power to grace the earth. / They knew not *enduring* nor *doing* of evil" (italics mine).[8] But the test of Milton's meaning is neither Caedmon nor a dictionary. We must turn to *Paradise Lost* and the poet's other works for a defining context. Though Milton in his epic "must needs adhere" to Genesis, his poem expands vastly on the spare biblical story. In the tradition of the exegetes (whose works he knew well), and by virtue of his own Protestant faith in responsible individual interpretation of the Scriptures, he explicates according to his own best lights the meaning of the events he takes as a framework for his poem.[9]

In *Paradise Lost* Milton does not alter the central fact of the Genesis version of the Fall: Adam and Eve fall from innocence by eating the fruit of "the Tree of the Knowledge of Good and Evil." In Genesis this act of disobedience to the explicit will of God *is* "simply to be accepted as having happened." We do not learn enough about Adam and Eve in the few verses between their creation and fall to understand any motivation or discover any cause for the act in antecedent circumstances. The eating of the fruit accounts for the entry of evil into the world of mankind and is the cause of all his subsequent miseries, but unless one accepts aetiological arguments which make the result into a cause, the Fall is essentially causeless. The narrative in Genesis is history, not poetry, according to Aristotle's distinction in the *Poetics* between an account of "what has happened" and "the sort of thing which might happen, the possible according to probability or necessity."[10] In Milton's poem, on the other hand, from Book IV to the middle of Book IX we are with the unfallen Adam and Eve in the Garden. They converse with each other and with their angelic visitor, Raphael. Together they hear Raphael's account of war in heaven and Adam learns of creation; their actions are described to us, and the narrator reflects on their state. In Book III, before they actually appear in the poem, God expounds their nature and previews for the Son (and the reader) the foreknown course of their life. By the time they actually eat the fruit we are quite fully acquainted with their nature and their situation. We are thus informed of the antecedent circumstances which must be known if there is to be a chance that the Fall may be seen as the climax of a possible or necessary sequence of events.

Among the circumstances concerning Adam and Eve which are revealed in this expanded narrative is one paradoxical fact of central importance to a proper understanding of innocence and the Fall: long before our first parents in turn taste the fruit, they already possess what we must in some sense call a "knowledge of good and evil."[11] On many occasions before the Fall they both hear and use the words *good* and *evil*, first heard when God announced to Adam the condition of life in the garden. They do not, as they did when Adam spoke of "death," wonder what the words might mean. Even before Raphael descends to warn them and educate them further in the history and ways of evil and the power of good, Adam shows not only that he knows what evil is, but also that he is aware of some of its ways and its current relation to Eve and him. Without such knowledge he could scarcely have responded as he does to Eve's satanically inspired dream, misliking it because "of evil sprung," wondering "yet evil whence," and assuring Eve that "Evil into the mind of God or Man / May come and go, so unapprov'd, and leave / No spot or blame behind" (V, 117–19). Calmed and comforted by Adam's words, Eve joins him in a morning hymn asking the continuance of good and the avoidance of evil:

> Hail Universal Lord, be bounteous still
> To give us only good: and if the night
> Have gathered aught of evil, or conceal'd,
> Disperse it, as now light dispels the dark.   (V, 205–08)

A knowledge of good and evil is surely demonstrated by speeches such as these; yet, at the conclusion of the hymn, the narrator notes that they "pray'd innocent" (V, 209).

Raphael, sent by God to warn Adam and Eve of Satan's plot

(though not of all its details), in his two discourses—on the War in Heaven and the Creation—provides further lessons in the unfallen knowledge of good and evil.[12] The story of Satan's revolt tells of the origin of evil as Michael addresses the Apostate as "Author of Evil, unknown till thy revolt" (VI, 262), and the deeds and fate of Satan are concrete examples of what evil is, of anger, pain, hypocrisy, and alienation from God. Evil is known, through Raphael's narrative, in the person of Satan and his followers, and Adam and Eve thereby know *of* evil (though it is not until their Fall that they know evil in the same sense as Satan does). The tale of the Creation has as its keynote the bountiful goodness of God, "whose wisdom had ordained / Good out of evil to create," and his works (VII, 187–88). In the eager strains of their hymns of praise Adam and Eve demonstrate their immediate and unforced perception of this goodness (IV, 720–35; V, 153–209). The contrast between the pain and disorder of revolt in Heaven and the blissful variety and marvelous order of the new creation puts the difference between good and evil in terms unmistakable even to one who has never himself felt the effects of that difference.

Unless one is willing to deny that knowledge may be acquired by a combination of direct admonition and concrete narrative example such as that which Raphael provides, and unless one refuses to accept as evidence of understanding the correct use of the words *good* and *evil* by Adam and Eve in their own speeches, it must be admitted that they already possess a "knowledge of good and evil" before they violate the tree which bears that name. Informed and sophisticated rather than naive or childlike, their innocence consists not of no acquaintance with evil but of no taint by it, of sinlessness rather than ignorance of sin.

A "knowledge of evil" and an awareness of the possibility of corruption are clearly not inconsistent with innocence as Milton conceives it: what then is to be understood by "the Tree of the Knowledge of Good and Evil"? If Adam and Eve already know evil, what sort of knowledge, if any, do they acquire as a result of violating God's prohibition regarding the tree? Milton preserves the name of the tree as it is given in Genesis, but in attempting to understand what the tree and the action around it signify in Milton's thought and in his epic, we face a situation rather like that with regard to his muse,

Urania: we should look to "the meaning, not the name." The "event"—
that is, the result for Adam and Eve of eating the fruit—reveals a
meaning which appears to be in conflict with the simple name.

In Book XI of *Paradise Lost,* announcing his decree that Adam
and Eve should be driven out of Paradise, God begins by describing
the effects of the forbidden fruit:

> O Sons, Like one of us Man is become
> To know both Good and Evil, since his taste
> Of that defended Fruit; but let him boast
> His knowledge of Good lost, and Evil got,
> Happier, had it sufficed him to have known
> Good by itself, and Evil not at all.   (XI, 84–89)

Adam, reviling Eve in Book IX after the fires of their first fallen lust
have been quenched, describes the effect of the tree in similar terms:

>   our Eyes
> Op'n'd we find indeed, and find we know
> Both Good and Evil, Good lost and Evil got,
> Bad fruit of Knowledge, if this be to know,
> Which leaves us naked thus.   (IX, 1070–74)

In *Areopagitica* and *The Christian Doctrine* Milton emphasizes that
as a result of the Fall good is no longer known by itself but only in
contrast or opposition to evil:

It was from out the rind of one apple tasted that the knowledge of good and
evil, as two twins cleaving together leaped forth into the world. And perhaps this is the doom which Adam fell into of knowing good and evil,
that is to say, of knowing good by evil.[13]

It was called the tree of the knowledge of good and evil from the event;
for since Adam tasted it, we not only know evil, but we know good only
by means of evil.[14]

All of these assertions about the tree and its effects make it difficult
to take as the meaning of the tree the plain sense which its name seems
to invite. Milton, furthermore, denies explicitly that there is anything
magical or even sacramental about the tree or its fruit: "The tree of
the knowledge of good and evil was not a sacrament; for a sacrament
is a thing to be used, not abstained from: but a pledge, as it were,
and memorial of obedience."[15] Only Satan in *Paradise Lost* promises
a magical transformation, that the tree will give "Life / To knowledge"

(IX, 686–87). When Adam and Eve eat the fruit, however, their intellectual powers are diminished, not heightened; their reason becomes "reasoning" as they spend the "fruitless hours" debating the blame for their change and mooting between themselves alternatives as futile as those we remember from the debate in Hell (IX, 1067–1189; X, 719–1006). Their love turns to lust, their honor to shame, and their innocence to guilt. Disobedience of God's express command, not any power intrinsic in the fruit, wreaks these changes.

That the Fall does not consist of an access of knowledge, as we usually conceive of it, but of a shift in the mode of man's knowledge of good and evil is shown by these changes. In the state of innocence, Adam and Eve live a total *experience* of good; their knowledge of evil, on the other hand, is conceptual. They know the word *evil*, what it has meant when the state so named has been actualized elsewhere, and what act could cause it to be actualized in their own existence. But so long as they remain faithful to God's command, evil remains only a potentiality in their lives: good alone is known as actual and innocence is preserved. When Adam and Eve fall, however, this actual-potential polarity is destroyed. By their disobedience evil is actualized as a part of their direct personal experience. The state of bliss in Paradise, a unique totality of good, is irrecoverably lost, so far as their unaided human capacity to recover it is concerned. Adam and Eve no longer may "know" evil in the guiltless way they did before the Fall. Their doom is not so severe as that of Satan and his rebellious cohorts for whom evil is not only the sole actual state but also their sole potentiality throughout eternity; good, by the grace of God, remains a potentiality for man, yet the actuality of evil predominates so much that good is known only by evil and in the midst of evil.

The mixed state of good and evil which man is to endure is defined concretely by Michael in the vision and narrative through which he prepares Adam for his entry with Eve into the post-Edenic world. The structure of his revelations contrasts markedly with that of the instruction offered Adam by Raphael before the Fall.[16] In Raphael's accounts the exemplification of evil in Satan's rebellion and the glorification of good in the Creation each had its separate place and was not mixed with the other (though the reader may note allusions to or foreshadowings of opposing things to come in each). One account supplies Adam with the conceptual knowledge of evil he needs to avoid falling into the experience of it; the other deepens his understanding of the experience he now enjoys. In Michael's account of man's future, on the other hand, in both vision and narrative good and evil are "as two twins cleaving together." The stories of the few "just men" are intermixed with the proliferating tales of disease, war, and tyranny, and Adam, as the responsive human audience, has great difficulty in sorting the good from the evil. He rejoices erroneously as the "sons of God" enjoy themselves with music, women, and feasting, and despairs prematurely when Christ is persecuted. The effects of the Fall are seen both in the events themselves and in Adam's inability to evaluate them clearly without Michael's guidance. For man the evil which was once a potentiality, localized, as in Raphael's narrative, in Satan and his followers, has now become the actuality described by Michael. The good that flowed through unfallen creation as a totality has become a more distant potentiality, preserved as possible through the promise of redemption in Christ and exemplified in those few "just men" who are his "shadowy types," but no longer that joyful actuality hymned by Raphael.

Michael's account of the future of man, as well as the painful and degrading immediate effects of the Fall on Adam and Eve, defines the "knowledge" acquired in the Fall as experiential knowledge of an actuality, rather than any intellectual enlightenment or increase in moral acuteness. In the face of the evidence that Adam and Eve knew evil before they fell, God's assertion that while unfallen they knew "good by itself, and Evil not at all" makes sense only if this interpretation is accepted. "Knowledge" in this sense is also the only sort which when acquired could lead to a diminution of man's freedom as a moral being. Having sinned, it is no longer possible for Adam and Eve to choose to remain sinless. They go not from ignorance to enlightenment or from naiveté to mature liberty, but from innocence to guilt. In the act of eating the fruit that evil which might otherwise "into the mind of God, or Man / . . . come and go" is "approv'd" in action and leaves, therefore, an indelible "spot or blame." The "meaning" of "knowledge" in the Genesis formula "the Tree of the Knowledge of Good and Evil" as Milton sees it in *Paradise Lost* is clearly closer to "being" or "becoming" than to what we would ordinarily call "knowing."

Such a definition of *knowledge* in this context, moreover, is not simply a result of Milton's idiosyncratic interpretation of Genesis: in connection with the prohibited tree "knowledge" retains some of the sense familiar to us in the biblical usage "carnal knowledge" (in this connection the number of metaphors of sexual violation surrounding the Fall in *Paradise Lost* should be noted). Other interpreters of Genesis have also found that "knowledge" in that context requires special treatment. O. A. Piper in *The Interpreter's Dictionary of the Bible*, under *Knowledge*, writes as follows:

For the Hebrews "to know" does not simply mean to be aware of the existence or nature of a particular object. Knowledge implies also the awareness of the specific relationship in which the individual stands with the object, or of the significance the object has for him.

The "tree of the knowledge of good and evil" (Gen. 2:17) is not to provide scientific or theosophic knowledge, or a purely theoretical knowledge of moral values. Rather, as the forbidden tree it will disclose the difference between good and evil to the first couple through their very act of eating the fruit. It is through trespassing God's prohibition that one will "know" what the wrong is like—viz. a *quality of one's own self in action*.[17] (italics mine)

Knowledge is no less complex a word in English than in Hebrew: the English word combines in itself two historical senses, that of knowing through sensuous perception (OE *kan*) and of knowing by the mind (Lat. *scire*). According to the *OED*, until 1896 a strong sense of the word was current, signifying "to have personal experience of (something) as affecting oneself, to have experienced, met with, felt or undergone." When "naming" the tree, as we have seen, Milton puts it in a context which focuses its meaning on this strong sense of "knowledge by experience" inherent in the Hebrew name and still current for him in the English.

This reading of "knowledge" as the "event" for which the tree is named also provides a clue to the understanding of God's ironic pronouncement that when Adam falls he "Like one of us . . . is become / To know both Good and Evil" (XI, 84–85). Adam, of course, has not become godlike by eating the fruit; the act lowers, rather than raises, him in the hierarchy of being. Yet, if the knowledge he acquires is the same as that possessed by the gods, must they not also be fallen? That the gods do in fact know good and evil is no less based on experienced actuality than that knowledge is among fallen men; evil, as is apparent in Michael's address to Satan quoted earlier, was "un-known" in Heaven before the revolt. But, though the faithful angels have seen evil actualized and have even suffered some of its effects during the War in Heaven, they themselves have not disobeyed God. Evil could be actualized in Heaven and yet leave the majority of angels untainted by it. On earth, however, Adam and Eve, because they were the only beings enjoying reason and free will, were the only beings capable of actualizing evil. Once Adam joins Eve in eating the fruit the possibility no longer exists that any portion of mankind could know evil as actual without sharing through their descent the guilt for having actualized it.

We must also remember that "actuality" in Heaven and the ex-perience of it are modified by the perspective of eternity and divine omniscience. In this respect the difference between man and the heavenly beings is like that pointed out by Raphael between the intuitive reason of the angels and man's discursive reason (V, 486–90); man's experience, as well as his reasoning, is a temporal process—one experience, one actuality, succeeds another in the passage of time. In the temporal universe the potentiality for evil which is implicit in the possession of free will becomes actualized through man's choice. Through God's grace and Christ's redemptive act the potential for good is restored, but the actualization of that new bliss will not occur until the centuries pass to the end of time. Man endures the actuality of evil in his temporal existence and can only seek comfort in the potentiality for ultimate good revealed in the eschatological promises of Scripture and typified by Christ. From God's "prospect high / In which past, present, future he beholds," this progression is reduced to a single moment; from that perspective, evil in its very moment of actualization has already been turned to good. In Heaven, then, the "knowledge of good and evil" is constantly and instantaneously re-solved to good alone. Through revelation and by reason and faith, man may perceive and believe in the time when and the way in which this resolution will also take place for him, and thus achieve a "paradise within," but unlike the heavenly beings he must live out-wardly and die in the actuality of his moment in time. Because he himself has actualized evil in the world, his experience cannot be of good *or* evil, but is of good *and* evil, or as Michael puts it, of "supernal Grace contending / With sinfulness of Men" (XI, 359–60). Both gods

and men "know" evil because it has been actualized in their experience, but only for the unfallen gods is the contention between
good and evil ended in its beginning and an experience made possible
in which the actuality of evil does not preclude an uncorrupted
eternity of good.

God's ironic statement reflects on the delusion fostered by Satan
that man could know good and evil in the way the gods in Heaven do.
Neither before nor after the Fall is this possible for Adam and Eve,
yet the knowledge of evil they do possess in their innocence is essential
to their status as free and responsible moral beings before the Fall.
"Uncloister'd" by their possession of that knowledge, they are also
dramatically exposed to choice by other aspects of their situation and
character. Though Paradise is a high place, palisaded by groves and
patrolled by God's angels, the author of evil is permitted easy entry;
throughout Books IV to IX we are constantly reminded of his lurking,
leering presence. The physical barriers of groves and guards can lock
out evil no more effectively than censorship, as Milton asserts in
Areopagitica, can remove "the matter of sin."[18] Adam and Eve not
only know evil and face an occasion for choice in God's command
regarding the tree, but are also further involved in a necessity for
action by the presence of a protagonist for the wrong choice.

The active moral status of the unfallen Adam and Eve is confirmed by the "passions within" with which they were created. In
Paradise Lost the difference between the state of innocence and the
life of fallen man is not one between passionless and passionate
existence, but between passions "rightly tempered" and "high
passions," between "sensual appetite" legitimately satisfied and that
"sensual Appetite, who from beneath / Usurping over sovran Reason
claim'd / Superior sway" (IX, 1129–31). Milton goes to lengths un-
precedented in hexaemeral literature to make clear his belief that
Adam and Eve were created with a full complement of human appetites. He turns his back on all interpretations of Genesis which hurry
Adam and Eve out of the Garden before they have a chance to
consummate their match, or which attribute to the Fall the existence
of human sexuality. Adam and Eve hunger and thirst, eat and drink;
Eve takes pains to make their diet not merely nutritious but pleasing
as well, "Taste after taste upheld with kindliest change" (V, 336).
Both of them feel the attraction of physical beauty in each other and

the Garden around them. Among the passions they possess must be
reckoned those of the mind as well as the senses. They are eager for
knowledge of themselves and the creation which they rule; they even
show signs of incipient egotism.[19] None of these passions, however, is
of itself incompatible with innocence: "rightly tempered," that is,
exercised according to the dictates of reason and not "sovran" over it,
the passions are the "very ingredients" of that virtue which defines
innocence. When Eve turns from her own reflection to acknowledge
the superior attractions of Adam's "manly grace / And Wisdom," she
has chosen to direct her passion toward the greater good recognized
by reason rather than remain entranced by the real but lesser good
which is her own soft beauty (IV, 477-91). Though her passions are
momentarily distempered by the dream which Satan insinuates into
her fancy, she rejects those promptings and accepts Adam's reasonable
counsel. If, when she remains adamant in her decision to labor away
from Adam for a morning, she does choose a lesser good over a greater,
it is to be known as such only by the outcome (which was not
necessitated by her choice to leave), and she departs forewarned by
Adam's last "reasoning words" (IX, 379). Adam passes the first test
of his rational freedom when he petitions God for a fit mate to match
his stature as a reasonable being instead of seeking mere sensual
gratification with a lower creature. Raphael's counsel persuades him
to refrain from speculation on "matters hid," and convinces him that
"to know / That which before us lies in daily life / Is the prime
Wisdom" (VIII, 192-94). When Adam lets Eve go on the fatal
morning, he neither forces her obedience nor yields his reason to her
beauty:

> Go: for thy stay, not free, absents thee more;
> Go in thy native innocence, rely
> On what thou hast of virtue, summon all,
> For God towards thee hath done his part, do thine. (IX, 372-75)

Innocence here is clearly no bar to morality but its support, and
Adam's acquiescence in this instance is very different from that at the
Fall, when he is "fondly overcome with femal charm" (IX, 999). Each
of the passions felt by Adam and Eve is indeed involved in their fall—
Satan and then the fallen Eve appeal not only to the sensual appetites
of hunger and sex, but also to the mental "appetites" of curiosity and

selfish egotism—but until the fruit is actually tasted these same passions, held in proper bounds, are the sources not of woe but of bliss.

Adam and Eve make a number of choices before the Fall; what distinguishes the decision which is the Fall is not that it is the first time they had a choice to make, but that it is the first time that they allowed passion to take the sway from reason in directing the will. That their passions do appear and that Adam and Eve recognize the difference between good and evil objects of passion are evidence that their freedom of the will is a genuine freedom. The strength of their passions also makes their choice not to be ruled by them a positive exercise of moral virtue. True freedom of the will could not exist or be demonstrated in the absence of that "liability to fall" with which Adam and Eve were created, but it is equally as manifest in a refusal to succumb to temptation as in acquiescence to Satan's blandishments.[20] The series of choices Adam and Eve make before the Fall in fact shows a series of victories over what Albert W. Fields calls "the darker side of self."[21] Had they not been created with a "darker side" as well as a self like God, they could not have been truly free. When they eat the fruit they pass not from a cloistered and immutable perfection to undeserved corruption, though corruption of their moral being is one of the results of the Fall, but from a free and joyous innocence to the straitened misery of guilt.[22]

To insist then, as many have, that man becomes faced with moral questions only when he is fallen, and thus lives an interesting and dramatic life only then, is to misunderstand not only the conception of innocence in *Paradise Lost*, but also the ideal of virtuous freedom and morality so eloquently set forth in *Areopagitica*. Defending the liberty of printing and reading, Milton never asserts that true moral choice requires the actual personal experience of evil: indeed, the opposite is the case. Through uncensored reading one may escape the confines of "cloister'd virtue" and "know the utmost which vice promises to her followers"; yet, because this knowledge is acquired without the necessity of actually partaking of vice, the reader may, like the unfallen gods, remain untainted, though not untested. The ideal is "to see and know and yet abstain."[23] In *Paradise Lost* the account of Satan's rebellion is in many respects the equivalent for Adam and Eve of a book which shows what "vice promises"; Eve's dream provides an even more striking example of a knowledge of vice acquired without cor-

ruption by it. The unfallen Adam and Eve, in fact, are held up in
Areopagitica as a model of morality for fallen man. Though the treatise is directed to man "in the field of this world," in arguing the futility of laws which seek to shelter man from the matter of or occasion
for sin, Milton describes Adam in terms which rule out any notion of
naive or cloistered innocence; any such notion would, of course, make
Adam's example irrelevant for fallen man:

> Many there be that complain of divine providence for suffering Adam to
> transgress, foolish tongues! when God gave him reason, he gave him free-
> dom to choose, for reason is but choosing; he had been else a mere artificial
> Adam, such an Adam as he is in the motions. We ourselves esteem not of
> that obedience, or love, or gift, which is of force: God therefore left him
> free, set before him a provoking object, ever almost in his eyes; herein
> consisted his merit, herein the right of his reward, the praise of his absti-
> nence. Wherefore did he create passions within us, pleasures round about
> us, but that these rightly tempered are the very ingredients of virtue?[24]

In *Paradise Lost,* as we have seen, Adam and Eve before the Fall are
no more like "Adam as he is in the motions" than is the Adam described in *Areopagitica.*

Far from describing what Milton's Adam and Eve should be but
are not in the state of innocence, Willey's definition of the exercise of
reason as "the choice of good by a free agent cognisant of evil" fits
precisely the behavior of unfallen man in the epic. This aspect of man's
primal nature is summarized by God in Book III in lines which echo
Milton's description of Adam in *Areopagitica:*

> I made him just and right,
> Sufficient to have stood, though free to fall.
> Such I created all th'ethereal Powers
> And Spirits, both them who stood and them who fail'd:
> Freely they stood who stood, and fell who fell.
> Not free, what proof could they have giv'n sincere
> Of true allegiance, constant Faith or Love,
> Where only what they needs must do, appear'd,
> Not what they would? what praise could they receive?
> What pleasure I from such obedience paid,
> When Will and Reason (Reason also is choice)
> Useless and vain, of freedom both despoil'd,
> Made passive both, had serv'd necessity,
> Not mee.   (98–111)

In addition, Raphael, just before the Fall, admonishes Adam that "to stand or fall / Free in thine own arbitrement it lies" (VIII, 640–41). Adam earlier admits to Raphael that he knows himself "to be both will and deed created free" (V, 549), and belief in the responsible freedom to choose their own fate underlies Adam's arguments to dissuade Eve from separate work in the garden, and is finally the reason why he lets her go. In their freedom Adam and Eve constantly face the possibility of sin. This freedom, with the "passions within" and the "provoking object" without making it a truly moral state, is seen by Milton as the glory of man's creation, and with the gift of reason, as the fundamental source of man's preeminent dignity among the creatures of the earth.

Milton's conception of life before the Fall, as I have attempted to outline it here, not only is satisfying as it endues Adam and Eve with a real freedom which is nonetheless consistent with innocence, but also as it makes possible a narrative rendering of the Fall which is coherent, credible, and dramatic. The change from innocence to corruption is no less sudden than it is in Genesis, no less a cataclysmic moment in history, but it is, as it is not in Genesis, the culmination of a clearly motivated and fully probable dramatic action. When Adam and Eve fall in *Paradise Lost* we need not merely "accept it as having happened": the history of Genesis is transmuted into the plot of *Paradise Lost*. In developing this plot Milton does not resort to "faking" or to delineating an Adam and Eve corrupt before the Fall; in the state of innocence they do not possess "some of the failings of the fallen."[25] They never actualize those failings, though they plentifully demonstrate a potential to do so. As the moment of the Fall draws closer through Books IV to IX of the epic, we as readers, through the hindsight of history, directed by the epic flashbacks in the poem's complex chronology, become increasingly aware that possibility is shading into probability, that potential is about to become actualized, but until the fruit is eaten, probability involves no necessity. The historical fact of the Fall, known by the reader and foreknown by God from his "prospect high" is what makes the Fall seem inevitable to us. This sense of the historical inevitability of the disobedience of Adam and Eve should not be confused with the possibilities and probabilities which operate in the narrative itself. Milton regularly reminds us that right up to the actual eating of the fruit Adam and Eve are "yet sinless." In the formula "sufficient to have stood, though free to fall," he sums up the potentialities with which man was created. Time and time again before the Fall Adam and Eve manifest the potentialities which prove them truly "free to fall"; yet, as H. V. S. Ogden has noted, were it not for the fact that they did fall, one would take such incidents as Eve's dream or Adam's rebuke by Raphael for uxorious tendencies as contributions to their sufficiency rather than portents of their fall.[26]

To understand the crucial relation between potential and actuality in the life of Adam and Eve, one must read *Paradise Lost* simultaneously from both eternal and temporal perspectives. The chronology of the narrative itself and the achronological structure viewed by God and the narrator must both be given full attention.[27] To focus only on the certainties foreknown by God is to ignore the genuine moral freedom enjoyed by Adam and Eve before they fall; to focus only on the human drama of Adam and Eve is to ignore the context which gives meaning to that drama. From the moment of their creation Adam and Eve are not puppets, nor, conversely, are they ever isolated individual egos adrift in an existential void. Both before and after the Fall they are thinking, knowing, feeling beings, endued with free will and faced by crucial choices in a world which has value and meaning. Milton in *Paradise Lost* is true both to his art and to his humanist ethos. The Fall of Adam and Eve is as truly dramatic and genuinely moral an action as that involving a "wayfaring [warfaring] Christian" in the fallen world or any hero of secular epic or tragedy.

Swarthmore College

NOTES

1. *Areopagitica*, in *John Milton: Complete Poems and Major Prose*, ed. Merritt Y. Hughes (New York, 1957), p. 733; *Paradise Lost* III, 108 "(Reason also is choice)." All references to *Areopagitica* and *Paradise Lost* are to Hughes' edition; further citations of *Paradise Lost* are in the text by book and line.

2. Millicent Bell, "The Fallacy of the Fall in *Paradise Lost*," *PMLA*, LXVIII (1953), 863. Miss Bell's essay gave rise to several responses: see Wayne Shumaker's reply in *PMLA*, LXX (1955), 1185 ff., and also H. V. S. Ogden, "The Crisis of *Paradise Lost* Reconsidered," *PQ*, XXXVI (1957), 1–19. For an argument with some similarities to mine, see Joseph H. Summers, *The Muse's Method* (London, 1962), pp. 149–50.

3. Bell, "The Fallacy of the Fall," p. 864.

4. E. M. W. Tillyard, "The Crisis of *Paradise Lost*," in his *Studies in Milton* (London, 1951), p. 11.

5. A. J. A. Waldock, *"Paradise Lost" and Its Critics* (Cambridge, Eng., 1947), pp. 18–24, 42, and passim: "What, after all, has Milton—the Milton of the great famous sayings in the prose works, the Milton who could not praise a fugitive and cloistered virtue unexercised and unbreathed—to do with the effortless innocence, the 'blank' virtue of prelapsarian man?" (p. 22). For a more strident extrapolation of the argument, see William Empson, *Milton's God*, rev. ed. (London, 1965).

6. To suggest the dual aspects of pilgrimage and struggle in Milton's idea of the Christian life one is tempted to conflate into one reading the "wayfaring" of the first edition of *Areopagitica* and the "warfaring" of subsequent editions.

7. *The Seventeenth Century Background* (1934; reprint, New York, 1955), p. 244. Cf. Samuel Johnson, "Milton," in *Lives of the English Poets.*

8. Watson Kirkconnell, ed. and trans., *The Celestial Cycle*, "The Caedmonian *Genesis*" (Toronto, 1952), p. 24.

9. See Arnold Williams, *The Common Expositor* (Chapel Hill, 1948), C. A. Patrides, *Milton and the Christian Tradition* (Oxford, 1966), and J. M. Evans, *"Paradise Lost" and the Genesis Tradition* (Oxford, 1968). Evans notes thoroughly the debt Milton owed to earlier interpretations of Genesis, but he also concludes that Milton "revolutionized the traditional view of Eden and pre-lapsarian Man" (p. 269).

10. *Poetics*, IX, 1451a.

11. Evans notes that a number of writers, including Philo Judaeus, loath to conceive of man created without moral prudence, assert that he possessed knowledge of good and evil before the Fall. These writers, however, then either posit some scientific rather than ethical knowledge as the fruit of the tree, or place the Fall elsewhere (p. 72).

12. For an extended analysis of these discourses as "tutorial narrative," see Jon S. Lawry, *The Shadow of Heaven* (Ithaca, 1968), pp. 183 ff.

13. Hughes, *John Milton*, p. 728.

14. *The Christian Doctrine*, ch. X, in *The Student's Milton*, rev. ed., ed. F. A. Patterson (New York, 1957), p. 986.

15. Ibid. Dennis H. Burden, in *The Logical Epic* (Cambridge, Mass., 1967), pp. 97–123, argues that the forbidden knowledge is of astronomy. Were this so, however, God (and Milton) could be justly accused by Satan of a capricious prohibition.

16. Lawry notes the parallel between Michael's mission and Raphael's which I develop here: "These books (V–VIII) concentrate the effort to define for man the essence of Paradise under the aegis of choice, balancing the postlapsarian definition of man and the world in Books XI–XII" (*Shadow of Heaven*, p. 183).

17. G. A. Buttrick, ed. (New York, 1962). Among the patristic and scholastic interpretations of the tree collected by Evans, two are of special relevance here: St. Augustine, *De Gen. Con. Man.* II. ix–xi, "the sin of the heart will bring its own punishment, for by *experience* it will learn the difference between the good it has forsaken and the evil into which it has fallen. And this will be to that soul the tasting of the fruit of the tree of the discernment of good and evil" (quoted in Evans, *"Paradise Lost" and the Genesis Tradition*, p. 75); Peter Comestor, *Hist. Schol., Lib. Gen.* xiii, "the tree of knowledge was named from

the event which followed the tasting of it. Before that man did not know what was evil, as he had not *experienced* it" (quoted in ibid., p. 170, all italics mine).

18. Hughes, *John Milton*, p. 733.

19. Eve's momentary narcissism at her first awakening, her dream when the guard of reason is down, the sexuality of her relations with Adam, and her desire to prove herself in solitary labor among the groves of Paradise, are all evidence of "passions within" and a lively sense of pleasures "round about." Adam's request for a proper mate, his curiosity about the heavens, and his tendency toward passionate overvaluation of Eve all attest to the presence within him of desires which could possibly catch the sway of his will from reason.

20. Milton's assertion that Adam and Eve were created with a "liability to fall" is found in *The Christian Doctrine*, ch. XI, in *The Student's Milton*, ed. F. A. Patterson, p. 997.

21. Albert W. Fields, "Milton and Self-knowledge," *PMLA*, LXXXIII (1968), p. 394.

22. Though I find Evans' argument in most respects compatible with mine, if different in emphasis, I cannot agree that "the difference between unfallen and fallen Man is simply the difference between a well and a badly tended Garden. It is a difference of degree, not of kind. That is why Paradise can be regained" (*"Paradise Lost" and the Genesis Tradition*, p. 271). This view ignores the guilt which must be atoned for if a Paradise both external and internal is to be restored. No matter how well a man may tend his spiritual and moral garden and with faith achieve a "paradise within," mankind must still live in the midst of "all our woe" until primal bliss is returned in "new Heaven and new earth" at the end of time.

23. Hughes, *John Milton*, p. 729.

24. Ibid., p. 733. Burden, *The Logical Epic*, pp. 125 ff., argues that Milton in the epic could not logically allow the tree to be provocative. I argue that it must be so if the logic of Adam and Eve's freedom is to hold.

25. Tillyard, "The Crisis of *Paradise Lost*," p. 10, accuses Milton of resorting to "some faking, perfectly legitimate in a poem, yet faking nevertheless," in order to make his narrative work.

26. Ogden, "The Crisis of *Paradise Lost* Reconsidered," p. 3: "The subsequent event determines our perspective, . . . experience could have strengthened innocence and confirmed rectitude as readily as in the event it destroyed them."

27. Lawry, in suggesting the proper "stance" for a reader of *Paradise Lost*, states neatly one-half of the dual focus I see as necessary: "Much of our difficulty with *Paradise Lost* arises from our failure to view lateral human history from this ultimately eternal stance. We usually isolate only one or another segment of time and event and rest all of our sense of God's meaning within it. We should instead utilize the stance of Book III in order that we place any particular segment within the perspective of Heaven, which is also that of epic" (*Shadow of Heaven*, p. 155). I suggest that the "perspective of Heaven" is one of the perspectives from which the poem should be read, but that the epic makes "lateral human history" equally important. The paradoxical relation of time to eternity, of man's perceptions to God's, is central to both the art and the theology of the poem.

ITERATIVE FIGURES AND IMAGES IN *PARADISE LOST*, XI–XII

Sister Mary Brian Durkin

Although lacking the epic power of the first books of *Paradise Lost*, Books XI and XII have significant merits. By panoramic visions and narration, Michael not only shows Adam the consequences of his disobedience, but teaches him how to live in a world unparadised; it is not the biblical events but their effect on the mind and heart of Adam that is noteworthy. Michael's terse counsels and Adam's references to him as guide, seer, and teacher emphasize the instructional importance of the books. Rhetorical figures, particularly anadiplosis, polyptoton, climax, *ploce*, anaphora, and epanalepsis, heighten lessons concerning aspects of life: war, peace; famine, plenty; freedom, slavery; thought and structure complement each other. Effectively employing alliteration, onomatopoeia, and assonance, Milton combines sound and sense with purpose and structure. Descriptions rich with metaphors, stated or implied, and references to color reveal the author's unimpaired aural and visual imagination.

AT THE opening of Book XI Adam and Eve are repentant: "the stonie from their hearts" has been removed; they are ready for regeneration. God, accepting their prayers offered to Him by His Divine Son, decrees their banishment from the Garden, and dispatches Michael with a twofold commission: he is to prepare the couple for exile; he is to impart wisdom, courage, and faith to Adam by revealing to him the future of his progeny. Michael shows Adam a panoramic vision of future events: Cain's slaughter of Abel, the sins of Seth's descendants, the destructive flood, God's Covenant with Noah. In Book XII Michael foretells significant episodes: the building of the Tower of Babel, the escape from Pharaoh's bondage, the formation of the Hebrew nation. Obedient to God's command that Adam is not to be overwhelmed by discouragement, Michael also tells of the glory of the Chosen Race, the birth of the Messiah.

Too much derogatory criticism has been aimed at this presentation of biblical events, revealed or recounted to Adam: the climactic episodes having ended, the biblical history of the last books is too familiar to sustain interest; Milton's gift of portraying memorable scenes, such as the abyss of Hell and the glories of Heaven, vanished before he completed these books.[1] Books XI and XII have intrinsic merit, not only because they contain the preview of future events which teach Adam rules for right living in a world no longer Paradise, but also because they show Milton's skill in utilizing rhetorical and prosodic techniques to intensify the instructional impact of the poem and to heighten the visual and auditory beauty of countless lines.

That Milton wished to emphasize the instructive quality of these books is evident from the numerous references to Michael's role as teacher, and the hortatory, instructional qualities of his admonitions. Of the former, Adam's invocations are significant, for he addresses Michael as "safe Guide" (XI, 372); "Celestial Guide" (XI, 785); "O Teacher" (XI, 450); "True opener of mine eyes" (XI, 598); "Heav'nly instructor" (XI, 871); "Enlightner of my darkness" (XII, 271); "O Prophet of glad tidings, finisher / Of utmost hope!" (XII, 375–76); "Seer blest" (XII, 553).[2]

Reproof and advice, tersely phrased by Adam's mentor, merit attention for their aphoristic wisdom. Succinct and consoling is Michael's counsel: "And one bad act with many deeds well done / Mayst cover" (XI, 256–57). In this doctrine of salvation, stated in eleven words, thought and structure complement each other. The contrast afforded by "one" and "many" is further heightened by "bad" and "well done" and the placing of the verb at the end. A warning against the false glamor of worldly rewards is pithily stated: "Thus Fame shall be atchiev'd, renown on Earth / And what most merits fame in silence hid" (XI, 698–99). A favorite idea of Milton's, that the individual not only creates, but carries within himself happiness or misery, heaven or hell, is stated twice:

> God attributes to place
> No sanctitie, if none be thither brought
> By Men who there frequent, or therein dwell.   (XI, 836–38)

> then wilt thou not be loath
> To leave this Paradise, but shall possess
> A Paradise within thee, happier farr.   (XII, 585–87)

Eve's awkward statement that she wishes to remain with Adam, even if it means that she must leave Paradise, reveals that she has not learned this lesson:

>   but now lead on;
>   In mee is no delay; with thee to goe
>   Is to stay here; without thee here to stay
>   Is to go hence unwilling; thou to mee
>   Art all things under Heav'n, all places thou,
>   Who for my wilful crime art banisht hence.   (XII, 614–19)

Marred by jerky rhythms and overstatement, her words are prompted by emotional tension rather than by rational thought, but no angelic instructor has taught her that true happiness cannot rest solely in another.

Brevity and profundity of thought characterize many passages. Recognizing Adam's contrition—"He sorrows, now, repents, and prayes contrite"—God, nevertheless, knows how vacillating Adam—and by implication all mankind—is. He comments: "how variable and vain / Self-left" (XI, 92–93). The position of "self-left" gives it dominance; the implications are many: man, alone, bereft of Divine Providence and saving grace, is indeed alone, shifting about like a weathercock; he is "self-left" because he has divorced himself from One who demands integrity, loyalty, love—service that leaves no room for self-love, vanity, inconstancy. Responsible for the step that separated him from his Creator, Adam is indeed without help, left to his own deserts, "self-left." The pun is unmistakable.

In Books XI and XII Adam learns many lessons from life's changing rhythms: systole, diastole; abundance, famine; labor, rest; goodness, corruption; peace, war; supremacy, slavery; sin, repentence; life, death. Frequently these ideas are emphasized by rhetorical figures: anadiplosis, polyptoton, climax, *ploce,* anaphora, epanalepsis. Scant attention has been paid to Milton's use of rhetorical figures to heighten the serious, instructional import of many lines.

Particularly effective is Milton's use of anadiplosis, the repetition of the last word of one clause or sentence at the beginning of the next:

who to surprize
One man, Assassin-like had levied Warr,
Warr unproclaim'd.   (XI, 218–20)

Anadiplosis accentuates the horrors of the plague sent to free those in bondage:

Thunder mixt with Hail,
Hail mixt with fire must rend th' Egyptian Skie.
                                       (XII, 181–82)

The following suggests the destructive force of the Flood, and the fury of God's vengeance:

Sea cover'd Sea,
Sea without shoar; and in thir Palaces
Where luxurie late reign'd, Sea-monsters whelp'd.
                                       (XI, 749–51)

The repetition of "foretold" in the following lines is a reminder that the longed-for Messiah fulfills a divine promise and ancient prophecy:

A Son, the Womans Seed to thee foretold,
Foretold to Abraham, as in whom shall trust
All Nations, and to Kings foretold.   (XII, 327–29)

Polyptoton, the repetition of words derived from the same root, not only adds solemn dignity to God's command to Michael, but also emphasizes the fallen state of Adam and Eve:

and from the Paradise of God
Without remorse drive out the sinful Pair,
From hallowd ground th' unholie.   (XI, 104–06)

The succinctness of Michael's advice to Adam in the following lines is achieved by the force of the antithetical words, "love," "hate"; "long," "short"; the repetition of "nor"; the shift of stress to the first word of the second line, with polyptoton intensifying the command:

Nor love thy Life, nor hate; but what thou liv'st
Live well, how long or short permit to Heav'n. (XI, 553–54)

Polyptoton effectively supports the hortatory tone of Michael's admonitions:

But prayer against his absolute Decree
No more avails than breath against the wind,
Blown stifling back on him that breaths it forth. (XI, 311–13)

And it adds trenchant force to Adam's expression of horror and revulsion when he beholds Cain's murder of Abel:

> O sight
> Of Terrour, foul and ugly to behold,
> Horrid to think, how horrible to feel!   (XI, 463–65)

It is particularly effective in lines denouncing evil:

> Sin, that first
> Distemperd all things, and of incorrupt
> Corrupted.   (XI, 55–57)

> by my foreknowledge gaining Birth
> Abortive, to torment me ere thir being,
> With thought that they must be.   (XI, 768–70)

Amorously aroused by "A Beavie of fair Women, richly gay / In Gems and wanton dress," the descendants of Seth succumb to temptation; polyptoton effectively suggests their sensuality:

> The Men though grave, ey'd them, and let thir eyes
> Rove without rein, till in the amorous Net
> Fast caught, they lik'd, and each his liking chose. (XI, 585–87)

Michael crushes Adam's delight in the scene, warning him that it is folly to be trapped by the senses:

> Judge not what is best
> By pleasure.
> . . . .
> Those Tents thou sawst so pleasant, were the Tents
> Of wickedness.   (XI, 603–04; 607–08)

Polyptoton frequently adds a poignant touch:

> Thy going is not lonely, with thee goes
> Thy husband.   (XI, 290–91)

> all places else
> Inhospitable appeer and desolate,
> Nor knowing us nor known.   (XI, 305–07)

> These two are Brethren, Adam, and to come
> Out of thy loyns; th' unjust the just hath slain. (XI, 454–55)

These lines are subtly reechoed when Michael speaks of expiation:

> they may conclude
> Some bloud more precious must be paid for Man,
> Just for unjust, that in such righteousness
> To them by Faith imputed, they may find
> Justification towards God.   (XII, 292–96)

The comforting assurance of spiritual guidance is marked by polyptoton which adds somber dignity to Michael's words:

> God is as here, and will be found alike
> Present, and of his presence many a signe
> Still following thee.   (XI, 350–52)

> and the Law of Faith
> Working through love, upon thir hearts shall write,
> To guide them in all truth, and also arm
> With spiritual Armour.   (XII, 488–91)

Also frequent is polyptoton combined with climax, carrying repetition through three or more clauses. The following repetition of "God's Image" or close variants intensifies the expression of Adam's distress over man's defacement of the "Divine similitude":

> Can thus
> Th' Image of God in man created once
> . . . .
> To such unsightly sufferings be debas't
> Under inhuman pains? Why should not Man,
> Retaining still Divine Similitude
> In part, from such deformities be free,
> And for his Makers Image sake exempt?
> Thir Makers Image, answerd Michael, then
> Forsook them, when themselves they villifi'd
> To serve ungovern'd appetites, and took
> His Image whom they serv'd, a brutish vice. (XI, 507–18)

The last "Image" refers, of course, to the image of Satan as Covetousness, Lust, and Gluttony. Climax effectively emphasizes the point that evildoers are "Disfiguring not Gods likeness, but thir own" (XI, 521) while they bring "Loathsom sickness" on themselves because "Gods Image [they] did not reverence in themselves" (XI, 525).

A marked caesural pause, frequent in climax, often increases the serious, instructional tone, as is shown in this example of climax, pleasingly combined with *ploce*, the speedy reiteration of a word with few words intervening:

> O goodness infinite, goodness immense!
> That all this good of evil shall produce,
> And evil turn to good.   (XII, 469–71)

Ploce, a figure termed by some *epanados* or *traductio,* frequently adds a sweeping effect of immediacy: "The Race of time, / Till time stand fixt" (XII, 554–55); "Subverting worldly strong, and worldly wise" (XII, 568); "Betwixt the world destroy'd and world restor'd" (XII, 3); "Forbidd'n knowledge by forbidd'n means" (XII, 279); "and bound his Reign / With earths wide bounds" (XII, 370–71).

Pleading for Adam and Eve, the Son addresses his Father with humility as becomes an intercessor, with compassion for the guilty as becomes their Saviour; *ploce* emphasizes this dual role:

> Unskilful with what words to pray, let mee
> Interpret for him, mee his Advocate
> And propitiation, all his works on mee
> Good or not good ingraft, my Merit those
> Shall perfet, and for these my Death shall pay.
> Accept me, and in mee from these receave
> The smell of peace toward Mankind.   (XI, 32–38)

The forceful repetition of "mee" suggests the uniquely personal relationship between fallen man and the Son, existing even before He assumed humanity. The following lines emphasize this relationship, and also the union between Father and Son to be enjoyed by redeemed mankind in the future life:

> where with mee
> All my redeemd may dwell in joy and bliss,
> Made one with me as I with thee am one.   (XI, 42–44)

Ploce characterizes the loving response of the Father:

> All thy request for Man, accepted Son,
> Obtain, all thy request was my Decree   (XI, 46–47)

but it adds a note of severity to his decree that the offenders must be ejected from Paradise: the repetition of "no" and "gross" emphasizes the Father's displeasure:

> Those pure immortal Elements that know
> No gross, no unharmoneous mixture foul,
> Eject him tainted now, and purge him off
> As a distemper, gross to air as gross.   (XI, 50–53)

Addressing the "Sons of Light," God reminds the angels of the folly of pride and disobedience; the repetition of the antithetical words "Good" and "Evil" starkly indicates Adam's offense:

> O Sons, like one of us Man is become
> To know both Good and Evil, since his taste
> Of that defended Fruit; but let him boast
> His knowledge of Good lost, and Evil got,
> Happier, had it suffic'd him to have known
> Good by itself, and Evil not at all.   (XI, 84–89)

The iterative stress of "for ever" stresses the enormity of their folly, and the finality of God's decree:

> Least therefore his now bolder hand
> Reach also of the Tree of Life, and eat,
> And live for ever, dream at least to live
> For ever, to remove him I decree.   (XI, 93–96)

Ploce adds a note of gravity to Michael's instructions to Adam:

> Obedience to the law of God, impos'd
> On penaltie of death, and suffering death,
> The penaltie to thy transgressions due,
> And due to theirs which out of thine will grow.
>   (XII, 397–400)

> The Law of God exact he shall fulfill
> Both by obedience and by love, though love
> Alone fulfill the Law.   (XII, 401–03)

> Not onely to the Sons of Abrahams Loins
> Salvation shall be Preacht, but to the Sons
> Of Abrahams Faith wherever through the world.
>   (XII, 447–49)

Anaphora, beginning a series of clauses or sentences with the same word, adds balanced formality to many passages:

> Part wield thir Arms, Part courb the foaming Steed.   (XI, 643)

> So many and so various Laws are giv'n;
> So many Laws argue so many sins
> Among them.   (XII, 282–85)

> Eve rightly call'd, Mother of all Mankind,
> Mother of all things living.   (XI, 159–60)

Excusing himself for not telling all the trials and troubles of Adam's progeny, Michael, by repeating the phrase "how many," implies that the wars were not only numerous but also too tedious to recount:

> the rest
> Were long to tell, how many Battels fought,
> How many Kings destroyd, and Kingdoms won. (XII, 260–62)

Wondering how the faithful, "left among th' unfaithful herd," will survive when the Son of God returns to Heaven, Adam plaintively inquires: "who then shall guide / His people, who defend?" (XII, 482–83). Anaphora adds a note of urgency as well as poignancy to his query; it gives pithy force to Michael's advice:

> onely add
> Deeds to thy knowledge answerable, add Faith,
> Add Vertue, Patience, Temperance, add Love (XII, 581–83)

and gives a note of formal dignity to Adam's expression of gratitude for Michael's lessons:

> Greatly instructed, I shall hence depart,
> Greatly in peace of thought.   (XII, 557–58)

Epanalepsis, beginning and ending a clause or sentence with the same word, and alliterative anaphora suggest the extent of the Flood in the lines: "Sea cover'd Sea, / Sea without shoar" (XI, 749–50). The echo quality, notable in epanalepsis, is appropriate for the foreboding tone of the following:

> Wolves shall succeed for teachers, grievous Wolves.   (XII, 506)

> Deaths Ministers, not Men, who thus deal Death
> Inhumanly to men.   (XI, 676–77)

Circumscribed in Books XI and XII by Scripture and tradition, Milton employs his imagination and poetic powers to develop with somber dignity and restraint concepts of the world's disorder after Adam's fall, man's perversity and his struggle to achieve salvation. The grandiose, sublime style which highlights earlier scenes, such as Satan's punishment, his council meeting, the temptation in the Garden, is not appropriate for the revelations made by Michael nor the lessons learned by Adam. In exhorting Adam to lead a life guided by reason and illumined by faith and love, Michael's words are grave, restrained, hortatory; when he shows Adam the waywardness of mankind, the result of man's disobedience, a tone of reproof and sorrow for the offense given to his Creator makes Adam realize the enormity of his guilt and its dire consequences for all mankind. Milton's judicious use of rhetorical figures in Books XI and XII creates a synthesis of religious thought and poetic power. These iterative figures, particularly polyptoton, *ploce*, and anaphora, invest many lines with balance, gravity, and a decorum appropriate for the thoughts expressed; frequently these devices add a graceful, lyrical beauty by chiming on key words: "Good or not good ingraft"; "Greatly instructed," "greatly in peace"; "add Faith, add Vertue."

Careful reading of Books XI and XII also reveals the notable effects that Milton achieves by alliteration, onomatopoeia, and assonance.[3] Noteworthy are the numerous alliterative lines which describe the trials and sufferings of future generations:

> Some, as thou saw'st, by violent stroke shall die,
> By Fire, Flood, Famin, by Intemperance more
> In Meats and Drinks, which on the Earth shall bring
> Diseases dire.   (XI, 471–74)

> Dire was the tossing, deep the groans, despair
> Tended the sick busiest from Couch to Couch;
> And over them triumphant Death his Dart
> Shook, but delaid to strike.   (XI, 489–92)

The consonantal harshness of "Fire, Flood, Famin" and "Dire," "deep," and "despair" reinforces the terror of awaiting death's unpredictable assault. Frequently when Milton wishes to recall the trickery of Satan in the Garden of Paradise, he effectively utilizes words that suggest the hissing of a serpent; "some," "spring," "Smoke," "Sin" (and its variants) achieve this in the following passage:

> Adam, now ope thine eyes, and first behold
> Th' effects which thy original crime hath wrought
> In some to spring from thee, who never touch'd
> Th' excepted Tree, nor with the Snake conspir'd
> Nor sinn'd thy sin, yet from that sin derive
> Corruption to bring forth more violent deeds.   (XI, 423–28)

In another passage repeated sibilants re-create the swirl and splash of the churning sea as it inundates the earth:

> Sea cover'd Sea,
> Sea without shoar; and in thir Palaces
> Where luxurie late reign'd, Sea-Monsters whelp'd
> And stabl'd; of Mankind, so numerous late,
> All left, in one small bottom swum imbark't.   (XI, 749–53)

An effective use of labials suggests the laborious pushing, pulling, and pressing down antecedent to the birth of giants: "Produce prodigious Births of bodie or mind" (XI, 688). The repetition of labials and sibilants accentuates the anguish of Adam and Eve expelled from Paradise:

> The brandisht Sword of God before them blaz'd.   (XII, 633)

Equally appropriate for the suffering described are the alliterative consonants:

> His Cattel must of Rot, and Murren die,
> Botches and Blains must all his flesh imboss,
> And all his people.   (XII, 179–81)

Some alliterative and assonantal patterns reinforce pleasing concepts, as is evident in this description of rural peace, disrupted by marauders:

> One way a Band select from forage drives
> A herd of Beeves, fair Oxen and fair Kine
> From a fat Meddow ground; or fleecy Flock,
> Ewes and thir bleating Lambs over the Plain.   (XI, 646–49)

Others suggest the emotion and pathos of scene or sufferer; Eve's wistful pleadings to be permitted to remain in Paradise are marked by alliteration and assonance:

> How shall I part, and whither wander down
> Into a lower World, to this obscure
> And wild, how shall we breathe in other Air.   (XI, 282–84)

Her comment, when Adam returns after his conference with Michael, is excessively alliterative:

> Whence thou returnst, and whither wentst, I know.   (XII, 610)

Is it possible that Milton wished to suggest Eve's sleep-drugged, witless confusion and dismay?

In the following passage the multiplication of *w* sounds suggests the force of the rising wind, an effect heightened by the alliterative sibilants, echoing the rushing downpour of the Flood:

> Meanwhile the Southwind rose, and with black wings
> Wide hovering, all the Clouds together drove
> From under Heav'n; the Hills to their supplie
> Vapour, and Exhalation dusk and moist,
> Sent up amain; and now the thick'n'd Skie
> Like a dark Ceeling stood; down rush'd the Rain. (XI, 738–43)

Onomatopoeia and alliteration suggest the fluid force of the Flood:

> but all the Cataracts
> Of Heav'n set open on the Earth shall powr
> Rain day and night, all fountains of the Deep
> Broke up, shall heave the Ocean to usurp
> Beyond all bounds, till inundation rise
> Above the highest Hills: then shall this Mount
> Of Paradise by might of Waves be moov'd
> Out of his place, pushed by the horned floud,
> With all his verdure spoil'd, and Trees adrift
> Down the great River to the op'ning Gulf
> And there take root an Iland salt and bare,
> The haunt of Seals and Orcs, and Sea-mews clang.
>
> (XI, 824–35)

The strident tone, and the irregularity of the rhythm achieved by the stress on the first syllable of some lines, are in harmony with the chaos and confusion represented. "Both rhythm and sound are handled in XI, 824–35, in such a way as to suggest the vigorous fluid strength which water has in a restricted space spending itself over a wider area and at last wasted to calm in the sea's expanse," states Mahood, impressed by Milton's ability to suggest the "primary qualities of matter, such as weight and projectile force."[4]

Mahood thinks that Milton's imagination was motile, and attempts to prove that the poet's concepts were tactile rather than aural or visual,[5] but a close study of Books XI and XII reveals that Milton's remarkable powers of aural imagination helped him to create countless lines harmonious in sound and sense. His skill in creating scenes strident with din and disorder is notable in the description of the confusion at the Tower of Babel when God

> in derision sets
> Upon thir Tongues a various Spirit to rase
> Quite out thir Native Language, and instead
> To sow a jangling noise of words unknown:
> Forthwith a hideous gabble rises loud
> Among the Builders; each to other calls
> Not understood, till hoarse, and all in rage,
> As mockt they storm; great laughter was in Heav'n
> And looking down, to see the hubbub strange
> And hear the din; thus was the building left
> Ridiculous, and the work Confusion nam'd.   (XII, 52–62)

"Jangling," "gabble," "hideous," "hubbub," "Din," and the heavier tones of "hoarse," "rage," "mockt" all suggest the senseless wrangling and mounting tension of the builders as the turmoil increased; the tumbling force of enjambment and rhythm accentuates the turbulent strife and chaos at the Tower of Babel. The scene is a sharp contrast to the opening of Book XII when Michael begins his prophetic narrative with a line suggestive of a whispered tale: "Then with transition sweet new Speech resumes" (XII, 5).

Fricatives and labials in the following passage add tremendous energy and emphatic denunciation:

> What will they then
> But force the Spirit of Grace it self, and bind
> His consort Libertie; what, but unbuild
> His living Temples, built by Faith to stand,
> Thir own Faith not anothers: for on Earth
> Who against Faith and Conscience can be heard
> Infallible?

As the passage ends, the force of the sibilants and the alliterative *r* intensifies the tone of anger and sorrow over the world's great folly:

> the *r*est, fa*rr* g*r*eate*r* pa*r*t,
> Will deem in outward *R*ites and *s*pecious fo*r*me*s*
> *R*eligion *s*ati*s*fi'd; T*r*uth *s*hall *r*eti*r*e
> Be*s*t*r*uck with *s*land*r*ous da*r*ts, and wo*r*ks of Faith
> *R*a*r*ely be found: *s*o *s*hall the Wo*r*ld goe on,
> To good malignant, to bad men benigne,
> Unde*r* he*r* own waight g*r*oaning.   (XII, 524–30; 533–39)

In denouncing Books XI and XII, critics often claim that these show a weakening of Milton's visual imagination: the metaphors are negligible; descriptions lack color and verve. Yet there are effective descriptions of nature, of movement, of spatial contrasts; and metaphors, implied or stated, add levels of meaning.

Some significant comparisons, particularly the multiple references to "fruit" and "seed," merit attention. The prayers and contrition of Adam and Eve are referred to by the Son as "first fruits" (XI, 22) and "fruits" again in line 26; the metaphor is extended by reference to the tears of the couple "manuring" the ground (XI, 28). God the Father alludes to their act of disobedience when He speaks of the "stol'n Fruit" (XI, 125) and the "knowledge of Good lost, and Evil got" when the couple tasted of that "defended Fruit" (XI, 85–86); Michael reminds Adam of "that false Fruit that promis'd clear sight" (XI, 413); earlier, Eve, not fully aware of the consequences of her disobedience, laments that they must leave Paradise, and queries: "how shall we breathe in other Air / Less pure, accustomed to immortal Fruits?" (XI, 284–85). Michael encourages Adam to lead a righteous life:

> So maist thou live, till like ripe Fruit thou drop
> Into thy Mothers lap, or be with ease
> Gatherd, not harshly pluckt, for death mature.   (XI, 534–37)

And towards the close of Book XII, Michael comforts Adam, telling him that at the end of the world God will raise

> From the conflagrant mass, purg'd and refin'd,
> New Heav'ns, new Earth, Ages of endless date
> Founded in righteousness and peace and love,
> To bring forth fruits joy and eternal Bliss.   (XII, 548–51)

It is significant that the last two references are no longer associated with man's disobedience, but refer instead to Adam purified, and the happiness of eternal life in Heaven.

The related image, "seed," first occurs when the Son addresses His Father on behalf of Adam and Eve:

> I thy Priest before thee bring,
> Fruits of more pleasing savour from thy seed
> Sow'n with contrition in his heart.   (XI, 26–28)

And the Father, bidding Michael to instruct Adam concerning the future, warns the angel to comfort the pair with the promise of a Saviour:

> intermix
> My Cov'nant in the womans seed renewd;
> So send them forth, though sorrowing, yet in peace.
>   (XI, 115–17)

Adam is indeed consoled by God's promise to Eve "that thy Seed shall bruise our Foe" (IX, 155); later he thanks his instructor for the assurance that mankind will survive even such perils as the Flood, and will "thir seed preserve" (XI, 873). This image occurs frequently in Book XII, particularly in reference to Abraham: "in his Seed / All Nations shall be blest" (125–26); and Michael continues:

> This ponder, that all Nations of the Earth
> Shall in his Seed be blessed; by that Seed
> Is meant thy great deliverer.   (146–49)

To emphasize the importance of the promised redeemer, Michael reiterates that future generations will be told

> of that destind Seed to bruise
> The Serpent, by what means he shall achieve
> Mankinds deliverance.   (233–35)

References to "Abraham and his Seed" occur in lines 260 and 273; from David, Michael asserts, shall rise "A Son, the Womans Seed, to thee foretold" (327); Adam is overjoyed when he realizes why the Messiah is called "The seed of Woman" (379). The Saviour, Michael tells Adam, will save mankind, not by destroying Satan, but by destroying "his works / In thee and in thy Seed" (394–95). Lines 543, 600, and 601 repeat the phrase, the "Womans Seed." Throughout the two books, "seed" has dual implications: it refers to all the faithful who have obeyed God's laws—

> Not onely to the Sons of Abrahams Loins
> Salvation shall be Preacht, but to the Sons
> Of Abrahams Faith wherever through the world;
> So in his seed all Nations shall be blest   (447–50)

—and it refers to the Saviour to be born of the Virgin Mary, evoking Eve's cry:

> though all by mee is lost,
> Such favour I unworthie am voutsaft,
> By mee the Promis'd Seed shall all restore.   (621–23)

Prayer, unheard by God, is compared to "Breath against the wind / Blown stifling back on him that breaths it forth" (XI, 312–13). It is significant that this is not breath forming a cold vapor, but a hot, stifling wind, suggesting the fiery pangs of guilt and remorse. The hardened heart of Pharaoh is compared to ice that has melted, then refrozen into a chunkier, more impenetrable mass (XII, 193–94). The angels guarding the gates of Eden are viewed by the departing couple as a gray haze:

> Gliding meteorous, as Ev'ning Mist
> Ris'n from a River o're the marish glides;
> And gathers ground fast at the Labourers heel
> Homeward returning.   (XII, 629–32)

When one considers that the outcasts are saddened, not only by their loss of Eden, but also by the necessity of earning their living by the sweat of their brows in a strange land, there is a significance, poignant and appropriate, in the sight of the angels, gray as clinging mist befogging the worker's progress homeward.

The angels' swords also are compared to a phenomenon of nature: "The brandisht Sword of God before them blaz'd / Fierce as a Comet" (XII, 633–34). The rainbow, which appeared after the Flood, is pictured as a border of flowers:

> But say, what mean those colourd streaks in Heavn,
> Distended as the Brow of God appeas'd
> Or serve they as a flowrie verge to bind
> The fluid skirts of that same watrie Cloud
> Least it again dissolve and showr the Earth?   (XI, 879–83)

There is a homey, visual beauty in this comparison of the bands of the rainbow bordering and binding the tilting clouds, reminding one of spacious English fields hedged by trees or stone walls, with the smaller fields within this enclosure separated from each other by hedges and rows of flowering bushes.

A study of the comparisons in Books XI and XII leads to a fuller appreciation of the poetic power of the final books and of Milton's use of color, which is so frequent that one questions the statement that his imagination was peculiarly "motile." From Book XI the following indicate his visual power: Morn's "rosie progress" (175); beauty that fades, "wither'd, weak and gray" (540); "Skie of Jasper" (209); an altar of "grassie Terf," and "Stone of lustre" (324–25); "starrie Helm" (245); "glistering Zodiac" (247); "in the Cloud a Bow / Conspicuous with three listed colours gay" (865–66); "now scatterd lies / With Carcasses and Arms th' ensanguind Field / Deserted" (653–55); "Cohort bright . . . Spangl'd with eyes" (127–30); "flaming Warriors" (101). Since in Book XII Michael is only narrating events, there are, appropriately enough, fewer visual images: "dawning light" (421) is repeated again in line 423; "Light out of darkness" (473); "flaming Sword" (592); and line 643 echoes this—"that flaming Brand."

References to colors and shades are numerous: in Book XI the following are notable: "the Golden Altar fum'd" (18); "this Golden Censer" (24); morning light, "a radiant white" (206); Michael's "vest of purple" (241); "First Fruits, the green Ear and the yellow Sheaf" (453); "Grey-headed men" (662); "Meanwhile the Southwind rose, and with black wings / Wide hovering, all the Clouds together drove" (738–39); "Green tree" (858); "O're the blew Firmament a radiant white" (206). In Book XII the following add vividness to Michael's narration: "black bituminous gurge" (40); Moses' rod is "palpable darkness" (18); "drie land between two christal walls" (197); "A darksom Cloud of Locusts" which swarm and eat, and "on the ground leave nothing green" (185–86); "Mount of Sinai, whose gray top / Shall tremble" (227–28); a Sanctuary "overlaid with Gold" (250); "A Mercie-seat of Gold" (253). Particularly striking for its multiple implications of pristine innocence, radiant holiness, and messianic dignity is the description of Noah: "One Man except, the onely Son of light / In a dark Age" (XI, 808–09).

By panoramic visions and narration, Michael revealed centuries of human error, sinfulness, repentance, and the paradox of the Fortunate Fall; by these and interpretative admonitions, Adam learned how to live in a world unparadised. Labor, poverty, penance, estrangement he will endure, but his redemption will come, not from these, but from self-transformation: exterior visions of ages to come have given him insights, a knowledge of self which enables him to see his guilt in the past and the redemptive way of life he must follow in the future. Paradise is no longer a garden, but an inner state of mind. Adam has indeed been "pierc'd / Ev'n to the inmost seat of mental sight" (XI, 417–18).

Milton's rhetorical and prosodic techniques intensify many passages in Books XI and XII, elevating them from oft-repeated biblical tales to episodes rich in dramatic, philosophical, and theological concepts which evoke our emotional and intellectual reactions. Milton never allows sound to take precedence over sense, but adroitly expresses both; consider the alliterative line which dramatically, syntactically, and rhythmically suggests Adam's horror and shock on learning that he must leave Paradise: "Heart-strook with chilling gripe of sorrow stood" (XI, 264). Iterative patterns, pervasive images, strident alliteration, assonance, and irregular rhythms heighten dramatic passages, such as the Flood scene, where form and structure express the chaos, confusion, and tumult of the event. In nondramatic passages, line after line is threaded with devices described in this essay; rhetorical patterns, prosodic structure, imagery, colorful metaphors—all support the sense and emphasize the themes of Books XI and XII, adding somber dignity and appropriate decorum, helping to clarify, compress, and synthesize thought and poetic beauty. The following is an example of Milton's achievement:

> Henceforth I learn, that to obey is best,
> And love with fear the onely God, to walk
> As in his presence, ever to observe
> His providence, and on him sole depend,
> Mercifull over all his works, with good
> Still overcoming evil, and by small
> Accomplishing great things, by things deemd weak
> Subverting worldly strong, and wordly wise
> By simply meek; that suffering for Truths sake
> Is fortitude to highest victorie,
> And to the faithful Death the Gate of Life.   (XII, 561–73)

In the extrinsic design, theme, and beauty of *Paradise Lost*, the last two books are essential to its structure and aim.[6] They merit praise and continued study, for the narrative, didactic, and rhetorical techniques in Books XI and XII are indisputable evidence of Milton's sustained power.

Rosary College

NOTES

1. C. S. Lewis, *A Preface to "Paradise Lost"* (London, 1942) regards Books XI–XII as "an untransmuted lump of futurity," but concedes that at the end of Book XII there is a "great recovery" (p. 125); M. M. Mahood, *Poetry and Humanism* (London, 1950), asserts: "'an age too late or cold Climat or Years' have rendered Milton's powers unequal to his purpose and the verse flags dismally" (p. 168); J. B. Broadbent, *Some Graver Subject: An Essay on "Paradise Lost"* (New York, 1960), states: "The decay of the poetry prevents us claiming it as the poem's crisis. . . . Books XI and XII try to open out the Domestic Fall and personal reconciliation into a dimension where they lose force" (p. 268); B. A. Wright, *Milton's "Paradise Lost"* (London, 1962), writes: "The last two books . . . have always been felt to be flat and disappointing. Addison mentions it as a common opinion" (p. 190); Louis L. Martz, *The Paradise Within* (New Haven, 1964), writes: "At every reading, the disappointment with the last two books returns. . . . The voice of the bard and seer has lost its vigor, and the writing has become . . . the Biblical paraphrase of an almost ordinary versifier" (p. 142).

Recent critical studies have found praiseworthy elements in Books XI–XII. The following contain significant comments: Robert Bryan, "Adam's Tragic Vision in *Paradise Lost*," *SP*, LXII (1965), 197–214; Larry Champion, "The Conclusion of *Paradise Lost*—A Reconsideration," *CE*, XXVII (1966), 384–94; Jackson I. Cope, *The Metaphoric Structure of "Paradise Lost"* (Baltimore, 1962); Barbara K. Lewalski, "Structure and the Symbolism of Vision in Michael's Prophecy: *Paradise Lost*, Books XI–XII," *PQ*, XLII (1963), 25–35; H. R. MacCallum, "Milton and Sacred History: Books XI and XII of *Paradise Lost*," *Essays in English Literature from the Renaissance to the Victorian Age Presented to A. S. P. Woodhouse*, ed. Millar MacLure and F. W. Watt (Toronto, 1964), pp. 149–68; William G. Madsen, "The Idea of Nature in Milton's Poetry," *Three Studies in the Renaissance: Sidney, Jonson, Milton* (New Haven, 1958), pp. 254–71; Virginia Mollenkott, "The Cycle of Sins in *Paradise Lost*, Book XI," *MLQ*, XXVII (1966), 33–40; F. T. Prince, "On the Last Two Books of *Paradise Lost*," *Essays and Studies, 1958* (London, 1958), pp. 38–52; John Reesing, *Milton's Poetic Art* (Cambridge, Mass., 1968), pp. 69–86, 87–104; Lawrence Sasek, "The Drama of *Paradise Lost*, Books XI and XII," *Studies in English Renaissance Literature*, ed. Waldo McNeir (Baton Rouge, 1962), pp. 181–96; Joseph Summers, *The Muse's Method* (Cambridge, Mass., 1962), ch. 7; Elbert Thompson, "For *Paradise Lost*, XI–XII," *PQ*, XXII (1943), 376–82; George Whiting, *Milton and This Pendant World* (Austin, 1958), ch. 5 and 7.

2. All quotations from *Paradise Lost* are taken from *The Complete English Poetry of John Milton*, ed. John T. Shawcross (New York, 1963).

3. F. T. Prince, in *The Italian Element in Milton's Verse* (Oxford, 1954), pp. 126–27, labors to show that Milton learned techniques of alliteration, onomatopoeia, and assonance from Tasso, but the passages cited by Prince to substantiate his theories may also serve as examples of Milton's familiarity with the parallelisms of the Psalms, the pensées in *Proverbs* and *Ecclesiastes*.

4. M. M. Mahood, *Poetry and Humanism*, p. 199.

5. Ibid., p. 201. I find myself more in agreement with Northrop Frye's statement: "The precision of Milton's poetry is aural rather than visual, musical rather

than pictorial. When we read, for instance, 'Immediately the mountains huge appear / Emergent, and their broad bare backs upheave,' the mountains cannot be *seen:* it is the ear that must hear in 'emergent' the splash of the water falling from them, and in the long level monosyllables the clear blue line of the horizon." *"Paradise Lost" and Selected Poetry and Prose,* ed. Northrop Frye (New York, 1951), xxix.

6. This paper does not attempt to examine Milton's reasons for rearranging his epic into twelve books, and the artistic gains achieved by this; a recent, rewarding study by John Reesing, "Essay for the Tercentenary of *Paradise Lost,*" in *Milton's Poetic Art* emphasizes the new resonances achieved by clearer relationships between V and XI, VI and XII.

MILTON'S GOD
IN COUNCIL AND WAR

Kitty Cohen

Milton's presentation of God and Heaven is poetically convincing if various Hebraic elements in the books describing Heaven are closely examined. Hebraic allusions convey the religious and moral justification of God in council and in war and provide the conceptual link between the various scenes in Heaven. The counterpoise of justice and mercy in the dialogue between God and the Son is expressed through verbal echoes from the dialogues of Abraham and Moses with their God. Milton's ironic use of Psalm ii and other Old Testament references enhances the liveliness and dramatic power of the council scene in Book V, and his use of Hebraic figures like the Son's chariot and the angel Abdiel expresses the poet's conception of the war between the heavenly host and the rebel angels in Book VI as a battle in which spirit overcomes force.

N o   a s p e c t   of *Paradise Lost* has been so harshly and frequently criticized as Milton's presentation of God and Heaven. Even critics of the school of Douglas Bush, who read the epic against its Christian humanist background, and staunch admirers of the poem's message and poetry like Marjorie Nicolson and Helen Gardner find it difficult to like Milton's God.[1] John Peter finds fault with Milton's "imperfectly anthropomorphic presentation" of God, and David Daiches finds that Milton fails to achieve his poetic intention because he is committing himself to logic in his description of God.[2] On the other hand, William Empson, completely ignoring Milton's religious beliefs, claims the poem is good precisely because God is so bad.[3] My objection to Empson's thesis is not only that it is unhistorical, but that it is not validated by what the poetry conveys.[4] The view I wish to advance here is that Milton's presentation of God and Heaven not only embodies his seventeenth-century theology, but is also poetically convincing if various Hebraic elements, thematic and metaphorical, that are incorporated in Milton's descriptions of God in council and in war are closely examined. An appreciation of Old Testament allusions and echoes is vital for the understanding of both the conceptual link between the various scenes taking place in Heaven and the analogical correspondence between Milton's circumference and the human center of the poem. The cosmic theme provides not only, as Helen Gardner says, "a comparison and a contrast to the story of man's creation, fall and restoration";[5] it also foreshadows the dramatic events in Eden which the poem holds in focus. The greatness of Milton's Heaven consists in the conceptual breadth and depth which it adds to the central theme of the poem rather than in any inherent rhetorical power. And this dimension depends upon biblical allusions and echoes interwoven in the poem. It is also the Old Testament allusions which give those parts of the poem dramatic intensity.

Milton uses Old Testament allusions not only for their poetic suggestiveness but also because the language of the Bible was the most appropriate for the description of God and Heaven. Like other Renaissance and seventeenth-century writers,[6] he believed:

When we speak of knowing God, it must be understood with reference to the imperfect comprehension of man; for to know God as he really is, far transcends the powers of man's thoughts, much more of his perception. . . . Our safest way is to form in our minds such a conception of God, *as shall correspond with his own delineation and representation of himself in the sacred writings.* For granting that both in the literal and figurative descriptions of God, he is exhibited not as he really is, but in such a manner as may be within the scope of our comprehensions, yet we ought to entertain such a conception of him, as he, in condescending to accommodate himself to our capacities, has shewn that he desires we should conceive.[7] (my italics)

Milton thus knew that it was best to avoid going "beyond the written word of Scripture," lest he "be tempted to indulge in vague cogitations and subtleties."[8] Helen Gardner believes that the theory of accommodation prevented Milton "from exercising his own power to suggest" and that "one reason why he 'wrote in fetters' when he wrote of Heaven is that there exist in Scripture images and fictions to describe Heaven which his own theory of Scripture told him were chosen by

God to illuminate our understanding."[9] It is true that Heaven and its characters are described almost exclusively in terms of Scripture, but this limitation is not necessarily constrictive. As a matter of fact, the scriptural passages Milton alludes to, and those taken from the Old Testament in particular, are powerfully suggestive and it is they which make his Heaven so effective.

To the Books of Moses and to the writings of the prophets Milton could turn for ideal models of poetic personifications of God, and in the unrhymed verses of the Psalms he could find the purest devotional poetry expressive of deep religious feelings. It is therefore natural that when he came to represent God, Milton turned to the verses of the Hebrew poet-prophets for inspiration. But the reason is not only poetic. Only the Hebraic omnipotent God of the Old Testament is morally strong enough to defeat the fallen angels associated with the idols and heathen gods mentioned in the Old Testament. A more merciful God, a less hard taskmaster, would not have been equal to his opponent in the poem. In the books on Hell Milton invoked the atmosphere of the conflict between the God of the Israelites and the false gods as represented in the Old Testament. In the books on Heaven, Milton very appropriately invokes the image of the powerful Creator, the God of Justice as he is revealed in his dealings with his most devoted believers—Abraham, Moses, and prophets like Isaiah and Ezekiel. This image of God and the recurrence of Old Testament allusions and motifs create the thematic and conceptual link between the scenes which take place in Heaven.

The first scene to be considered is the heavenly council in Book III. Here Milton was faced with the problem of representing God as at once the powerful ruler of the universe, the Lord of Hosts, and as the essence of goodness and light. In terms of style, God had to be simultaneously idealized and rendered concrete. Milton achieves this end in the council scene, where God's first speech reveals his identity:

> Only begotten Son, seest thou what rage
> Transports our adversary, whom no bounds
> Prescrib'd, no bars of Hell, nor all the chains
> Heapt on him there, nor yet the main Abyss
> Wide interrupt can hold; so bent he seems
> On desperate revenge, that shall redound
> Upon his own rebellious head.   (III, 80–86)[10]

This is the divine wrath of the Old Testament God that is also heard in the words of St. Paul and Revelations. And divine justice is turned against those who are wicked. God's attitude to man, who broke the "Sole pledge of his obedience," is not only that of a judge punishing evil; it is mixed with paternal care:

> So will fall
> Hee and his faithless Progeny: whose fault?
> Whose but his own? ingrate, he had of mee
> All he could have; I made him just and right,
> Sufficient to have stood, though free to fall.   (III, 95–99)

These lines imply more than the mere affirmation of justice; they imply the hope that man might live up to the moral nature he has been endowed with as well as a deep disappointment at his failure to do so. The eagerness to see man in his perfection and the regret at his moral fall are common to Milton and to the Old Testament prophets. Moreover, the sentiment expressed in Milton's lines here resembles that of the prophets blaming Israel for ingratitude to the Creator, for example: "I have nourished and brought up children, and they have rebelled against me. The ox knoweth his owner, and the ass his master's crib: but Israel doth not know, my people doth not consider" (Isaiah i, 2–3).[11]

Although God's first speech ends with the promise, "Mercy first and last shall brightest shine" (III, 134), God's relationship to most of mankind is that of the Old Testament God of Justice and Milton forcefully expresses this in the words of the prophets. For those who "pray, repent, and bring obedience due" He promises His "ear shall not be slow," His "eye not shut," "for I will clear thir senses dark, / . . . and soft'n stony hearts." But mercy is extended only to those who repent, and the words are harsh. It may be significant that the same metaphors are used by Isaiah in an opposite context: "Make the heart of this people fat, and make their ears heavy, and shut their eyes; lest they see with their eyes and hear with their ears, and understand with their heart, and convert, and be healed" (Isaiah vi, 10). Milton's God, too, has no mercy for the sinners:

> my day of grace
> They who neglect and scorn, shall never taste;
> But hard be hard'n'd, blind be blinded more,
> That they may stumble on, and deeper fall.   (III, 198–201)

Patrick Hume notes (on III, 200) that the allusion is to Pharaoh, the example of a sinner hardened by God's remitting his punishment, and he quotes Exodus viii, 15: "But when Pharaoh saw that there was respite, he hardened his heart, and hearkened not unto them; as the Lord had said."[12] The correspondence between the sinners and Pharaoh has a double function here. The sinners are as proud and obstinate as Pharaoh, and like him their hearts are hardened. But the recurring allusions to Pharaoh also have another significance, for throughout the Old Testament there are references to God's victory over the Egyptians and to the liberation of the Hebrews from Egyptian slavery. The recurrence of these references makes the Egyptians an archetype of God's enemies, secondary perhaps only to 'Amaleq.

When Milton expresses the irrevocability of God's punishments, the "desperate revenge, that shall redound / Upon his own rebellious head" (III, 85–86), the words as well as the concept are reminiscent of many Old Testament verses.[13] Milton's lines also reveal another important attribute of God—his jealousy, for Milton knew that only the jealous Lord of Hosts, the Almighty God who demands sacrifices from his prophets and who cruelly chastises his enemies could be the counterpart to the evil adversary and the pagan deities described in the first two books.[14]

The first speech of God, the Son's reply and the ensuing speeches have been the subject of heated critical dispute, focusing on God's logical arguments, on his rigid concept of justice, and on the Son's more emotional plea for mercy. With respect to Milton's intention in presenting God as he does, two questions have to be clarified: the first is whether the distinction between the Old Testament God of vengeance and the merciful Jesus is coextensive with the theme of the dialogue or, in other words, whether there is an argument here between Milton's God (that is, Justice) and the Son (Mercy); the second is what concept of God emerges from the scene as a whole.

In one of the most recent critiques of the council scene Hughes considers the tension between justice and mercy to be part of the tradition to which *Paradise Lost* belongs, for in the morality plays justice and truth plead for the prosecution, mercy and peace for the defense, and in the moralities "Mercy always prevailed with God for the repentant sinner."[15] Hughes believes that by "abandoning the debate between Justice and Mercy over fallen Man in favor of the

dialogue between the Almighty Father and the Son, Milton found
the way to a dialogue of distinct persons." He rightly rejects the
theories of those modern critics who tend to polarize the Son and the
Father by contrasting their characters. His thesis is that the debate
on justice versus mercy is a "dialogue in a more or less Platonic sense:
the quest of truth" and that the "counterpoise of justice and mercy
in the debate which Milton inherited from the theologians as well as
from the morality plays was itself a forensic metaphor."[16]

The conversation between God and the Son is indeed a dialogue,
but it seems that Milton was less inspired by theologians or by the
dramatic justice versus mercy antinomy found in so many morality
plays than by two dialogues in the Old Testament—between God
and Abraham and between God and Moses—in which the dichotomy
between justice and mercy does not exist. Hughes recognizes the
biblical allusions but fails to appreciate their significance. He writes,
for example, that Milton "understood the difficulty of reconciling the
passions of the anthropomorphic God of the Old Testament to the
standards of human decency."[17] I believe the opposite is true, namely
that precisely by verbally echoing the dialogues of Abraham and
Moses with their God, Milton was able to convey the true nature of
his God, a God who stands for much more than "human decency,"
a God who loves His creatures, whose aim is to protect and save mankind as well as the moral principles of justice and righteousness He
stands for. In these biblical episodes Milton very probably also found
a model for what Hughes calls "a dialogue of distinct persons."

When the council scene in Heaven opens we see God as the
supreme and beneficent Creator and Father of the Universe: "High
Thron'd above all highth, bent down his eye, / His own works and
their works at once to view" (III, 58–59). We then hear God explain
two great truths that are paradoxes only to nonbelievers: good is
creative and powerful but not powerful enough to destroy evil; the
greatest good that was bestowed upon man ("All he could have"—
III, 98) is also the source of the greatest evil that may befall him.
This good is reason, man being "just and right, / Sufficient to have
stood, though free to fall" (III, 98–99).

When the Son answers God's speech he neither argues with God
nor does he flatter Him, but—relying on God's partiality for His

creation—he tries to soften man's sentence. His speech expresses mercy and goodness, but his words are those of another son of God who asks, in the name of divine justice, that God have mercy on his creatures. Abraham says: "That be far from thee to do after this manner, to slay the righteous with the wicked: and that the righteous should be as the wicked, that be far from thee: Shall not the Judge of all the earth do right?" (Genesis xviii, 25). So the Son in Milton pleads:

> For should Man finally be lost, should Man
> Thy creature late so lov'd, thy youngest Son
> Fall circumvented thus by fraud, though join'd
> With his own folly? that be from thee far,
> That far be from thee, Father, who art Judge
> Of all things made, and judgest only right.   (III, 150–55)

Milton not merely borrows Abraham's words and rhetoric; he assimilates them and subordinates them to the controlling idea of the Son's speech:

> Or shall the Adversary thus obtain
> His end, and frustrate thine, shall he fulfill
> His malice, and thy goodness bring to naught. (III, 156–59)

No clash is intended between the God of Abraham and Milton's God here, for in the Son, as in his patriarchal prototype, love of justice and mercy are fused with a boundless devotion to God. We might add that just as there is no true clash between Abraham and God, so there is no debate, no argument between God and the Son. Like Abraham's intercession for the innocent people of Sodom, the Son's intercession for sinful man is motivated by absolute faith in God and a deep love for humanity. That he "believed in the Lord" (Genesis xv, 6) is one of the leitmotifs of Abraham's life from the day God ordered him to "Get thee out of thy country, and from thy kindred" (Genesis xii, 1) until the moment of the supreme test: "Take now thy son, thine only son Isaac, whom thou lovest, and get thee into the land of Moriah" (Genesis xxii, 2). God understands Abraham's plea for Sodom, which is a plea for justice as well as a plea for Abraham's own faith which needs to be reasserted. And just as God answers Abraham and spares the innocent family of Lot, so Milton's God readily complies with the Son's request, which also expresses His own will:

> O Son, in whom my Soul hath chief delight,
> Son of my bosom, Son who art alone
> My word, my wisdom, and effectual might,
> All hast thou spok'n as my thoughts are, all
> As my Eternal purpose hath decreed:
> Man shall not quite be lost, but sav'd who will,
> Yet not of will in him, but grace in me
> Freely voutsaf't.   (III, 168–75)

When the Son offers himself for the redemption of mankind—

> Behold mee then, mee for him, life for life
> I offer, on mee let thine anger fall;
> . . . I for his sake will leave
> Thy bosom, . . .
>
> . . . .
> . . . on me let Death wreck all his rage   (III, 236–41)[18]

—his words echo those spoken by Moses when he pleads with God to have mercy on the people who sinned against Him. Moses, like the Son, argues that the enemy would achieve his aim, vengeance, if God destroyed his own people.[19] Later on, when Moses realizes how great is the sin which the Israelites have committed, he again intercedes with God and offers himself as a scapegoat to save the people: "Yet now, if thou wilt forgive their sin—; and if not, blot me, I pray thee, out of thy book which thou hast written" (Exodus xxxii, 32). God's reply to Moses reflects an austere but moral concept of justice which is less harsh than the "rigid satisfaction" mentioned by Milton's God at the outset of the dialogue between Himself and the Son. David Daiches has pointed out that this rigid satisfaction is very far from the Christian doctrine of atonement.[20] It is equally far, however, from the Old Testament concept of justice which is rigorous but righteous.

While Abraham the patriarch was the father of the chosen people, Moses was their political and spiritual leader. Two of his most significant character traits are revealed in the episode of the burning bush (Exodus iii): the first is his humility—"And Moses said unto God, who am I, that I should go unto Pharaoh?" (Exodus iii, 11); the second is his complete identification with his mission. Both these traits are reflected in Exodus xxxii. Like Abraham, Moses is concerned about God's own truth and justice and selflessly offers himself for the sake of God's people, just as Abraham is ready to sacrifice his son to God.

Now Hughes recognizes that "in Milton's scene [in heaven] the level is above fear or any passion except the love of mankind, of truth, and of God's self," and he contrasts it with Charlemagne's prayer to God in Ariosto. On the other hand, he writes that one of the reasons why "Milton went as far as he did in developing the ambivalence of the suppliant figure of the Son" is that his "Italian studies had introduced him to the compound of severity and mercy which T. M. Greene recognizes as characteristic of the poetry and painting of the age which produced Vida's *Christiad* (1535) and Marino's *Gerusalemme Distrutta* (1632), with its painful portrayal of the Virgin pleading for God's mercy on the city."[21] I would argue that Milton's dialogue between God and the Son derives its power from verbal echoes in the dialogues of Abraham and Moses with their God, for these two episodes, as well as many others in the Old Testament in which God reveals Himself to His patriarchs or to the prophets, are permeated with a vision of God both as the benevolent and merciful Creator and as a just and moral God. It is in such poignant revelation scenes that men like Abraham and Moses are inspired with the spiritual courage to fulfil their moral duties in the spirit of their God. In such revelation scenes Milton found the "counterpoise of justice and mercy" that is, indeed, the keynote to his dialogue in Book III.

But there is also another reason the seventeenth-century prophetic poet turned to these Old Testament episodes for inspiration, and that is the personal relationship between man and God which they exemplify. Milton felt the need to convey this sense of personal relationship in the scene between God and the Son, and in these Old Testament scenes he found the perfect example of a relationship of man to God based upon absolute faith and devotion but not lacking the spiritual daring to search for justice and truth. Here Milton found what Hughes calls "the dialogue in a more or less Platonic sense: the quest of truth" and here he also found a dialogue of "distinct persons," a dialogue "above fear or any passion except the love of mankind, of truth and of God's self." Milton was certainly familiar with the traditional debate in the morality plays as well as with similar scenes in Italian literature, as Greene suggests, but he believed it "is better . . . to contemplate the Deity, and to conceive of him, not with reference to human passions, that is, after the manner of men, who are never weary of forming subtle imaginations respecting him, but after the manner of Scripture, that is, in the way in which God has offered himself to our contemplation."[22]

Further evidence that Milton's dialogue between God and the Son was inspired by these Old Testament dialogues may be found in his resorting to many other verses from Exodus related to Moses throughout Book III. When the Son expresses the hope that he will see his Father's face upon his return to Heaven (III, 262), the reference is again to Moses, for to him was it given to behold God's face. Milton had the figure of Moses as intercessor in mind, for he silently appropriates another allusion in his final description of the council:

> Thee next they sang of all Creation first,
> Begotten Son, Divine Similitude,
> In whose conspicuous count'nance, without cloud
> Made visible, th'Almighty Father shines,
> Whom else no Creature can behold.   (III, 383–87)[23]

The shining of the Almighty Father is expressed in even stronger terms in lines 375–82: "Fountain of Light, thyself invisible / Amidst the glorious brightness where thou sit'st" (III, 375–76).[24] About the sources of these lines Harding writes that "the *Bible* contains many passages which associate God with intense light. . . . But nowhere in the *Bible* is the radiance about God described as being so intense that the eye cannot bear it."[25] We find, however, a very intense light shining not from God but from Moses' face, who himself possessed a divine quality when he descended from Mount Sinai: "And when Aaron and all the children of Israel saw Moses, behold the skin of his face shone; and they were afraid to come nigh him. . . . And till Moses had done speaking with them, he put a veil on his face" (Exodus xxxiv, 30, 33). The episode of Moses' shining face is likely to be an additional source of lines 380–83, besides the *Metamorphoses* and Isaiah vi, mentioned by Harding:

> Dark with excessive bright thy skirts appear,
> Yet dazzle Heav'n, that brightest Seraphim
> Approach not, but with both wings veil thir eyes.

A final comment. God can neither be described nor conceived of in terms of any other character. Therefore, in the council scene, we have no long similes, no classical allusions and metaphors as we have in Hell or Paradise. Milton's concept of God emerges from this scene— as it does from the whole poem—through the Old Testament allusions, images, and phrases that have a definite poetic function, stressing God's righteousness, his might and the certainty of his victory over his enemies. They reveal both the similarity and the difference between Milton's Christian God and the jealous but just Old Testament Lord of Hosts.[26] If, indeed, we read the council scene with the Old Testament in mind, we see that Milton's God is a Hebraic God though nonetheless consistent with the Christian view.

The next scene to be considered is the council scene in Book V. It is less austere and even more dramatic than the scene in Book III. It is my contention that the liveliness and dramatic power of this scene has its origin in various Old Testament passages such as Genesis xviii, Exodus xix, Micaiah's vision in I Kings xxii, 19 and in the council scene described in Psalm ii. Whereas in the description of the council scene in Book III Milton conveys the sublime and the ethereal, Raphael's account to Adam of a previous council of God in Book V and of the war in Heaven in Book VI is mainly rendered in human terms expressing the correspondence between Heaven and Earth:

> By lik'ning spiritual to corporal forms,
> As may express them best, though what if Earth
> Be but the shadow of Heav'n, and things therein
> Each to other like, more than on Earth is thought? (V, 573–76)

Milton's intention here is not, as in Book III, to contrast Heaven and Hell, but to compare Heaven and Earth.

After the meal, the seraph answers Adam's question about Heaven and describes the council which incited Satan to rebel against God. This council is more dramatic than the one described in Book III, because Satan and his consort play an active part in it, and because it explains the cause of Satan's fall while foreshadowing the fall of Adam and Eve. Here we see Satan as he, for the first time, openly disobeys God by refusing to accept the principles God lays down. The theological issues of Book III are thus clearly dramatized. The council scene as related by Raphael is also stylistically dramatic.

As in the council of God described in I Kings xxii, 19, there is an impressive "Empyreal Host" standing by the throne of God. The throne itself appears "Amidst as from a flaming Mount, whose top / Brightness had made invisible" (V, 598–99). The invisibility of God's brightness is extensively found in ancient epics as well as in medieval, Renaissance, and baroque poems. But it is in the first instance a biblical concept. In *Paradise Lost* it is part of the light versus darkness imagery which derives its power from Milton's biblical sources. The fallen angels had described God "with the majesty of Darkness" round his throne (II, 266). The flaming mount whose top is invisible is associated with the mount of Exodus xix, 16: "And it came to pass on the third day in the morning, that there were thunders and lightnings, and a thick cloud upon the mount, . . . so that all the people that was in the camp trembled." Milton's description here does not produce fear, but the vision is nonetheless awe-inspiring.

The simplicity and directness of God's speech derive a dramatic immediacy from a biblical passage; God's speech is almost a paraphrase of Psalm ii:

Why do the heathen rage, and the people imagine a vain thing? The kings of the earth set themselves, and the rulers take counsel together, against the Lord, and against his anointed, saying, Let us break their bands asunder, and cast away their cords from us. He that sitteth in the heavens shall laugh: the Lord shall have them in derision. Then shall he speak unto them in his wrath, and vex them in his sore displeasure. Yet have I set my king upon my holy hill of Zion. I will declare the decree: the Lord hath said unto me, Thou art my Son; this day have I begotten thee. Ask of me, and I shall give thee the heathen for thine inheritance, and the uttermost parts of the earth for thy possession. Thou shalt break them with a rod of iron; thou shalt dash them in pieces like a potter's vessel. Be wise now, therefore, O ye kings: be instructed, ye judges of the earth. Serve the Lord with fear, and rejoice with trembling. Kiss the Son, lest he be angry, and ye perish from the way, when his wrath is kindled but a little. Blessed are all they that put their trust in him.

Milton had translated this psalm in August 1653.[27] Now in *Paradise Lost*, his account of God's decree and the origin of Satan's rebellion is a dramatization based upon this psalm, revealing the way he used Scripture for his poetic and dramatic purposes. In the psalm the rebellion of "the kings of the earth" precedes God's decree, but Milton's God does not declare his will to vex his enemies. The decree is the cause and not the result of the rebellion. The effect is thus one of dramatic irony, for if we remember verses 6 and 7 of the psalm, we also remember the evil pride and the futility of those who "rage" and invent a "vain thing." The "unsleeping eyes of God" then witness the rebellion and he takes counsel with the Son.[28] The Son's answer is not to be taken as a "jeering . . . as coarse as his Father's,"[29] nor as representing an Epicurean God, equally indifferent to good and evil:

> Mighty Father, thou thy foes
> Justly hast in derision, and secure
> Laugh'st at thir vain designs and tumults vain,
> Matter to mee of Glory, whom thir hate
> Illustrates, when they see all Regal Power
> Giv'n me to quell thir pride.   (V, 735–40)

In reality God's laughter reflects neither vindictiveness nor philosophical indifference; it rather reflects, in anthropomorphic terms, the utter futility and vanity (Milton repeats "vain" twice in line 737) of the rebels' efforts. Milton also alludes to Psalm ii to enhance the moral significance of the council scene in Book V, for the message of the psalm is: "Blessed are all they that put their trust in him." By referring to this psalm, Milton conveys his concept of an omnipotent but not vindictive God, a God against whom it is "vain" to rage. Thus the scene very dramatically ridicules the vain attempts of the fallen angels in the war in Book VI to which we turn next.

Saint John's revelation about "a great red dragon" whose "tail drew the third part of the stars of heaven and did cast them to the earth" (Revelation xii, 3–4) was Milton's authority for the rebellion in Heaven and for the historical truth of the war he described in Book VI. The war itself, however, is in the classical tradition of the battle between the Olympian gods and the Titans as told by Hesiod.[30] Milton was thus following the allegorical tradition which saw in the revolt of the Titans a pagan version—that is, a shadowy reflection—of the revolt of the angels, and which identified the victorious Zeus with God.[31]

But Milton's particular conception of this war in Heaven is reflected in his use of various Old Testament allusions throughout Book VI. These allusions are a unifying element in the account of the war. Milton's attitude toward the war itself is not that of a classical poet glorifying heroism in battle. In Book XI Michael condemns the futility of war:

> For in those days Might only shall be admir'd,
> And Valor and Heroic Virtue call'd;
> To overcome in Battle, and subdue
> Nations, and bring home spoils with infinite
> Man-slaughter, shall be held the highest pitch
> Of human Glory, and for Glory done
> Of triumph, to be styl'd great Conquerors,
> Patrons of Mankind, Gods, and Sons of Gods.   (XI, 689–96)

While Book VI glorifies God's host and the Son overcoming the rebellious angels, there is no doubt as to the outcome of the war. Abdiel's words foretell it:

> fool, not to think how vain
> Against th'Omnipotent to rise in Arms;
> Who out of smallest things could without end
> Have rais'd incessant Armies to defeat
> Thy folly.   (VI, 135–39)[32]

And his stroke defeats Satan momentarily:

> a noble stroke he lifted high,
> Which hung not, but so swift with tempest fell
> On the proud Crest of *Satan*, that no sight,
> Nor motion of swift thought, less could his Shield
> Such ruin intercept.   (VI, 189–93)

This is more than a "Presage of Victory," for Abdiel is "in word mightier than they in Arms" (VI, 32), mightier than Satan who achieves here, as in Book I, gigantic dimensions:

> ten paces huge
> He back recoil'd; the tenth on bended knee
> His massy Spear upstay'd; as if on Earth
> Winds under ground or waters forcing way
> Sidelong, had pusht a Mountain from his seat
> Half sunk with all his Pines.   (VI, 193–98)

The battle is thus not only between the heavenly host and the rebel angels. It is a reflection of the war taking place in the soul of man in that it is primarily a battle in which spirit overcomes force. This is the theme that is at the core of the war in Heaven and an examination of it reinforces Joseph Summers' thesis about the significance of Book VI.[33]

The Old Testament motif, "Not by might, nor by power, but by

my spirit, saith the Lord of hosts" (Zechariah iv, 6) is the key to
Book VI and it is best revealed in Milton's literary treatment of the
chariot throughout Book VI, for in *Paradise Lost* chariots come to
mean more than part of the conventional equipment used in ancient
warfare.[34]

In the first two books of *Paradise Lost* the fall of Satan's host is
already associated with the destruction of Pharaoh's chariots, for
Satan's fallen host is likened to the Egyptian "floating Carcasses /
And broken Chariot Wheels" (I, 310–11).[35] These chariots are conventional ones but they are symbolic of Pharaoh's futile warfare and
defeat. In Book III we learn that the Son of God overcame his
enemies in a unique chariot, a flaming one:

> thou that day
> Thy Father's dreadful Thunder didst not spare,
> Nor stop thy flaming Chariot wheels, that shook
> Heav'n's everlasting Frame, while o'er the necks
> Thou drov'st of warring Angels disarray'd.   (III, 392–96)[36]

But we do not yet know how the Son overcame the warring angels
or how his chariot differs from the conventional war chariots. The
two kinds of chariots, that of the Son of God on the one hand, and all
the others on the other hand, are, however, clearly contrasted in
Book VI.

On his way to the Mount of God, Abdiel beholds

> all the Plain
> Cover'd with thick embattl'd Squadrons bright,
> Chariots and flaming Arms, and fiery Steeds
> Reflecting blaze on blaze.   (VI, 15–18)

This description is Homeric and although the chariots are those of
armed saints, they do not seem to differ from the chariots of the
warriors in the *Iliad*.[37] As for Satan,

> High in the midst exalted as a God
> Th' Apostate in his Sun-bright Chariot sat
> Idol of Majesty Divine.   (VI, 99–101)

The chariot is that of the Sun God and Satan's exaltation is like that
of the ambitious Phaeton. He is, significantly, described as an "Idol"
of divine majesty. His chariot is thus associated with that other one
which brought about chaos and destruction to the world until its

proud charioteer was struck down by Jove's thunderbolt.[38] But Satan's rash ambition is humbled for he can, no more than Phaeton, "equal God in power" (VI, 343) and, wounded by Michael's sword, he is borne back to his chariot (VI, 338). The first day of battle ends,

> all the ground
> With shiver'd armor strown, and on a heap
> Chariot and Charioteer lay overturn'd
> And fiery foaming Steeds.   (VI, 388–91)

Satan still thinks that God can be deemed fallible (VI, 428) and he plans, the next day, to send forth

> Such implements of mischief as shall dash
> To pieces, and o'erwhelm whatever stands
> Adverse, that they shall fear we have disarm'd
> The Thunderer of his only dreaded bolt.   (VI, 488–91)

At first it seems that Satan is overcoming God's host, for "down they fell / By thousands, Angel on Arch-Angel roll'd" (VI, 593–94). And Milton adds, "The sooner for thir Arms" (VI, 595), since force alone cannot overcome evil. It is thus significant that on the third day of battle God sends forth, not Michael and his host with implements from the "Armory of God" (VI, 321), but his Son:

> Go then thou Mightiest in thy Father's might,
> Ascend my Chariot, guide the rapid Wheels
> That shake Heav'n's basis, bring forth all my War,
> My Bow and Thunder, my Almighty Arms
> Gird on, and Sword upon thy puissant Thigh.   (VI, 710–14)

These lines echo the descriptions of Homeric battles, but they also include a biblical element, and whereas Phaeton did wrong in insisting upon riding Apollo's chariot, Milton's God invites his Son to "ascend my Chariot." The contrast between the God-Son and the Apollo-Phaeton situation is the more striking for the similarity of the vocabulary God uses to that attributed to Apollo by writers from Homer to Ovid: "bring forth all my War, / My Bow and Thunder, my Almighty Arms / Gird on." Moreover, since the Son rides the chariot at the request of his Father, it is not—as in the hands of Phaeton—an instrument of destruction and chaos; it brings about peace and order in Heaven:

> At his command the uprooted Hills retir'd
> Each to his place, they heard his voice and went
> Obsequious. (VI, 781–83)

And when the Son appears Milton does not describe another battle scene. Instead he describes a spiritual revelation:

> forth rush'd with whirl-wind sound
> The Chariot of Paternal Deity,
> Flashing thick flames, Wheel within Wheel, undrawn,
> Itself instinct with Spirit, but convoy'd
> By four Cherubic shapes, four Faces each
> Had wondrous, as with Stars thir bodies all
> And Wings were set with Eyes, with Eyes the Wheels
> Of Beryl, and careering Fires between;
> Over thir heads a crystal Firmament,
> Whereon a Sapphire Throne, inlaid with pure
> Amber, and colors of the show'ry Arch.
> Hee in Celestial Panoply all arm'd
> Of radiant Urim, work divinely wrought,
> Ascended. (VI, 749–62)

This revelation is the climax of Book VI as well as of the war in Heaven. It deserves some consideration.

As has been indicated by previous editors, the chariot revelation is inspired by the vision of the prophet Ezekiel (i, 4–28).[39] Milton, as well as the hexaemeral poets before him,[40] had the authority of St. John for identifying the divine image of the chariot with Christ, but Milton's description is much closer to the original revelation of the Old Testament poet-prophet. Although his lines condense the Ezekiel chapter, at times he slightly diverges from it and emphasizes, as we shall see, those elements that are necessary for his poetic purposes. For example, Milton's chariot "forth rush'd with whirl-wind sound," whereas Ezekiel first beholds a whirlwind coming out of the north and in the midst of it he then sees a chariot (i, 4). Ezekiel sees a cloud, a brightness about it and "out of the midst thereof as the colour of amber, out of the midst of the fire" (i, 4), while Milton expresses the brightness and the fire in the onomatopoeic phrase, "Flashing thick flames" (VI, 751). Milton follows Ezekiel when he emphasizes that the chariot has "Wheel within Wheel, undrawn, / Itself instinct with Spirit": "and their appearance and their work was as it were a wheel in the middle of a wheel. When they went, they went

upon their four sides; and they turned not when they went. . . .
Whithersoever the spirit was to go, they went, thither was their spirit
to go: and the wheels were lifted up over against them: for the spirit
of the living creature was in the wheels" (i, 16, 17, 20). Milton's four
"Cherubic shapes" (VI, 753), however, are an idealized form of the
"living creatures" of Ezekiel (*hayyot*) as well as of the beasts which
appear in St. John's revelation (iv, 6). Milton may well have been influenced by Isaiah's initiatory vision, for the beasts in Revelation
have six wings like the "seraphims" (the plural of Hebrew *seraph* is
seraphim) in Isaiah (i, 2). The living creatures of Ezekiel have wings
as well, but only four. It is also possible that the "Cherubic shapes"
of Milton were suggested to him by chapter x of Ezekiel, where we
find cherubim in a similar vision at the center of which is the "likeness
of a throne": "This is the living creature that I saw under the God
of Israel by the river of Chebar; and I knew that they were the
cherubims" (Ezekiel x, 20). The "four Faces each / Had wondrous"
(VI, 753–54) are like the four faces each "living creature" had in
Ezekiel's vision, whereas in Revelation each of the beasts has a
different face (iv, 7).

The light, radiance, and fire predominant in Milton's lines are
also derived from Ezekiel's chapter. The wings as well as the wheels
are set with eyes, but the sight is not as dreadful as Ezekiel's vision:
"As for their rings, they were so high that they were dreadful; and
their rings were full of eyes round about them four" (i, 18); nor is the
"crystal Firmament" over Milton's chariot (IV, 757) the "terrible
crystal" of Ezekiel i, 22. But all about the chariot of the Son is re-
splendent with light: the wheels are of Beryl (VI, 756) as in Ezekiel
i, 16, the throne is of Sapphire (VI, 758) as in Ezekiel i, 26. The
"careering Fires" (VI, 756) are like the flashes of fire and lightning
of Ezekiel i, 13–14.[41] The Son is armed with bow and quiver and
"three-bolted Thunder" (VI, 764), but the nature of his divine armor
is symbolized by the ancient and radiant "*Urim*" worn on the breastplate by the Hebrew high priests.[42]

We may conclude, then, that if Milton had wanted to present a
powerful Lord of Hosts destroying and routing his enemies, he could
easily have found authoritative sources for such a conception.[43] But
as long as the battle between Heaven and Hell was described in terms
of war, no poetic distinction was possible between the forces of

Heaven and the forces of Hell. So Milton chose to present the manifestation of God's might not in terms of power but in a scene intense with light and spirit, radiant with glory. The very splendor of the Son's chariot and the light it radiates denigrate Satan, exalted as a God in his sun-bright chariot, and render all the devilish machinations (VI, 504) powerless. The great thematic image of the chariot thus emphasizes the key theme of Book VI, for the power of Ezekiel's as well as Milton's fiery chariot is that it is instinct with spirit and moved by divine force, and it is this divine force which renders the power of God's enemies futile. The chariot scene thus serves, by its very nature, as the poetic distinction between the powers of Heaven and the powers of Hell. Here, rather than in the council scene of Book III, Milton becomes, like the Hebrew prophets and like Dante, a visionary of God.

The essence of the divine chariot having been revealed, Milton turns to the actual war, for the wrath of the jealous Lord of Hosts is now turned against his enemies. The "smoke and bickering flame, and sparkles dire" (VI, 766) are like a raging fire that consumes everything in its path.[44] The divine chariot is no longer alone; it is now part of the multitude of chariots forming God's host. The description is reminiscent not only of Homer but also of Psalm lxviii, which is echoed by Revelation vii:

> Attended with ten thousand thousand Saints,
> He onward came, far off his coming shone,
> And twenty thousand (I thir number heard)
> Chariots of God, half on each hand were seen.
>
> (VI, 767–70)[45]

When the Son appears on the battlefield, the metaphor of the throne merges with that of the God, who like Baal riding the clouds, is described by David as he "rode upon a cherub, and did fly: and he was seen upon the wings of the wind" (II Samuel xxii, 11). But he does not, at first, manifest his wrath by destruction and his appearance is not described in destructive terms as that of the Babylon prophecy (Isaiah xiii), for "At his command the uprooted Hills retir'd / Each to his place, they heard his voice and went / Obsequious, Heav'n his wonted face renewed" (VI, 781–83). Order and harmony are thus the manifestation of God's might.

Yet the "hapless Foes" (VI, 785) are still insensate, "obdur'd"

and, like the Egyptians, "hard'n'd more" against the might and glory
of God. And it is at this stage that the Son's appearance becomes that
of the wrathful God of Deuteronomy (xxxii, 35),[46] for "Vengeance is
his, or whose he sole appoints" (VI, 808). And "since by strength /
They measure all, of other excellence / Not emulous" (VI, 820–22),
he reveals his might in battle:

> and into terror chang'd
> His count'nance too severe to be beheld
> And full of wrath bent on his Enemies.   (VI, 824–26)

Like the jealous God of Israel, Milton's God punishes and destroys
those who disobey him. The enemy now "all resistance lost, / All
courage; down thir idle weapons dropp'd" (VI, 838–39) and "wish't
the Mountains now might be again / Thrown on them as a shelter
from his ire" (VI, 842–43). Their fear is like that of the kings of the
earth (in Revelation vi, 15–16) and also echoes the fear of the sinners
on the Day of Judgment described by Isaiah (xiii, 7–8): "Therefore
shall all hands be faint, and every man's heart shall melt: and they
shall be afraid." When the Son vanquishes his enemies the chariot is
again the element Milton emphasizes and he effectively echoes the
awe-inspiring passages of the Ezekiel chapter:

> from the fourfold-visag'd Four
> Distinct with eyes, and from the living Wheels,
> Distinct alike with multitude of eyes;
> One spirit in them rul'd, and every eye
> Glar'd lightning.   (VI, 845–49)[47]

Thus the power of God is mostly represented in spiritual terms recalling Ezekiel's vision, and to the chariot itself, both as reality and
as symbol, is attributed a new significance in the mythical war in
Heaven. Thus whenever the might of God is manifested in terms of
war, the allusions echo Old Testament passages where a jealous but
righteous God punishes those who persist in their sins, so that although
the war in Heaven follows classical tradition, its religious and moral
justification is poetically expressed through Hebraic allusions.[48]

One set of such allusions functions through one of Milton's angels
who is a unique Miltonic figure. He is different from the others in that
he is an original creation of Milton. His name is not reminiscent of
any biblical or Hebraic figure.[49] It is, however, a Hebrew name mean-

ing the "Servant of God" (VI, 29). Abdiel's character and zeal for
God suggest why Milton chose a Hebrew name for him. In his faith
in the Son and his loyalty to the Son of God, Abdiel is a Christian
figure. His words to Satan (V, 835-45), for example, about the creation
through the Son echo, as Hughes indicates, Colossians i, 15-17; but the
terms in which Abdiel conveys his zeal for the Son are often Hebraic.
In his speech to Satan, for instance, he warns that

> That Golden Sceptre which thou didst reject
> Is now an Iron Rod to bruise and break
> Thy disobedience.   (V, 886–88)

This iron rod, as Hume points out (II, 327), is an allusion to Psalm ii,
9: "Thou shalt break them with a rod of iron." It also reminds us of
the words of Beelzebub when he warns the fallen angels that God

> In highth or depth, still first and last will Reign
> Sole King, and of his Kingdom lose no part
> By our revolt, but over Hell extend
> His Empire, and with Iron Sceptre rule
> Us here, as with his Golden those in Heav'n.   (II, 324–28)

Beelzebub has learned that Abdiel's warning has become reality. As
Newton remarks (quoted by Todd on V, 835) Abdiel's first speech
ends on the note of Psalm ii, 10–12:

> Cease then this impious rage,
> And tempt not these; but hast'n to appease
> Th' incensed Father, and th' incensed Son,
> While Pardon may be found in time besought.   (V, 845–48)

The second speech also ends with an Old Testament allusion. Abdiel's
zeal could not save the rebel angels just as Moses' warning could not
prevent the just punishment that befell another faithless band destroyed by God's ire:

> Well thou didst advise,
> Yet not for thy advice or threats I fly
> These wicked Tents devoted, lest the wrath
> Impendent, raging into sudden flame
> Distinguish not.   (V, 888–92)[50]

The words of God to Abdiel show best how Milton infuses Old Testament allusions in Christian contexts:

> Servant of God, well done, well hast thou fought
> The better fight, who single hast maintain'd
> Against revolted multitudes the Cause
> Of Truth, in word mightier than they in Arms;
> And for the testimony of Truth hast borne
> Universal reproach, far worse to bear
> Than violence: for this was all thy care
> To stand approv'd in sight of God, though Worlds
> Judg'd thee perverse.   (VI, 29–37)

As Hughes indicates (VI, 29) the greeting to the man in the parable of judgment (Matthew xxv, 21) mingles here with St. Paul's cry, "I have fought a good fight," but these lines also silently appropriate Isaiah's description of God's servant: "He is despised and rejected of men; a man of sorrows, and acquainted with grief: and we hid as it were our faces from him; he was despised, and we esteemed him not" (Isaiah liii, 3). To Milton's Abdiel, the fervent defender of the Son, are thus attributed some qualities associated with prefigurations of Christ, yet, significantly, he is more Hebraic than Christian. He is, like the Old Testament Messiah, God's instrument for the punishment of the wicked. The character of the angel "in word mightier than they in Arms" embodies the Old Testament concept of spiritual superiority over physical strength which is the central theme of the war in Heaven. This Hebraic element of spiritual might lives again in Milton and is one of the elements which keeps the balance between the humanist and the Puritan in his thought. It is spiritual might which is made evident in Book III, in the scenes describing the Son in battle, God in council, and in figures like the chariot and the angel Abdiel.

Tel-Aviv University

NOTES

1. Marjorie Nicolson writes that "a modern reader of Book III feels rebuffed and repelled when he first meets Milton's God." She voices the opinion of many critics when she asks, "Great poet of light and sound as Milton was, could he not have made his God an awesome Presence, unmoved and unmoving, whom we feel, but whom our eyes—weaker than those of the Seraphim—cannot and should not see?" (*John Milton: A Reader's Guide to His Poetry* [New York, 1966 (1963)], pp. 224–25). Helen Gardner, too, reluctantly admits that "it is impossible to deny

that Milton's presentation of the Adversary and of Hell is far more impressive than his presentation of God and Heaven" (*A Reading of "Paradise Lost"* [Oxford, 1965], p. 55).

2. Peter's first impressions of God are "strangely unfavourable" (*A Critique of "Paradise Lost"* [New York and London, 1960], pp. 12 and 18). See also David Daiches, *Milton* (London, 1961 [1957]), p. 181.

3. William Empson, *Milton's God* (London, 1965), rev. ed., pp. 11 and 13.

4. In his essay, "Literary Criticism," in *The Aims and Methods of Scholarship in Modern Languages and Literatures,* ed. James Thorpe (New York, 1963), p. 59, Frye writes that academic criticism should be "partly historical, studying past literature in its original context, and partly an attempt to express what past literature can communicate beyond its own time to ours." Empson indeed claims a historical basis for his thesis. He believes that "the main European revolt against Christianity does not date from the Romantic Movement but from more than two centuries earlier, and the first name that occurs to one is Montaigne. . . . A person aware of this tradition . . . is not likely to be 'embarrassed' by the wickedness of Milton's God" (Empson, *Milton's God,* p. 14). This thesis is not substantiated by the text.

5. Gardner, *A Reading of "Paradise Lost,"* p. 52.

6. In his chapter, "The Filiations of Milton's Celestial Dialogue," Merritt Y. Hughes indicates that the theory of accommodation, as expressed by St. Augustine for example, was familiar to seventeenth-century readers. *Ten Perspectives on Milton* (New Haven, 1965), pp. 123–25. See also William G. Madsen, "Earth the Shadow of Heaven: Typological Symbolism in *Paradise Lost,*" in *Milton: Modern Essays in Criticism,* ed. Arthur E. Barker (New York, 1965), pp. 246–63. Madsen reads Raphael's narrative in light of Christian interpretations of the "shadow" metaphor.

7. *The Christian Doctrine,* I, 2, in *John Milton: Complete Poems and Major Prose,* ed. Merritt Y. Hughes (New York, 1957), p. 905. All citations of Milton's works refer to Hughes' text.

8. Ibid.

9. Gardner, *A Reading of "Paradise Lost,"* p. 55.

10. A. J. A. Waldock believes that these lines contradict Milton's own statement that Satan and his mate escaped the Stygian flood through the "sufferance of supernal Power." It is, however, difficult to accept his feeling of "impatience" with a poet "who, not content with a God who must, however matters are contrived, appear somewhat vindictive, goes out of his way to convict him on his very first appearance of flagrant disingenuousness and hypocrisy" (*"Paradise Lost" and Its Critics* [Cambridge, Eng., 1964 (1947)], p. 101). Waldock seems unaware of the conceptions of God and Satan prevalent in the seventeenth-century audience for which Milton wrote.

The lines which Waldock objects to so strongly have been commented upon more justly by Christopher Ricks, who examines their diction and syntax, showing how they "compress [God's] knowledge of Satan's single motive with his observation of his escape from Hell" (*Milton's Grand Style* [Oxford, 1963], p. 60).

11. Also Isaiah v, 1–7; Jeremiah ii, 5–iii, 10; iii, 20–21; Ezekiel v, 5–6; Micah vi, 2–8, and others.

12. *Paradise Lost,* ed. P[atrick]. H[ume]. (London, 1695).

13. For instance: Ezekiel xvii, 19; ix, 10. In his second speech (III, 178–82)

God promises that He will once more vouchsafe his grace to man. As Hughes' note indicates, line 180 echoes Psalm xxxix, 4: "Lord, make me to know . . . how frail I am."

14. Lines 178–82 also express the idea of Exodus xx, 3. Verbally they echo the verses of the poet-prophet to whom Milton alludes so often: Isaiah xlv, 5–6, 22.

15. In his learned analysis, "The Filiations of Milton's Celestial Dialogue," Hughes reminds us that Milton had sketched the dramatic situation of the council (III, 80–343) in an outline for a tragedy on the theme of *Paradise Lost* (*Ten Perspectives*, pp. 104–35).

The distinction between the Old Testament God of Justice and the merciful Jesus is well rooted in English literature from the time of the mystery cycles, the plays of John Bale and onward. See M. Roston, *Biblical Drama in England* (London, 1968), pp. 60 ff.

16. Hughes, *Ten Perspectives*, pp. 111, 113, 128, 134.

17. Ibid., p. 123. Hughes admits that the "Scriptural substrate of the speeches vindicated both their theology and their style," adding that "the unmistakable Scriptural echoes . . . give every line the semblance of authentic divine utterance" (p. 122).

18. In his 1801 edition of *The Poetical Works of John Milton* (London), Todd (on III, 236) quotes Newton who noted that the frequent and vehement repetition of *mee* is very like Virgil when Nisus bravely offers himself and cries: "*Me, me:* adsum qui feci: in *me* convertite ferrum" (*Aeneid* IX, 427).

Isaiah offers a perhaps more relevant prototype of the volunteer who is willing to sacrifice his own life for the sake of others, but whereas the Son steps forward to "be mortal to redeem Man's mortal crime," Isaiah accepts a mission to the people to warn and heal them. Both act in answer to God's call:

> Say Heav'nly Powers, where shall we find such love,
> Which of you will be mortal to redeem
> Man's mortal crime.   (III, 213–15)

"Also I heard the voice of the Lord, saying, Whom shall I send, and who will go for us?" (Isaiah vi, 8).

19. See III, 156–66 and Exodus xxxii, 12.

20. Daiches, *Milton,* p. 182.

21. *Ten Perspectives*, pp. 118 and 120.

22. *The Christian Doctrine,* I, 2 (Hughes, *Complete Poems and Major Prose*), p. 906.

23. "And there arose not a prophet since in Israel like unto Moses whom the Lord knew face to face" (Deuteronomy xxxiv, 10).

24. See Todd, ed., *Poetical Works,* on III, 377.

25. Davis P. Harding, *Milton and the Renaissance Ovid* (Urbana, Ill., 1946), pp. 91–92.

26. There are also many biblical allusions the function of which is to project New Testament beliefs into Old Testament episodes, but these are not to be considered Hebraic. The best example of this category is Isaiah's prophecy (vii, 14) echoed by Milton in III, 283–86.

27. Hughes, *Complete Poems and Major Prose,* p. 162. See also Milton's reference to Psalm ii in chapter V of the *Christian Doctrine,* ibid., p. 933. Newton (quoted by Todd in *Poetical Works*) on V, 602 says: "In this particular speech the

reader will easily remark how much of it is copied from Holy Writ, by comparing it with the following texts: *Psalm* ii. 6. 7; *Gen.* xxii. 16. *Phil.* ii. 10.11." It is true that these texts are in the background of God's speech, but I shall try to show that Milton does more than merely "copy" from "Holy Writ."

28. Todd (*Poetical Works*) on V, 647, quotes Newton, who suggests that "the unsleeping eyes of God" echoes Psalm cxxi, 4—"He that keepeth Israel shall neither slumber nor sleep"—and adds that "the author had likewise Homer in mind, *Iliad.* ii.1."

29. Empson, *Milton's God*, p. 96.

30. Hesoid, *Theogony*, trans. Norman O. Brown (Indianapolis, 1953), pp. 53–82. See also Hughes, *Complete Poems and Major Prose*, p. 178.

31. For an account of the didactic and allegorical interpretations of Ovid, for instance, see Harding, *Milton and the Renaissance Ovid*, pp. 22 ff.

32. The certainty of God's victory is a Hebraic element (adopted by all monotheistic religions), for in Greek mythology none of the deities was assured of victory from the outset.

33. Joseph H. Summers, *The Muse's Method* (London, 1962), pp. 112–37.

34. For the cabalistic treatment of the Merkabah vision and its influence on Milton's chariot episode through Christian Platonists like Reuchlin and Pico, see J. H. Adamson, "The War in Heaven: Milton's Version of the Merkabah," *JEGP*, LVII (1958), 690–703. Chariots, in their conventional meaning, occur often in *Paradise Lost*—e.g., II, 885–87.

35. This episode (Exodus xiv) is mentioned again by Michael (XII, 210).

36. Another flaming chariot is alluded to in Book III. When Satan is on his journey to Earth, he sees the gates of Heaven and

> underneath a bright Sea flow'd
> Of Jasper, or of liquid Pearl, whereon
> Who after came from Earth, sailing arriv'd,
> Wafted by Angels, or flew o'er the Lake
> Rapt in a Chariot drawn by fiery Steeds. 　　　(III, 518–22)

The vision is reminiscent of the one Elisha had when there appeared "a chariot of fire, and horses of fire, and parted them both asunder; and Elijah went up by a whirlwind into heaven" (II Kings ii, 11).

37. See, for example, *Iliad* VIII, 562–65, trans. Richmond Lattimore (Chicago, 1951), p. 197. Todd, on VI, 18, refers to Homer and adds: "But it is probable, that Milton had in view a very magnificent description of this kind in I *Maccabees*, vi. 39."

38. *The Metamorphoses of Ovid*, trans. Mary M. Innes (London, 1955), pp. 54–63. See also Harding, *Milton and the Renaissance Ovid*, p. 88.

39. See Hume, *Paradise Lost*, and Newton and Todd, *Poetical Works*. Todd, on VI, 749, refers to Ezekiel i and, quoting Newton, adds: "Or perhaps Milton here drew Isaiah likewise to his assistance, lxvi. 15." On VI, 755, Todd quotes Ezekiel i, 16 and 13 and adds: "Milton has again described this part of the prophetick vision, and with additional sublimity, ver. 848."

40. Referring to G. McColley's *Paradise Lost*, pp. 36–38, Hughes (on VI, 750–59) notes that at least one hexaemeral poet before Milton, Rupert of Deutz in the twelfth century, had used the vision of Ezekiel as a symbol of Christ triumphing spiritually over the rebel angels.

41. On VI, 751, Hume quotes the Ezekiel chapter "out of which Chapter this noble Description is taken." Milton's lines indeed follow the order of Ezekiel's description, which begins with the chariot, the living creatures, and ends with the throne. In Revelation iv, the description begins with "a throne was set in heaven, and one sat on the throne" (iv, 2) and ends with the description of the beasts and the elders worshipping the Lord. There is no chariot in the vision.

42. As Todd indicates (VI, 760), Milton has the authority of Ephesians vi, 11, for the Son's divine armor, but the mysterious Urim are those we find on Aaron's breastplate (Exodus xxviii, 30). See also Hume on VI, 760.

43. See, for example, the fierce description of the Day of Judgment of Joel ii, 1–11.

44. See Nahum i, 6; Isaiah ix, 18–19 (Hebrew canon: Isaiah ix, 17–18); II Samuel xxii, 9. Hume's annotation to VI, 766, refers to Psalm xviii, 8 (xviii, 9 in the Hebrew canon) and to Psalm i, 3.

45. Newton, quoted by Todd on VI, 767, refers to both Psalm lxviii, 17, and Revelation vii, 4, and, characteristically, observes: "Let it be remarked how much of his sublimity, even in the sublimest part of his works, Milton owes to Scripture."

46. See Hume and Todd on VI, 808.

47. See Hume on VI, 848.

48. Todd stresses the idea that the Son "meant / Not to destroy," and on VI, 853 ("Yet half his strength he put not forth"), he writes: "This fine thought is somewhat like that of the Psalmist lxxviii. 38. 'But he, being full of compassion, forgave their iniquity, and destroyed them not; yea, many a time turned he his anger away, and *did not stir up all his wrath.*' And it greatly exceeds Hesiod, who makes Jupiter, upon a like occasion, exert *all* his strength, *Theog.* 687."

49. The name *Abdiel* appears only once in the Old Testament (I Chronicles v, 15), referring to a human being. Another version of the same name—Abd'el—is also mentioned once (Jeremiah xxxvi, 26) with reference to another person. See also Hughes on *PL* V, 805. On Abdiel see also Robert H. West, *Milton and the Angels* (Athens, Ga., 1955), pp. 124, 152–54; G. Davidson, *A Dictionary of Angels* (London, 1968), p. 4; M. Schwab, *Vocabulaire de l'Angélologie* (Paris, 1897), p. 207; *Sefer Raziel* (Amsterdam, 1701), f. 4b, 34b; J. Goldman, "Insight into Milton's Abdiel," *Philological Quarterly* XLIX (1970), 249–54.

50. Newton (quoted by Todd on V, 890) points out the allusion to Numbers xvi, 16: "And he [Moses] spake unto the congregation, saying, Depart, I pray you, from the tents of these wicked men, and touch nothing of theirs, lest ye be consumed in all their sins."

MILTON'S SAMSON
AND THE JEWISH TRADITION

Samuel S. Stollman

Milton's Samson is significantly different from the Samson of
Jewish tradition. The rabbinic interpretation depicts Samson
as a sensualist, but one who observed the Law by converting
Dalila to Judaism before marrying her. His passion for Philistine women was punished by "an eye [blinding] for an eye"
(sensuality). Milton's Samson, on the other hand, is guided by
"intimate impulse," associated with "right reason" and the "law
of nature," rather than Mosaic Law. He married Dalila in her
gentile state (contrary to the Law). His sin was the failure
of reason, and led to the loss of liberty. He is regenerated when
he recovers his reason. His fellow Israelites, however, are depicted as bound by the Mosaic Law and as incapable of com-
prehending the import of freedom. Milton did not borrow from
the Rabbis; his organizing principle in *Samson Agonistes* is
his antinomian view of the Mosaic Law. Milton reads the Mosaic Law as superseded by reason—equated with liberty—
with Samson as the Old Testament precursor of Christian
liberty.

A COMPARATIVE study of Milton's Samson and the Jewish tradition, supplementing F. Michael Krouse's *Milton's Samson and
the Christian Tradition* (Princeton, 1949), should be useful in exploring Milton's reputed use of Jewish materials, his conception of a
Jewish hero and the Jewish ethos, and for the light it might throw on
the interpretations—Christian, Hellenic, Hebraic, and other—in which
Samson Agonistes is "copiously enroll'd."[1] Milton's frequent references
to the Jewish tradition and his stated adherence to the requirements
of "verisimilitude and decorum" in the composition of his Old Testa-

ment drama suggest the validity of a fresh appraisal of the materials and organizing principles of *Samson Agonistes*.

I

The Talmud,[2] the *locus classicus* for the Jewish Samson, interprets his physical endowment to be virility: "His physique was like that of other men, but his virility was like a flowing stream." His weakness was carnal desire: "Samson rebelled [against God] with his eyes, as it is said, 'And Samson said unto his father, "Get her for me, for she is pleasing in my eyes" (Judges xiv, 3)'." Dalila elicited Samson's secret at the height of his passion: "She . . . urged him" (Judges xvi, 16) is a euphemism for "At the time of consummation she detached herself from him."

In the rest he was a faithful judge and a selfless deliverer of his people, who "judged Israel as their Father in heaven, as it is said, 'Dan [Samson being of the tribe of Dan] shall judge his people as One [the One being God Who judges man with justice tempered with mercy]'" (Genesis xlix, 16); Samson was "called by the name of the Holy One, blessed be He, as it is said, 'For the Lord God is a sun and a shield [the Hebrew word for sun is *shemesh* which is related to *Shimshon*, Samson's name]' (Psalms lxxxiv, 11). As the Holy One, blessed be He, shields the world, so did Samson shield Israel in his generation."

Samson was guided by God: "The *Shechinah* [the Divine Presence] rang before him (Judges xiii, 25) like a bell [to lead him]." He fulfilled "Jacob's prophecy . . . as it is written, 'Dan shall be a serpent in the way' [attacking the Philistines] (Genesis xlix, 17)." He remained humble, despite his exploits, praying at the end of his life: "Sovereign of the Universe, remember on my behalf the twenty years I judged Israel and that I never ordered a man to carry my staff from one place to another." He was God-fearing; even Dalila "knew that this righteous man would not utter the Divine Name in vain."

The rabbis saw the retributive law of measure for measure operative in three instances in Samson's career: in his dependence on the ritually unclean jawbone from which he had to drink—"He desired that which was unclean [Philistine women]; therefore his life was made dependent upon an unclean thing"; in his degeneration which began in Gaza—"therefore he was punished in Gaza"; and in his blinding—Samson "followed his eyes; therefore the Philistines put out his eyes." Ironically, Samson himself was motivated by this same principle in choosing foxes to burn the Philistine crops: "Why foxes? . . . Let the animal come which turns backward [which runs in circles when pursued] and exact punishment of the Philistines who went back on their oath [Abimelech's word to Isaac, who covenanted with the former 'That thou wilt not deal falsely with me, nor with my son, nor with my son's son' (Genesis xxi, 23)]."

The ritual problem of Samson's defilement by contact with the dead—an act forbidden a Nazarite—is dealt with by the rabbis in the framework of the Mosaic and the Oral Law: a "lifetime Nazarite" was exempt from the restriction, according to one view in the Talmud. Samson's final prayer (Judges xvi, 28) was for vengeance and also for life in the hereafter: "Master of the Universe, reward me for one eye in this world, and may the compensation for my other eye be reserved for me in the world-to-come."

Another important Jewish source (more so for Milton than for the rabbis) is the historian-apologist Josephus Flavius (37–95 C.E.), who, unlike the Talmud, faults Samson for pride: "Yet Samson, unduly proud of this feat [smiting a thousand Philistines], did not say that it was God's assistance that had brought it to pass, but ascribed the issue to his own valour." Samson's thirst was allayed not from the ass's jawbone (as the rabbis state) but from a fountain which the Lord opened for him at Ramat-Lehi. Josephus implies that Samson did not marry Dalila; she was a concubine (contrary to the rabbinic tradition). Samson's fall is attributed in part to his breaking the vow of abstinence: "She [Dalila] posted some soldiers in ambush within and while Samson was drunken bound him."[3]

A third major source for the Jewish interpretation of the Samson chapters is the "Rabbinic Bible," which contains, in addition to the Jonathan Targum (an ancient paraphrase of the Hebrew Scriptures, ascribed to Jonathan ben Uzziel), the glosses of Rashi (Rabbi Solomon ben Isaac; Troyes, France; 1040–1105), Radak (or Kimchi: Rabbi David Kimchi; Narbonne, Provence, France; 1160–1235), and Ralbag (Ben Gerson or Gersonides: Rabbi Levi ben Gerson; Avignon, France; 1288–1344), commentators alluded to by name or by implication (according to Harris Francis Fletcher) in Milton's prose.[4] These commentaries incorporate many of the talmudic views in addition to independent observations.

The oldest of these, the Jonathan Targum, expands the Hebrew for "the spirit of the Lord" (Judges xiii, 25, and xiv, 6) into "a spirit of might from before the Lord, to give him strength," incorporating the talmudic comment that Samson's strength was supernatural and superimposed.

Rashi, whose method is to give "the plain meaning of the text," as well as to note pertinent exegetical views of the rabbis, offers the following: "The spirit of the Lord" (Judges xiii, 25) descended upon Samson "from time to time." To the words of the men of Judah who say, "Why are ye come up against us?" (Judges xv, 10), Rashi adds: "Are we not as bondsmen to you?" When Samson prayed for water, "God cleaved the hollow place" in the jawbone itself, "and there came water thereout" (Judges xv, 19). Rashi notes the divine justice in Samson's downfall in Gaza. He observes also that Samson never made demands upon his fellow Israelites. Samson's final prayer was for life in the hereafter.

Radak, or Kimchi, offers the most elaborate and rationalistic gloss on Judges. Regarding Samson's ritual defilement Kimchi suggests that since Samson had not personally taken a vow to abide by the Nazarite code, he was bound only by those restrictions specified by the angel to his parents—to abstain from strong drink and to refrain from cutting his hair. Furthermore, he avoided touching the Philistines after they were slain. Kimchi cites the two traditions regarding Samson's assuaging of his thirst—the jawbone and the fountain—but indicates no preference. Samson converted the women whom he married. Although his first motives had been to do God's will, "afterwards desire seized him when he saw the Philistine woman of Timna, and the divine intention was submerged in his physical desire." Kimchi cites Jonathan's "spirit of might" as the source of Samson's strength and also explains this spirit to be divine inspiration.

Ralbag, or Ben Gerson (Milton: "Ben Gersom"), is also of the rationalistic school. Samson was destined to be a Nazarite since God knew that Samson would be tempted by women. Therefore God commanded that Samson avoid wine and that Samson's mother, while pregnant, practice temperance to influence her unborn son in the ways of holiness. The prohibition against the cutting of his hair was to teach him discipline. His locks were not the source of his prowess; his strength was divinely endowed. Ben Gerson agrees with the older tradition that Samson converted his wives to Judaism. He concludes that the Israelite bondage was punishment for their sins and that they were liberated after they had repented; that one must not reveal a secret even to one's wife; that one should not "cleave" to the daughters of the Philistine, even if they are converts; that a leader must defend his people regardless of personal danger; that God performs miracles through the agency of mortals, though they be bound and weaponless; that Samson's punishment was just; and that God reestablished His glory in destroying Dagon.

The last of the Jewish authorities for our purposes (but chronologically before Kimchi) is Maimonides (Rabbi Moses ben Maimon, foremost medieval Jewish philosopher and talmudist; Fez and Cairo; 1135–1204), who is of the view that Samson converted the Philistine women whom he married, but that they did not convert in good faith.[5]

The Jewish sources give us the following composite: Samson was a selfless leader, humble, just, and God-fearing, divinely guided and endowed but weak in the flesh. The tradition postulates a hereafter, the operation of divine justice, and the framework of Jewish Law (the Mosaic and the Oral Law) governing Samson's marriages and ritual conduct. The theme of servitude is submerged. Josephus deviates from the rabbinic tradition in assigning to pride and intemperance contributory roles in Samson's fall and in regarding Dalila's relationship as concubinage.

II

Turning to *Samson Agonistes* (and limiting our investigation to those aspects of the drama that may be juxtaposed with the Jewish tradition), we find: Samson married Dalila (as all the rabbinic commentators agree),[6] but she was not converted to Judaism—the prohibition against a gentile marriage was suspended for Samson. Here then we have a major difference between Milton and the rabbis in respect to the Mosaic Law. Milton is of the view that the Mosaic Law, in Old

Testament times, could be rescinded by divine fiat or by the criterion of reason. Thus the chorus avers that the law forbidding marriage with a non-Jew was abrogated for Samson by God Himself,

> Who made our Laws to bind us, not himself,
> And hath full right t' exempt
> Whom so it pleases him by choice
> From National obstriction, without taint
> Of sin, or legal debt;
> For with his own Laws he can best dispence.   (309–14)[7]

Later, when Samson agrees to accompany the Philistine officer, he confirms the choric thesis:

> Yet that he may dispense with me or thee
> Present in Temples at Idolatrous Rites
> For some important cause, thou needst not doubt. (1377–79)

The divine dispensation is denoted in Milton's poeticization of "And the spirit of the Lord began to move him" into Samson's "intimate impulse" (223). The Mosaic Law may also be superseded by reason, which is equated with the moral law:

> Reason here aver[s]
> That moral verdit quits her [Dalila] of unclean:
> Unchaste was subsequent.   (323–25)

And so his last words: "Hitherto, Lords, what your commands impos'd / I have perform'd, as reason was, obeying" (1640–41). In addition, Milton incorporates his doctrinal position that the "law of nature, law of nations," is universally binding—for Philistine and Jew—and equated with "right reason" and the moral law:

> Being once a wife, for me thou wast to leave
> Parents and countrey; nor was I their subject,
> Nor under their protection but my own,
> Thou mine, not theirs: if aught against my life
> Thy countrey sought of thee, it sought unjustly,
> Against the law of nature, law of nations.   (885–90)[8]

This is not to say, of course, that Samson has abandoned the Law or is above it. In keeping with Old Testament decorum—and when no overriding directive of "intimate impulse" or reason is present—Samson is law-abiding:

> I with this Messenger will go along,
> Nothing to do, be sure, that may dishonour
> Our Law, or stain my vow of *Nazarite.*   (1384–86)

To appreciate fully Milton's conception of the Mosaic Law, it is necessary to remember that the normative Jewish view of the Mosaic Law (and the Oral Law, for that matter) is that the Law is eternal and immutable, and that it transcends "the law of nature" and "right reason." Changes in the Law may be made only within the framework of the Law. Milton, on the other hand, subscribes to the Pauline antinomian doctrine and to the canonical view of the Church Fathers that the *ius naturale* precedes the Mosaic Law, and in its "moral" aspects is equated with it.[9]

A second major feature of Milton's interpretation of Samson is that the protagonist's spiritual conflict takes place in the arena of reason and wisdom versus folly and sophistry. The action of the drama centers on the ascendancy in Samson of "plain Heroic magnitude of mind" (1279) and his perception of the meaning of liberty found in following the dictates of reason and the divine impulse. The confrontations with Manoa, Dalila, and Harapha are basically a regenerative process for Samson whereby he perceives his errors and his sins and emerges from the darkness of folly and servitude to the light of wisdom and liberty.[10] Throughout, Milton stresses the eclipse of Samson's reason, rather than the dominance of sensuality, as the cause of his downfall:

> O impotence of mind, in body strong!
> But what is strength without a double share
> Of wisdom?   (52–54)

> Immeasurable strength they might behold
> In me, of wisdom nothing more then mean.   (206–07)

A life of voluptuousness contributed to his fall, but his sin was yielding his "fort of silence to a Woman" (236) and his "Shameful garrulity" (491). Samson's admission becomes a confessional refrain:

> But I
> Gods counsel have not kept, his holy secret
> Presumptuously have publish'd, impiously,
> Weakly at least, and shamefully: A sin
> That Gentiles in thir Parables condemn.   (496–500)

He has sinned not against the Mosaic Law but against the law of nature and of nations. It is Manoa—who is presented as spiritually less perceptive than Samson—who attributes to temptation the beginning of Samson's fall; but even Manoa sees Samson's sin as the dethronement of reason: "thou the sooner / Temptation found'st, or over-potent charms / To violate the sacred trust of silence" (426–28).

Nowhere does Milton suggest that Samson's blinding was divine punishment for his wandering eyes. Only once does Milton echo the rabbinically amplified motif of measure-for-measure: "servil mind / Rewarded well with servil punishment!" (412–13), but not once with the biblical metaphor of "an eye for an eye." In one figure only, in an inversion of the "eye for an eye" principle, does Milton obversely recall the image: "and that blindness worse then this, / That saw not how degenerately I serv'd" (418–19). Thus, the theme of sensuality, central to the rabbinic interpretation, is muted throughout by Milton. Samson's motives in both marriages are pure (while the rabbis see them as mixed)—

> The first I saw at *Timna*, and she pleas'd
> Mee, not my Parents, that I sought to wed,
> The daughter of an Infidel: they knew not
> That what I motion'd was of God; I knew
> From intimate impulse, and therefore urg'd
> The Marriage on   (219–24)

—although, with Dalila, Samson deduces rather than intuits: "I thought it lawful ["law" and "intimate impulse" are equated] from my former act" (231). Significantly, Samson (contrary to the view of Josephus) has kept his vow of abstinence: "Desire of wine and all delicious drinks, . . . Thou couldst repress" (541–43). He is portrayed as once having loved Dalila (878) but never as having merely desired her carnally. While he admits to having been "Soft'n'd with pleasure and voluptuous life" (534), only Dalila's attachment is denounced as lust (837). Nowhere do we find that Dalila elicited his secret at the height of sexual passion (as the rabbis psychologize) but after sexual union:

> With blandisht parlies, feminine assaults,
> Tongue-batteries, she surceas'd not day nor night
> To storm me over-watch't, and wearied out.
> At times when men seek most repose and rest,
> I yielded, and unlock'd her all my heart.   (403–07)

The sin that led to Samson's eclipse of reason was hubris. He had no personal ambition (similar to the rabbinic view): "I . . . / Us'd no ambition to commend my deeds" (246–47), but he was tainted with the sin of pride (echoing Josephus): "like a petty God / I walk'd about admir'd of all" (529–30); and "swoll'n with pride into the snare I fell" (532).

It is clear that Milton's interpretation differs radically from that of the rabbis. Milton's formulation of Samson's spiritual conflict elevates Samson to the plane of the elect, distinguishes him from his peers—Jewish and Philistine—and associates the theme of reason with that of liberty, as folly has been associated with servitude. The theme of servitude versus liberty (briefly alluded to by Rashi and Ben Gerson) is therefore another—the third—major element in Milton's treatment of Samson. Beginning with Samson's plaint, "my task of servile toyl" (5), the least of his restrictions, the theme of bondage becomes a swelling refrain:

> But foul effeminacy held me yok't
> Her Bond-slave; O indignity, O blot
> To Honour and Religion! servil mind
> Rewarded well with servil punishment!
> The base degree to which I now am fall'n,
> These rags, this grinding, is not yet so base
> As was my former servitude, ignoble,
> Unmanly, ignominious, infamous,
> True slavery, and that blindness worse then this,
> That saw not how degenerally I serv'd.   (410–19)

Similarly, Samson has condemned the servility of Israel:

> But what more oft in Nations grown corrupt,
> And by thir vices brought to servitude,
> Then to love Bondage more then Liberty,
> Bondage with ease then strenuous liberty.   (268–71)

While he has been the victim of uxorious servitude, he has never lost sight of his divine role to achieve political liberty for Israel. The Jews, however, "love Bondage more then Liberty" (270), to the extent, Samson says, that

> their servile minds
> Me their Deliverer sent would not receive,
> But to thir Masters gave me up for nought.   (1213–15)

Milton's interpolation of the theme of servitude versus freedom in the story of Samson, while an innovation in emphasis, is not contrary to the values ascribed to freedom in the normative Jewish tradition and in Jewish history, although the Jewish and Miltonic ideologies differ as to the nature and the source of liberty.[11] What is significant here is Milton's characterization of the Jewish ethos as servile. Nowhere does the Jewish tradition suggest that servility is a Jewish characteristic. The explanation that offers itself for Milton's attribution of this trait to the Jews—here and elsewhere—is that he is reading the Old Testament as a whole—and here the Samson chapters —as the antithesis of the New Testament, with the Law and the Israelites representing bondage, as opposed to the Gospel and the Christians, who represent liberty.[12] If this Pauline doctrine is being applied here—and it is a recurring motif in Milton's work—then we may have another major Christian interpolation in *Samson Agonistes* (in addition to Milton's Christian interpretation of the Mosaic Law), with Samson, as the protagonist of freedom, prefiguring the Christian Messiah. On this basis a typological reading of *Samson Agonistes* may be possible.

In addition to these three major differences between Milton and the rabbis, several sundry details that remain to be noted include Milton's denial of the afterlife to Samson (not the Jewish view):

> All otherwise to me my thoughts portend,
> That these dark orbs no more shall treat with light,
> Nor th' other light of life continue long,
> But yield to double darkness nigh at hand:
> So much I feel my genial spirits droop,
> My hopes all flat.[13]   (590–95)

The semichorus suggests an immortality for Samson but it is an immortality of fame, not a personal immortality:

> So vertue giv'n for lost,
> . . . .
> Like that self-begott'n bird
> . . . .
> though her body die, her fame survives,
> A secular bird ages of lives.[14]   (1697–1707)

Another point: Manoa refers to the quenching of Samson's thirst at Ramat-Lehi with a description that does not tally with that of the Talmud and Rashi, who interpret "the hollow place" as the jawbone itself (but that accords with Josephus' view and one opinion in Kimchi's gloss): "God . . . caus'd a fountain at thy prayer / From the dry ground to spring" (581–82). Lastly, the simile of Samson as "an ev'ning Dragon" (read: "serpent," 1692 ff.) echoes the talmudic tradition that Samson fulfilled Jacob's prophecy regarding the tribe of Dan, who would be "a serpent in the path."[15]

III

We began our study with several questions: Did Milton borrow from the Jewish tradition in composing *Samson Agonistes?* How did he conceptualize an Old Testament hero and the Jewish people? Do our findings throw any light on the organizing principles of *Samson Agonistes?*

Regarding the first inquiry, we have found little evidence for Milton's use of rabbinic lore. Of the ten or so points of comparison between the Jewish tradition and Milton's interpretation, we found that the rabbis and Milton differ in the treatment of the Mosaic Law, the role of sensuality and pride (although here Milton agrees with Josephus), and in the belief in an afterlife for Samson. They also differ in respect to the jawbone and the "eye for an eye" motif. Milton treats servitude versus liberty as a central theme while only Rashi and Ben Gerson touch upon it. Milton concurs with the rabbis in their insistence upon Samson's marriages but not for their reasons. He also agrees with the rabbis in regard to Samson's abstinence (contrary this time to Josephus), alludes perhaps to a rabbinic tradition in the "ev'ning Dragon" simile, and parallels Ben Gerson in Samson's garrulousness. The differences are major; the parallels are few and minor and are primarily rationalistic concurrences. The evidence or lack of it adds nothing to the claims of those who believe that Milton dipped into Jewish lore for the embellishment of his Old Testament themes.

As to our second inquiry, it is apparent, first of all, that Milton (and the Christian tradition: Epistle to the Hebrews xi, 32–34) has a higher opinion of Samson than the one held by the rabbis.[16] For the Jewish tradition the story of Samson reflects insights regarding the *Yetzer ha-ra,* "the evil inclination," which has to be controlled or sublimated by the *Yetzer ha-tov,* "the good inclination," which is associated with the study and observance of the Torah, the Law. Samson is the proverbial strong man who capitulates to his libido. "Who is mighty?" ask the rabbis, and they answer: "He who subdues his 'evil inclination,' as it is written: 'He that is slow to anger is better than the mighty; and he that ruleth his spirit than he that taketh a city' (Proverbs xvi, 32)." As the rabbis had reservations concerning the athlete, so did they withhold full praise from the ascete, the Nazarite, who, though dedicated to God, wrongfully abjures the lawful pleasures of this world (the drinking of wine), given to man to be enjoyed in moderation.[17] On the other hand, sexual morality is for Judaism the discipline of holiness. Samson, of course, is a hero in the Jewish Bible, but he is not the saint or elect that he is for Christianity, which is partisan to the ascete.

Whatever the reasons for Milton's choice of Samson for his last (or penultimate) work, he conceived of him as a being apart from his fellow Israelites in at least two ways: Samson is a champion of freedom, and he is guided by the divine impulse and reason, whereas his people accept bondage and are ruled by the Mosaic Law. Samson belongs to the Old Testament but Milton reads him in the light of the Christian canonization of Old Testament saints whose spiritual calling and conversion is not far different from the experience of the regenerate.[18] By having Samson dispense with the Mosaic Law ("for some important cause"), by distinguishing him from his fellow Jews in his advocacy of liberty, his denunciation of all forms of servitude, and his condemnation of his people, Milton projects a hero who is emancipated from the constraints of the Law and the servility of Israel. While Samson is not clearly a typological figure,[19] and he seems to represent something more affirmative than the antithesis (according to Madsen) of Jesus in *Paradise Regained,* he does embody those spiritual perceptions and dimensions that Milton associates with the "manly liberty worthy the sons of God."[20] In this respect, then, Milton has Christianized Samson. This is more than an allegorical echo but less than a typological construction—although the latter cannot be entirely ruled out. Milton's interpretation is one which makes Samson compatible with Christian doctrine and at the same time Hebraically decorous. Samson is "between the pillars," as it were, of the Old and the New Testaments.

Our third objective was to ascertain the motifs or organizing principles—if any—that bear upon Milton's attitude towards or use of the Jewish tradition. These motifs and organizing principles, in turn, might throw some new light on *Samson Agonistes* or corroborate extant interpretations. The juxtaposition of the Jewish and Miltonic portrayals of Samson has, I believe, led to the adumbration of certain basic concepts in the drama, namely, reason and liberty. These two motifs have already been isolated (by Basil Willey) in *Paradise Lost,* where Michael tells Adam,

> Since thy original lapse, true Libertie
> Is lost, which always with right Reason dwells
> Twinn'd, and from her hath no dividual being:
> Reason in man obscur'd, or not obeyd,
> Immediately inordinate desires
> And upstart Passions catch the Government
> From Reason, and to servitude reduce
> Man till then free.[21]   (XII, 83–90)

These two motifs are no less central in the organization of *Samson Agonistes* than they are in *Paradise Lost.* Indeed, Arthur E. Barker has argued for the centrality of the motif of liberty in *Samson Agonistes*[22]—a view in which we concur and to which we would join the theme of reason. In *Samson Agonistes* we see reason as the handmaid of liberty—its servant and its peer. Reason underlies and qualifies the Mosaic Law. Reason reduces and modifies the role of sensuality. And reason is the principle of Milton's scriptural herme- neutics and his rationalistic reading of the Book of Judges. Or to ap- proach the drama from the other pole, liberty is Samson's vision and preoccupation. Liberty is the springboard of his outbursts against personal, domestic, religious, and political servitude. Liberty is equated with reason and defines the Law, both as the Law's source and as its yardstick. Utilizing Willey's formulation of the fall of Adam as "the obscuration of Reason and the loss of liberty,"[23] we may define Samson's regeneration as the reinstitution of reason and the restoration of liberty.

These twin motifs, which can be traced throughout Milton's prose and poetry, emerge from, or are related directly to, Milton's con- ception of the Mosaic Law, the scriptural pivot that divides the Jewish and Miltonic ideologies and their interpretations of Samson. I think it can be demonstrated, by citing (apart from the Samson ma- terial) both from the rabbis and from Milton, that they do not differ radically in their moral (not philosophical) evaluation of servitude, reason, discipline, sensuality, and pride: the rabbis condemn servi- tude, folly, and pride as they do sensuality. Milton condemns sensual- ity as he does servitude and pride. On the other hand, the rabbis apotheosize reason and freedom as they do discipline. And Milton praises discipline as he does reason and liberty.[24] But Milton and the rabbis do differ substantively in their analysis and evaluation of the Mosaic Law. The rabbis regard the Law as both written and oral; as eternal and immutable in its externalized, legal form; as transcending (human) reason; and as epitomizing the source of true liberty. Milton, on the other hand, regards the Law as Mosaic (written) only (the Oral Law is human tradition); as abrogated for the Christian and dispensable (on certain occasions) for the Jew of the Old Testament; as equated with right reason and nature, confirmed by the Holy Spirit in the heart of believers;[25] and as representing a form of bondage for a people (Jewish) inclined to bondage. Milton's conception of the Mosaic Law turns, of course, on the Christian belief that the Gospel has superseded the Law, on Paul's antinomianism, and on the reading of the Law and the Gospel as antitheses. Milton's interpretation and doctrine are buttressed by the classical Greek influences of the supremacy of reason and the dichotomy of the flesh and the spirit.

Samson Agonistes contains little or none of "copious Legend," be it Christian (as Krouse has shown) or Jewish (as our study shows). Milton's rationalistic interpretation of Samson indicates that his critical requirements of "verisimilitude and decorum" involve a "unity and consistency"[26] of dramatic and philosophic presentation rather than a conformity with any exegetical (as opposed to doctrinal) tradition, whether Christian or Jewish. Samson Agonistes is a dramatization of an Old Testament story that is consistent from within as well as with Milton's general doctrinal views. Samson faithfully champions Milton's vision of reason and liberty, which rest on Milton's conception of the Mosaic Law.

University of Windsor

NOTES

1. Even the Hebraic interpretations deal either with the "spirit" of *Samson Agonistes*, e.g., Sir Richard C. Jebb, "*Samson Agonistes* and the Hellenic Drama," *Proceedings of the British Academy, 1907–1908* (London, 1908), pp. 341–48; or with Hebraic elements, e.g., Ann Mary Gossman, "The Synthesis of Hebraism and Hellenism in Milton's *Samson Agonistes*" (Ph.D. diss., The Rice Institute, 1957). Arnold Stein, *Heroic Knowledge* (Minneapolis, 1957), pp. 227–28, n. 2, observes: "We could use a modern study of Milton's 'Hebraism'—not an assessment of his knowledge but of his understanding."

2. The Talmud is the vast compendium of the Jewish oral tradition from which I have cited, in my own translation, Samson lore to be found in the Babylonian Talmud, tractate Sotah, 9 and 10; tractate Nazir, 4b; and the Jerusalem Talmud, Sotah I, 8. For additional Samson legends and interpretation, see Louis Ginzberg, *Legends of the Jews* (Philadelphia, 1938), 7 vols., esp. vol. IV.

3. *Jewish Antiquities, Books V–VIII*, trans. H. St. J. Thackeray and Ralph Marcus, vol. V of *Josephus*, ed. T. E. Page et al. (London and Cambridge, Mass., 1926–63), pp. 125 ff.

4. Fletcher, *Milton's Rabbinical Readings* (Urbana, 1930), passim, argues that Milton had access to the Buxtorf Rabbinical Bible of 1618–19 from which he borrowed certain hexaemeral details to embellish *Paradise Lost*. I have utilized the Mikraot Gedolot Rabbinic Bible (New York, 1951), VII, folios 63b–69a, which is similar to the Buxtorf. Milton, in *Doctrine and Discipline of Divorce, Prose Works of John Milton*, ed. Don M. Wolfe et al. (New Haven, 1953—), II, 335–36, refers to Radak as "Kimchi" and to Ralbag as "Ben Gersom." Further references to Milton's prose, except for *Christian Doctrine*, are to this edition.

5. Mishne Torah, Book of Holiness, vol. V, ch. xiii, 14.

6. Contrary to Merritt Y. Hughes, ed. *John Milton: Complete Poems and Major Prose* (New York, 1957), p. 534, who states that Milton made Dalila "his wife instead of the mistress that she is in the biblical story and in most Jewish . . . commentaries."

7. All citations of *Samson Agonistes* refer to *The Complete English Poetry of John Milton*, ed. John T. Shawcross (New York, 1963), pp. 149–95. For other Old Testament dispensations, see *Tetrachordon*, II, 588.

8. Cf. *Reason of Church-Government*, I, 764. The continuing validity of the moral law, Milton argues in *Doctrine and Discipline of Divorce*, II, 292, 306, is the law's identity with "Reason" and "Nature" and that which is "Moral." See also Arthur E. Barker, *Milton and the Puritan Dilemma, 1641–1660* (Toronto, 1956), p. 169.

9. Adrian Fortescue, "Law (Christian, Western)," *Encyclopaedia of Religion and Ethics*, ed. James Hastings and John Selbie (New York, 1928), VII, 832. See also *Christian Doctrine*, in *The Works of John Milton*, ed. Frank A. Patterson et al. (New York, 1931–1942), XVI, 273. All references to *Christian Doctrine* are to this edition.

10. See also F. Michael Krouse, *Milton's Samson and the Christian Tradition* (Princeton, 1949), p. 100; and E. M. Clark, "Milton's Conception of Samson," *Texas University Studies in English*, VIII (1928), 88–89.

11. "When Law came into the world, freedom came into the world" (Bereshith Rabbah, Va-Yairah, liii, 7). "No man is free but he who labors in the Torah" (Aboth, VI, 2). W. E. H. Lecky has observed: "It is at least an historical fact that in the great majority of instances the early Protestant defenders of civil liberty derived their political principles chiefly from the Old Testament and the defenders of despotism from the New. The rebellions that were so frequent in Jewish history formed the favourite topic of the one—the unreserved submission inculcated by St. Paul, of the other" (*The Rise and Influence of the Spirit of Rationalism in Europe* [New York, 1895], II, 168).

12. "The Gospell is the end and fulfilling of the Law, our liberty also from the bondage of the Law I plainly reade" (*Reason of Church-Government*, I, 763). See also *Christian Doctrine*, XVI, 103, 125 ff.

"I shall not repeat for you [Salmasius] the words of Aristotle and Cicero, who are surely our most reliable authorities, and who said in the *Politics* and the speech *On the Provinces* respectively that the peoples of Asia readily endure slavery, while the Jews and Syrians were born for it" (*A Defence of the People of England*, IV, pt. 1, 343). See also *Commonplace Book*, I, 440; *Christian Doctrine*, XIV, 153; XV, 169; *Tetrachordon*, II, 664.

13. This is probably in accord with the Christian view (*Christian Doctrine*, XVI, 111, 113) that there was no hope of eternal life in the Old Testament. Milton, however, also subscribed to the theory of "mortalism." See ibid., XV, 39 ff., 219.

14. This observation is made by William G. Madsen, *From Shadowy Types to Truth: Studies in Milton's Symbolism* (New Haven, 1968), p. 198.

15. See my "Samson as 'Dragon' and a Scriptural Tradition," *ELN*, VII (March 1970), 186–89.

16. Krouse, *Milton's Samson*, pp. 29–30. For the rabbinic view, see Ginzberg, *Legends*, VI, 201, n. 101.

17. Aboth, IV, 1; Yebamoth, 6b.

18. *Christian Doctrine*, XV, 367.

19. Madsen, *From Shadowy Types to Truth*, pp. 181–202, reads *Samson Agonistes* typologically, with Samson as the antithesis of Jesus in *Paradise Regained*. On the other hand, it has been observed that Samson is not one of the "personal" types recognized by Milton as prefiguring Jesus, and that Milton recognizes only six—Moses, Aaron, Melchizedec, Joshua, David, and Solomon—out of a total of seventy-one types listed by the Latin Fathers. Milton's typological conservatism and the "notable omission" of Samson from the basic types are attributed to Milton's "hermeneutical principle of relying upon the New Testament to pronounce all types" (Theodore Long Huguelet, "Milton's Hermeneutics: A Study of Scriptural Interpretation in the Divorce Tracts and in *De Doctrina Christiana*" [Ph.D. diss., University of North Carolina, 1959], pp. 162–63, 168, 170).

20. *Christian Doctrine*, XVI, 105.

21. Cited by Basil Willey, *The Seventeenth Century Background* (1934; reprint Garden City, N.Y., 1953), p. 249.

22. "Structural and Doctrinal Patterns in Milton's Later Poems," *Essays in English Literature from the Renaissance to the Victorian Age Presented to A. S. P. Woodhouse*, ed. Millar MacLure and F. W. Watt (Toronto, 1964), pp. 169–94, esp. 175–79. I came across Barker's essay after I had written the major part of my essay.

23. Willey, *Seventeenth Century Background*, p. 247.

24. "Rabbi Simeon ben Yohai said: Pride is equivalent to idolatry. Rabbi Johanan said: The proud man is as sinful as if he had committed every kind of unchastity. . . . Rabbi Hisda said: God declares, 'The proud man and I cannot live in the world together'" (Sotah, 4b–5a). Milton writes: "For there is not that thing in the world of more grave and urgent importance throughout the whole life of man, then is discipline" (*Reason of Church-Government*, I, 751). However, see n. 5 ad loc. Cf. "Rabbi Hanina said: It is finer to do what is commanded than to do the same thing when it is not commanded" (Kiddushin, 31a).

25. *Christian Doctrine*, XVI, 265, 273, 275.

26. Thomas Kranidas, *The Fierce Equation: A Study of Milton's Decorum* (Hague, 1965), p. 156.

COMUS
AND THE CASTLEHAVEN SCANDAL

Barbara Breasted

The cuts made for the first performance of *Comus* tend to reduce the explicit sexual content of the Lady's and Comus' speeches. This decorum, and the "cleansing family ritual" of the masque itself, were probably designed to repair the Bridgewater family's reputation, damaged by the trial and execution, three years before, of the Earl of Castlehaven and two of his servants for sexual crimes. Testimony and reports of the trial in diaries and letters describe the rape and promiscuity of the Earl's wife (sister to the Countess of Bridgewater), homosexuality between the Earl and his servants, and the conversion of Elizabeth Audley (Alice Egerton's twelve-year-old cousin) into a "whore." Letters of the Countess Dowager of Derby, for whom Milton wrote *Arcades,* reveal her distress over the scandal and her efforts to obtain pardons for her daughter and granddaughter. For the first audience, seeing Lady Alice Egerton act out her resistance to sexual temptation, *Comus* affirmed the Bridgewaters' possession of the aristocratic virtues which their relatives so notoriously lacked.

I N T H E early seventeenth century the king and queen and the peers were, ideally, still meant to define all virtues and so to exert a superior moral authority over the rest of England's population. Masques, like other literary entertainment created for the aristocracy, respected and flattered this ideal by extravagantly portraying aristocrats as exerting such moral authority. Milton's only masque is no exception to other Stuart masques in its use of the traditional complimentary device of masques: the triumph of aristocratic virtue over vice. When Milton's "Mask," which has come to be called *Comus,* was first performed on September 29, 1634, it defined anew the nobility of the Bridgewater family for an aristocratic audience. Like other Stuart masques, this one provided an elegant framework for a particular party. The occasion of the party on that September evening at Ludlow Castle was the celebration of the Earl of Bridgewater's accession to his new viceregal position as Lord President of the Council of Wales.

Comus has always been read as a lovely compliment to the family of the Earl of Bridgewater, whose three youngest children performed in it for their parents' pleasure. I, too, think Comus is a lovely compliment, but I think it is one which has not been fully appreciated before. Besides providing an opportunity for the Bridgewater children to display their skills at memorizing poetry, singing, and dancing, Comus may also have expressed the family's need to see its last unmarried daughter enact sexual virtue and restraint. The Bridgewaters' cousins had, three years before, been exposed as the central figures in one of the most outrageous sexual scandals of the early seventeenth century. I would like to argue that this scandal provided a context for Comus that may have influenced the way the masque was written, the way it was cut for its first performance, and the way it was received by its first audience in 1634. My paper will consider Comus in the light of this well-publicized family scandal, involving rape, homosexuality, and the conversion of an apparently innocent aristocratic child into a "whore," as Lady Alice Egerton's cousin Elizabeth is described in letters. Milton's masque may not have been intended simply to celebrate the reunion of the Bridgewater children with their father in Wales. It may also have been intended to help repair the reputation of the entire family by making the last unmarried Egerton daughter act out her resistance to dangerous sexual temptation.

The aristocratic audience enjoying Comus on that September night in 1634 would have experienced many court masques in London and would have expected this masque, like those at court, to culminate in beautiful formal dances as the prelude to their favorite kind of party. They would have expected this masque, like others, not to be about the shunning of all sensuous and amorous pleasure, but simply to be about the shunning of dangerous or unseemly pleasure. Comus is then, appropriately, about discriminating among different kinds of pleasurable experience. It is about discriminating between Comus' "liquor," sumptuous food, and sexual invitations on the one hand, and the gentle amorousness of the masque's songs and even the approaching party at Ludlow Castle on the other hand. The masque displays the Earl and Countess of Bridgewater's three youngest and still unmarried children being guided out of an imaginary danger toward the right and safe sort of pleasure, toward, in fact, the actual evening of dancing and celebration about to begin at Ludlow Castle.

That imaginary danger, particularly in the uncut version of *Comus* (which is the version we commonly read) is the sexual temptation of an aristocratic virgin. In the beginning of the masque, three aristocratic children, the Lady, the Elder Brother, and the Younger Brother (acted by fifteen-year-old Lady Alice, eleven-year-old John, and nine-year-old Thomas Egerton) are lost in a wood. The virgin has become separated from her brothers. She is discovered by an enchanter, Comus, who tempts her to drink his magical liquor and to submit to his sexual offers. The Lady easily refuses his offers because she knows so little about the pleasures described in them.

Until 1637, when Henry Lawes had *Comus* published, there are no recorded opinions of the masque. Henry Lawes himself, the Bridgewater children's music teacher who composed music for *Comus* and acted in it, then gave the piece nothing but praise. In his dedication to this first edition of the masque, he implies that it had satisfied its first audience completely and continued to satisfy readers, being "so lovely, and so much desired." Yet neither Lawes himself nor literary historians have emphasized one important reason why the masque may have proved so satisfactory.

In the winter of 1630–1631, the Earl of Bridgewater's brother-in-law, the Earl of Castlehaven, was indicted and imprisoned for raping his own wife and committing sodomy with one of his servants. After a trial, the transcripts of which sound like notes for pornographic fiction, Mervyn Touchet, Lord Audley, the Earl of Castlehaven, was beheaded for these sexual crimes in May 1631. His odder and more outrageous acts, revealed during his trial, consisted in extreme treachery to his heir. The Earl had apparently threatened to disinherit his eldest son in favor of a servant whom the Earl had persuaded to become the lover of his son's twelve-year-old bride. (The girl was also the Earl's own stepdaughter.)

News of his crimes and other more bizarre behavior may have

FIGURE 1

THE DERBY-BRIDGEWATER-CASTLEHAVEN FAMILY

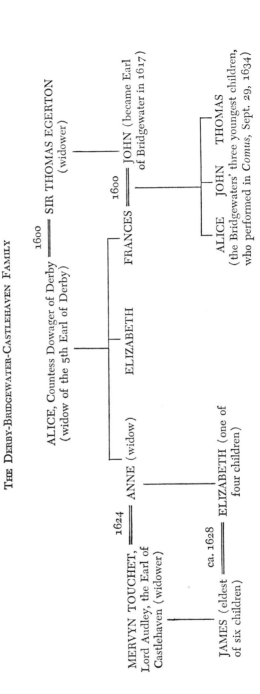

been kept from the public at first. But soon enough the stories were well known. Two of the Earl of Castlehaven's male servants were hung at Tyburn in July 1631 for their participation in his orgies. Before the crowd of onlookers, these two men confirmed the tales of the earl's homosexuality and of his efforts to persuade his favorite servant to beget an heir upon his twelve-year-old daughter-in-law and step-daughter. The "allurements" which he supposedly offered this young girl (who was only three years older than her cousin, Lady Alice Egerton) in urging her to become the mistress of his servants and an accomplice in disinheriting his own son, were as shocking to the public and to his relatives as the sexual crimes committed upon his wife and servants.

Read in the light of the Castlehaven scandal, the threats to the Lady's "honor" in *Comus* may have been a more pointed allusion to events in the family's recent history than has been thought by literary historians who have dealt with the formal masque conventions used in *Comus,* or by critics who have recorded their complex readings of the masque. Even a critic such as David Wilkinson, who suggested that *Comus* must have been responded to as a cleansing family ritual, does not suspect why such a cleansing family ritual might have been particularly appropriate for *this* family.[1]

I would like to argue that the audience at the first performance of *Comus* may have acknowledged, in the Lady's resistance to Comus' allurements and sexual offers, an implicit contrast between Lady Alice Egerton and her cousin, Lady Elizabeth Audley, even though three passages emphasizing those sexual offers were cut from that per-formance. I think this speculation is justified because Lady Alice Egerton's role in *Comus* is not meant to make us forget who she is, but, like other masque roles aristocrats played, was intended to be a glorified, idealized version of her public identity. By creating an imaginary sexual temptation for the Bridgewaters' last unmarried daughter, Milton may be alluding to the circumstances through which her cousin was reputed to have become by the age of fifteen such a "whore" that her husband never lived with her again after 1631.[2]

THE CUTS IN THE BRIDGEWATER MANUSCRIPT

Of the two extant manuscript versions of *Comus,* the Bridgewater manuscript is assumed to be much closer to the version of the masque performed at Ludlow than the Trinity manuscript. As Milton's most recent biographer says of the Bridgewater manuscript:

Its many cuts . . . remind us that the audience heard a version shorter than the text which we commonly read—and probably a version, as with the Bridgewater Manuscript, in which some of the lengthy discussions of chastity were lacking.[3]

The passages cut from the Bridgewater manuscript of *Comus* were restored to the text when the masque was first published in 1637, six years after Castlehaven's trial and execution.[4]

The reasons for the selection of these cuts in the Bridgewater manuscript have never been adequately explained. Why, in particular, were the "discussions of chastity" cut from the text in 1634? Diekhoff is the only twentieth-century critic who has entertained David Masson's speculation that the selection of these cuts was due to social rather than technical scruples:

Masson guesses that some of these lines [cut from the Lady's first speech], and lines 697–700 . . . are such as the Earl and Countess "would hardly have liked to hear their young daughter speaking aloud" and that they would have preferred other lines (omitted from Comus's speeches) not to be addressed to her.[5]

But neither Masson nor twentieth-century Milton scholars who have written about the cuts in *Comus* (such as Diekhoff, Shawcross, Tillyard, and Stevens) have explained the masque, with or without the cuts, in terms of the recent sexual scandal in the Bridgewater-Derby-Castlehaven family.

The cuts in the Bridgewater manuscript are evidence of Milton's or Henry Lawes' great attention to decorum in the text.[6] These cuts are clearly evidence of one or both of them having taken pains not to let Lady Alice Egerton appear in an improper light. Possibly, the cuts are also evidence of Milton or Lawes taking care not to evoke memories of the Castlehaven scandal too vividly. I believe that the impropriety of requiring Lady Alice to speak in public about chastity and seduction, not to mention the impropriety of making too explicit a comparison between this presumably innocent young noblewoman and her ruined cousin, explain three of the five principal cuts in the Bridgewater manuscript more adequately than previous explanations have.

Formerly, readers remarking upon these cuts have suggested that they were made simply because the performers had enough to memorize and the masque may have been a little too long. The five principal cuts, lines 195b–225, 632–37, 697–700, 735–55, and 1000–11, amount to under eighty lines in a masque of about a thousand lines.[7] Yet it seems odd that such vivid passages as these were cut from the working text. Three of the five cut passages, the first, third, and fourth (lines 195b–225, 697–700, 735–55) show that the sexual dangers threatening the Lady were toned down for the initial performance.

Almost half of the Lady's first speech (lines 195b–225), in which she talks about being alone in the wood, is cut from the Bridgewater manuscript. It is in this deleted second half of her speech that the Virgin (as Comus has already called her) accuses Night of having some "felonious" purpose in shutting out the stars. Fearing this danger, the Lady hopes that her mind possesses the strengths of "the virtuous mind," strengths which she soon confidently summons before her imagination:

> O welcome pure-ey'd Faith, white-handed Hope,
> Thou hov'ring Angel girt with golden wings,
> And thou unblemish't form of Chastity,
> I see ye visibly, and now believe
> That he, the Supreme good . . .
> Would send a glist'ring Guardian, if need were,
> To keep my life and honor unassail'd.   (213–20)

I do not think that this first principal cut of the thirty lines surrounding and including this passage was made, as literary historians have suggested before, because Lady Alice Egerton had trouble memorizing long speeches. This accomplished young woman, who was remembered later by her music teacher Lawes as having been an excellent pupil, and who had already participated in court masques, would hardly have been incapable of learning more lines. But even if she had been incapable, this fact would not explain the decision to cut these particular lines rather than others. I think, instead, that it is possible that Lawes or Milton cut this passage and two others from the performance because he thought it indecorous to require a young unmarried noblewoman to talk in public about sex and chastity, particularly when her cousin's loss of honor was probably still one of the most scandalous stories in England. Although Lawes and Milton wanted the masque to emphasize the Lady's virtue, the person who cut the text apparently did not want the masque to make the Lady's anxiety about her honor too embarrassingly open.

After the Lady has been led offstage by Comus (disguised as a shepherd), we hear the two brothers speaking about their lost sister. At this point, even in the cut version of the masque, our attention is again focused upon the sister's chastity. The Elder Brother tries to convince the Younger Brother of their sister's safety, innocently asserting that a girl of "Virgin purity," of virgin "chastity . . . is clad in complete steel." After he creates a vision of supernaturally protected virginity that comforts only himself, he describes with equal fervor lust's effect upon the "soul":

> but when lust
> By unchaste looks, loose gestures, and foul talk,
> But most by lewd and lavish act of sin,
> Lets in defilement to the inward parts,
> The soul grows clotted by contagion.   (463–67)

Apparently Milton or Lawes did not feel it indecorous for a *boy* to speak such lines, for they were not cut from the Bridgewater manuscript.

When we next see the Lady we discover that the Attendant Spirit's fears about her are justified. Comus has begun to control her body by making her powerless to leave the chair in which she sits. Comus himself now becomes more explicit about the sexual nature of his offers to the Lady, particularly in the uncut version of the masque. What he does not realize is that she is not yet fitted to appreciate the pleasures with which he is tempting her. Comus offers her refreshment which she is not old enough to desire:

> Why should you be so cruel to yourself,
> And to those dainty limbs which nature lent
> For gentle usage and soft delicacy?
> But you invert the cov'nant of her trust,
> And harshly deal like an ill borrower
> With that which you receiv'd on other terms,
> Scorning the unexempt condition
> By which all mortal frailty must subsist,
> Refreshment after toil, ease after pain,
> That have been tir'd all day without repast,
> And timely rest have wanted; but, fair Virgin,
> This will restore all soon.   (679–89)[8]

The third principal cut in the Bridgewater manuscript appears now. Four lines were cut from the Lady's reply to this speech of the "false traitor," the man whom she knows has already deceived her by enchanting her instead of leading her to her brothers. The four deleted lines imply that although the Lady cannot respond to Comus' pleasures, she is beginning to catch on to the "trap" they threaten to construct for her:

> Hast thou betray'd my credulous innocence
> With vizor'd falsehood and base forgery,
> And wouldst thou seek again to trap me here
> With lickerish baits fit to ensnare a brute? (697–700)

As with the first principal cut, I think it possible that Milton or Lawes chose to cut these lines because they make the Lady's sexual predicament too explicit. Besides, there was no longer an excuse for these four lines since they were dropped together with the fourth principal cut of nineteen other lines in which Comus does proffer "lickerish baits."

The fourth principal cut made in the Bridgewater manuscript occurs when Comus responds to the Lady's repeated refusals with his famous speech about enjoying Nature's bounties. In the last nineteen lines cut from this speech Comus refers bluntly to his captive's virginity and extends an open sexual invitation to her. Again, this passage may have been cut because it was thought inappropriate that the Lady be propositioned so openly, in view of her position as an unmarried noblewoman and possibly also in view of her cousin's history, as I have said before. These final nineteen lines compose a traditional poem of persuasion in themselves and, had they been left in the text, would have allowed the first audience no doubt about what Comus had in mind:

> List Lady, be not coy, and be not cozen'd
> With that same vaunted name Virginity;
> Beauty is nature's coin, must not be hoarded,
> But must be current, and the good thereof
> Consists in mutual and partak'n bliss,
> Unsavory in th' enjoyment of itself.
> If you let slip time, like a neglected rose
> It withers on the stalk with languish't head.
> Beauty is nature's brag, and must be shown
> In courts, and feasts, and high solemnities

Where most may wonder at the workmanship;
It is for homely features to keep home,
They had their name thence; coarse complexions
And cheeks of sorry grain will serve to ply
The sampler, and to tease the housewife's wool.
What need a vermeil-tinctur'd lip for that,
Love-darting eyes, or tresses like the Morn?
There was another meaning in these gifts,
Think what, and be advis'd; you are but young yet. (737–55)

The first half of the Lady's reply (lines 779–99) to this speech of
Comus is missing both in the Bridgewater and the Trinity manuscripts,
and was therefore probably added to the text three years after the
masque was performed, when *Comus* was first being prepared for the
press. These twenty added lines compose the famous passage in which
the Lady insists that Comus lacks the "Ear" to apprehend the sublimity
and mystery of Virginity. In response, Comus only tempts her with
the cup again, saying, "Be wise, and taste." Before there is time for
her to hesitate over the drink, the Lady's brothers rush up and drive
Comus away. They find their sister silent and fixed to her chair, even
after Comus has disappeared. They and the Shepherd must summon
another virgin to release her from her enchantment. With the nymph
Sabrina's help, "ensnared chastity" is soon freed from the magic spell,
and is invited to "return" to Ludlow Castle, from which the children's
father (called in the beginning of the masque "A noble Peer of mickle
trust and power") rules the western part of England.

The Lady, her two brothers, and the Shepherd pretend to move
from the wood to Ludlow Castle where the *right* sort of party is
about to begin, where they will celebrate their masque triumph "o'er
sensual Folly and Intemperance" by dancing! The Shepherd invites
the Lady to be guided back to her parents' house and to its health-
giving pleasures which will not threaten her life or honor:

Come Lady . . .
Let us fly this cursed place . . .
And not many furlongs thence
Is your father's residence,
Where this night are met in state
Many a friend to gratulate
His wish't presence, and beside
All the Swains that there abide,
With Jigs and rural dance resort

. . . .
And our sudden coming there
Will double all their mirth and cheer.   (938–55)

Within the Great Hall of Ludlow Castle the scenery now changes
to present a painted view of "Ludlow Town and the President's
Castle." Country dancers enter and dance until the Shepherd re-
appears to sing a song and speak his concluding lines. The second
verse of his song presents the three children to their father and mother,
who would have been sitting in the center and front of the audience,
the conventional place for the guests of honor at a masque:

> *Noble Lord, and Lady bright,*
> *I have brought ye new delight,*
> *Here behold so goodly grown*
> *Three fair branches of your own.*
> *Heav'n hath timely tri'd their youth,*
> *Their faith, their patience, and their truth,*
> *And sent them here through hard assays*
> *With a crown of deathless Praise,*
>   *To triumph in victorious dance*
> *O'er sensual Folly and Intemperance.*   (966–75)

By thus presenting the Lady, the Elder Brother, and the Younger
Brother to their actual parents in the audience, the Shepherd confirms
the public identities of the three children that the masque has been
idealizing all along. By idealizing these last three unmarried Egerton
children and their relationship with their parents, Milton invites us to
regard the masque as a ritual purification of the entire family.

We have reviewed *Comus* in order to look at the three passages
cut from the speeches of Comus and the Lady which indicate that
social decorum governed the terms of that purification in the first
performance (though not in the published version of the masque). In
the following two sections of my paper I will briefly explore the historical evidence for the Castlehaven scandal having provided a context for that performance in 1634, and for its possibly giving Milton
and Lawes more reason than the obvious requirements of decorum
to tone down the sexual terms of *Comus*.

THE DERBY-BRIDGEWATER-CASTLEHAVEN FAMILY
AND THE SCANDAL

The scandalous sexual and dynastic troubles of the Castlehaven
family began when the Earl married Anne Stanley in July 1624.

Anne was the Countess Dowager of Derby's eldest daughter, and therefore was the aunt of the Lady in *Comus*. (Frances, the Countess of Bridgewater, was the Countess Dowager's second daughter.)[9] Anne was already the widow of Grey Lord Chandos, by whom she had had two sons and two daughters. The Earl of Castlehaven was himself a widower with children. Anne and he were to have no children together. But in 1628 he and Anne became doubly related to one another through the marriage of his eldest son James to his wife's eleven- or twelve-year-old daughter, Lady Elizabeth.[10]

The Castlehaven troubles did not become common knowledge, and thus a matter of great shame for the rest of the family, until they were exposed during the Earl of Castlehaven's trial in April 1631. By that time, Mervyn's son James had hardened himself to the thought of the inevitable publicity, and had appealed to the king for justice.[11] On Monday, April 25, 1631, the Earl of Castlehaven was arraigned, tried, and sentenced to death for crimes of rape and sodomy.[12] The personal testimonies of witnesses which were read during the trial disclosed not only instances of the crimes of which he was accused, but also stories of Mervyn's efforts to deprive his son James of his bride and of his inheritance, while engaging in voyeuristic sexual behavior with James' bride. These testimonies are important not because they established the "truth" about the Earl but because they were believed. (The Earl himself pleaded "not guilty" to the charges brought against him.)

As the testimonies are repetitive, I will give only four principal ones. The first is that given by the Countess of Castlehaven:

The first or second night after we were married, *Antil* [former servant and a present son-in-law of the Earl] came to his bed side whilest we were in bed, and the Lord spake lasciviously to her [the Countess of Castlehaven], and told her, her body was his, and that if she loved him, she must love *Antil*, and if shee lay with any man with his consent, it was not her fault, but his. Hee would make *Skipwith* [a servant] come naked into her chamber, and bed, and delighted in calling up his servants, making them shew their privities, and her looke on, and commended those that had the largest. *Broadway* [a servant] lay with her whilst she made resistance, and my Lord held her hands, and one of her feet, and she would have killed herselfe afterwards with a knife, but that hee tooke it from her; and before the act of *Broadway* shee had never done it. He delighted to see the act done, and made *Antil* come into the bed to them, and lye with her whilst he might see it; and that she cryed out.[13]

A servant, Fitzpatrick, later executed for committing sodomy with the Earl, gave the next testimony:

That *Henry Skipwith* was the speciall favourite of the Lord, and that he usually lay with him; and that *Skipwith* sayd, the Lord made him lye with his owne Lady *Awdley,* and that he saw *Skipwith* in his sight doe it, my Lord being present; and that he lay with *Blandina* [a prostitute, residing temporarily in the household] in his sight, and foure more, and afterwards he himselfe in their sights.[14]

The testimony of Henry Skipwith, the servant most favored by the Earl, was then given:

That the earl often solicited him to lie with the young lady, and persuaded her to love him; and to draw her thereunto, he urged that his son loved her not; and that in the end he usually lay with the young lady, and that there was love between them both before and after; and that my lord said, he would rather have a boy of his begetting than any other; and that she was but twelve years of age when he first lay with her, and that he could not enter her body without art; and that the Lord Audley fetched oil to open her body, but she cried out, and he could not enter; and then the earl appointed oil the second time; and then Skipwith entered her body, and he knew her carnally; and that my lord made him lie with his own lady, but he knew her not, but told his lord he did.—That he spent 500 *l.* per ann. of the lord's purse, and, for the most part, he lay with the said earl. That the earl gave him his house at Salisbury, and a manor of 600 *l.*—That Blandina lay in the earl's house half a year, and was a common whore.[15]

Fitzpatrick was asked to give a second testimony:

That the lord Audley made him lie with him at Founthill [Castlehaven's principal estate in Wiltshire] and at Salisbury, and once in the bed, and emitted between his thighs, but did not penetrate his body; and that he heard he did so with others.—That Skipwith lay with the young lady often, and ordinarily; and that the earl knew it; and encouraged him in it, and wished to have a boy by him and the young lady.—That Blandina lived half a year in my lord's house, and was a common whore.[16]

The chronology and nature of the events described in these four testimonies are slightly different in the *MS Ashmolean* 824 version of the trial. In this version the Countess claims the Earl offered her money as a means of persuasion, Skipwith suggests he seduced Lady Elizabeth by himself, and Edmund Scot (another servant) claims that James' and Elizabeth's marriage was a happy one at first.[17]

On May 14, 1631, the Earl of Castlehaven was executed on Tower Hill, his sentence having been changed from hanging to beheading, due to his rank as a peer.

The Castlehaven family's first public response to the trial was to try to have the Earl pardoned. The Bridgewater family responded by silence, while the person at the center of both families, the old Countess Dowager of Derby, responded by trying to obtain pardons for her daughter's and granddaughter's sexual offenses, and by trying to mend the wretched marriage of James and Elizabeth Audley.

As one of the thirty-four functioning members of the Privy Council in the year 1630–1631, the Earl of Bridgewater was in a position to know all about the legal arrangements being made for his brother-in-law and for the various members of his brother-in-law's family.[18] Though the Earl of Bridgewater held the highest public office in his family, he made no effort that has been recorded to have Castlehaven pardoned. Bridgewater seems to have believed in his brother-in-law's guilt. Between the fifteenth of February and the tenth of June, 1631, the months during which Castlehaven's trial was prepared and accomplished, the shocking testimonies revealed, and the Earl beheaded, Bridgewater appears not to have attended any meetings of the Privy Council. Nor did the king ask him to attend the trial in April along with twenty-seven other peers who were all members of the Privy Council. Since other evidence is lacking, might it not be possible to explain Bridgewater's absence from official duties during this period as a measure of his distress about the family scandal? His stepuncle, the sixth earl of Derby, did attend the trial. But people knew that the king, either out of a sense of tact or out of a sense of justice, spared Bridgewater from having to judge the innocence of a man so closely related to himself.[19] Those who had tried to free the Earl were his sisters, his sister Eleanor's husband, and even his son James.[20]

The only member of the Bridgewater-Derby half of the family whose responses to the whole calamity are recorded is Alice, the Countess Dowager of Derby. She was painfully shocked, and by no means willing to forgive her daughter and granddaughter as being merely the victims of Castlehaven's lascivious designs. From the first, she refused to take them into her home until the king had pardoned them, and until there was some hope of their reform.

In the last week of April 1631, Alice wrote to the king's Secretary, the eminent Viscount Dorchester, explaining her refusal to take her daughter Anne in, though the king did not oppose the idea:

neither [will I] dare, nor will I venture to take her from y.ᵉ Byshop of Winchesters house till I may heare further from yoᵘ whether I may Receive her before the Tryall of y.ᵉ othe[r] offenders be past.

Alice hopes that Castlehaven's son and his wife, her fifteen-year-old grandchild, can yet be reconciled. The girl, her grandmother continues, could in the future regain some of her honor by proving "a vertuous good & louing wife to him." She prays

that neither my daughter nor she will euer offend either God or his Ma[jes]ᵗⁱᵉ againe by their wicked Courses, But redeeme what is past, by their reformation and newnesse of life.

Alice concludes her letter by asking for help in obtaining official pardons for her daughter and granddaughter from the king:

further more I must entreat yoʳ Lo[rdshi]ᵖˢ: favour, that when yoᵘ. thinke the time drawes neere fo:ʳ y:ᵉ obtaining their pdons (w:ᶜʰ as yet yo.ᵘ say cannot be granted) you will not be unmindfull, when yo.ᵘ see it stand wᵗʰ the Conveniency of time to be an humble Suiter to his Ma[jes]:ᵗⁱᵉ from me in Solliciting him for it.²¹

The Countess Dowager's grief and distaste for the whole business are more apparent in her next letter to Secretary Dorchester, written a month later. The stronger terms of this letter make it probable that in the interval the elderly aristocrat either had decided Secretary Dorchester needed to be addressed more urgently or had learned more details of the family scandal. Though the Earl of Castlehaven had now been executed, the Countess Dowager's daughter and grandchild were still not pardoned by the king. In addition, Alice was particularly stung by her granddaughter's refusal to obey her command to return to her husband. Alice makes clear in this letter to Dorchester that she has been so "perplexed and afflicted wᵗʰ griefe for my daughter Castlehaven, and Grandchilde Audlie, in that they have so Infinitlie offended God, & the King, by their wicked Crimes," that she still simply cannot take the grandchild, particularly, into her house. Alice was already taking care of Lady Elizabeth Audley's remaining brothers and sister at Harefield. For this reason she is especially unwilling to receive their sister whose influence might be very corrupting:

I doe Earnestlie entreate yor Lo[rd]:$^{s[hi]p}$ to plead my Cause, [and] beseech his Ma[jes]^{tie}: to excuse me (yet a while) for [i.e., from] taking my Grandchilde Audlie. . . . I am fearefull least there should be some sparkes of my Grand-childe Audlies misbehauiour remaining, w^{ch}: might giue ill Example to y.^{e} young ones w^{ch}: are wth: me.[22]

If the Earl of Bridgewater's stepmother was as explicit as this about the possible corrupting effect of Lady Elizabeth Audley upon her brothers and sister in 1631, is it not possible that the Bridgewaters, too, might have been particularly anxious about the girl's effect upon the moral education of their own children? Wouldn't the Bridgewaters, whose household still included four unmarried daughters and two little boys in 1631, also continue to be anxious for a few years lest their niece's spectacular example of promiscuity and disobedience contaminate the remaining children in their family?

Alice continues, in her letter of May 21, 1631, to Secretary Dorchester, to remind him how much the pardons mean to her and to say that she believes her grandchild might yet respond to education. She hopes the king will help arrange and finance this education.[23] But she is still firmly convinced of the propriety of her refusal to see her two scandalous relatives until they have been pardoned. The Bridgewaters, who never even offered to take their notorious cousins in, though they could have afforded the extra expense much better than Alice, probably responded to the scandal even more extremely than she, who at least proposed practical solutions to it:

And if his Ma[jes]^{tie}: shall like thereof to provide a place where she may be wth: som good Gentlewoman that shall Instruct her in y^e: feare of God w^{ch}: she had need of, And when I see her Reformation I shall wth more Joy expresse my kindnes to her and her Lo[rd]: if there may be an Attonement betwixt them. And that my daughter and she may be so happie to receive their pardon from the King. and till such time I shall never willinglie yeeld to see either of them. for the sight of them would but Increase my griefe whoese heart is almost wounded to death already w.th thinking of so fowle a business.[24]

After July 6, 1631, there could be no question that the most shocking details of the family scandal were common knowledge. On that day two of the Earl of Castlehaven's servants were hung at Tyburn for sexual offenses committed with him. Fitzpatrick's and Broadway's open discussion at their hanging of the Castlehavens' sexual behavior must have given the entire family its most distasteful dose of publicity yet.[25] Not until November 1631, six months after Castlehaven's execution and four months after the executions of Fitzpatrick and Broadway, did the king finally pardon the Countess of Derby's daughter and grandchild. Her daughter was pardoned first, on November 14:

This bill contayneth yo[r] Ma[jes][te] gracious pardon unto y[e] Countess of Castlehaven of all offences, of Adulterie, fornication and incontinency, heretofore comĩtted by her.[26]

Two weeks later, on November 30, Attorney General Noy was directed to prepare a similar pardon for the Countess of Castlehaven's daughter. In Secretary Dorchester's warrant for the preparation of this pardon, he implies that a young person's moral frailties are easier to forgive than an older person's. He writes that the excuses made for the Countess of Castlehaven "are made more considerable [for her daughter] by her tender years apt to be [. . .] by the allurements w[ch] were used to misleade her."[27] We should keep in mind that in *Comus* Milton assumes that the young may be more easily deceived than adults by "allurements" and that therefore their ability to withstand temptation is always a matter of anxiety.

In the light of these private and public responses to the family scandal, it is difficult to believe that *Comus* could have been written and performed with no thought in anyone's mind of how it might allude to that scandal. Would it have been possible to watch even the cut version of the masque performed and not be reminded of the members of the family who *had* yielded to "fowle" temptations? By 1634, the family as well as the public had for three years been able to point to a vivid example of an aristocratic girl (not to mention her aristocratic mother) who had yielded to sexual offers of an illicit and potentially sadistic sort, and whose honor, marriage, and chance to live a normal life had been ruined as a result.

Milton and the Castlehaven Scandal

Milton would have been more likely to learn of the Castlehaven scandal (and the family's responses to it) by virtue of the people he knew than simply by virtue of where he lived.[28] In this respect, the most important piece of information we have about him before he wrote *Comus* is that he was invited to compose an "entertainment" for the Countess Dowager of Derby some time between 1631 and 1633.[29] It seems likely that some of Alice's relatives who performed in *Arcades* at Harefield were those children of Anne Castlehaven whom Alice had taken into her home. If Milton were told anything about Alice's household he would probably have been told about these children and why they lived there.

Among Milton's acquaintances who knew of the Castlehaven scandal, the person most qualified to speak of its effect upon the Bridgewater family was Henry Lawes, Milton's collaborator on *Arcades* as well as on *Comus*. By 1634 Lawes had been the children's music teacher in the Bridgewater household for at least seven years.[30] Of course Milton need not have waited for Lawes or the Bridgewaters to inform him of the Castlehaven scandal. It seems, as we might expect, to have been common knowledge. Besides, the year 1630–1631 was a plague year when official business in London was reduced to a minimum, and court and city life slowed. It must have been a duller year than usual for gossip until the Earl was imprisoned.

London gossip about Castlehaven fed diaries, poems, personal letters, and the more formal letters called news-letters.[31] The Marchioness of Winchester's death and the preparations for Castlehaven's trial were discussed in the same week, and the Marchioness' death occasioned a poem by Milton, which suggests he probably knew about the other event as well. At least three short poems were written about Castlehaven that Milton might possibly have heard of or read: a mock epitaph "by" the Earl himself,[32] an answer to the mock epitaph spoken "by" the Countess,[33] and a third poem, "Upon the Lord Audley's Conviction," signed "Jo: R:."[34] The one lengthy contemporary account of the Earl that does not turn him completely into a "monster" (the favorite term for him) is part of a folio, never published, describing the trial.[35]

The shocked fascination with which people responded to the stories of Castlehaven and his family is displayed in a private letter sent on May 19, 1631, to Doctor Ward, Public Professor of Divinity and Master of Sidney-Sussex College in Cambridge:

Worthy S^r

Yo^{rs} of May 3 came hither in mine absence. . . . On Saturday last was the Earl of Castlehaven beheaded publikely, on the Toure-hil, dieng in profess[ing?] a Protestant, & cleering himself to the death of ye crimes y^t he suffred for. Some think, y^t he had hope of reprival to ye last. . . . His sonnes wife (it seemeth) is not yet 16 yeeres old, whome before 12. he made a whore. It is wel y^t the land is cleered of so vile a monster: & y^t the pack of them is discovered & dissolved. Ffor horrible things are acknowledged to have been comonly practised among them, & much more in likelyhood was then is disclosed.[36]

How rich are the terms of this letter in the light of *Comus* which was to be performed three years later! Fifteen-year-old Elizabeth Audley is called a "whore," Castlehaven a "vile . . . monster," and the members of his household a "pack." Such terms represented the common public reaction to this scandal which had violated the essential sexual and dynastic codes of English society.

That Milton successfully entertained the Bridgewaters in 1634 is evident from the mere fact that Lawes was later allowed to publish *Comus*. Apparently, in its cut version, Milton's masque had not offended the taste of its first audience at all. *Comus*, then, remains a perfect compliment to the Bridgewater family, a compliment which I hope seems enhanced by its possible connection with the Castlehaven scandal. The Bridgewater manuscript of *Comus* gives evidence of cuts made in order to tone down for the first performance the sexual temptations offered to the Lady. I have tried to suggest plausible reasons for these adjustments in the text. I have argued that either Milton or Henry Lawes or both men realized that the uncut text posed embarrassing problems of theatrical propriety, including the danger of alluding too strongly to the Castlehaven scandal. It seems unavoidable that this family scandal was part of the historical context of *Comus*.

Nine months before the performance at Ludlow Castle, a man named Dr. Dee gave a sermon on virginity before the king. One of the listeners commented later that the doctor had chosen a poor topic for the court:

[Dr. Dee] spake so much in commendation of virginity, as I do verily believe all those women that heard him, that have wicked husbands, or are aged, wish themselves virgins and young again.

Sure this doctor made no good choice of the court to commend virginity in.[37]

The writer of this letter does not allow for another possibility in his wry remark: the possibility that Dr. Dee (and later Milton) made the very best choice of the court to recommend virginity in. Although aristocrats, like other people, could not live perfectly, their masques show how they loved for an evening to act capable of that perfection.

Wellesley College

NOTES

1. "The underlying [compliment] . . . concerns the whole family, being involved in a conflict with evil, suffering and overcoming (at least nominally), and finally being blessed, all which action is identical with that communal re-enactment of significant moral experience which we call ritual. One can scarcely believe that the Egerton family . . . emerged from the evening no whit affected in their 'sense of family.' " David Wilkinson, "The Escape from Pollution: A Comment on 'Comus,' " *Essays in Criticism*, X (1960), 34.

There are several plays and masques that have been pointed to as possible models for Milton's masque about the temptation of a virgin: Tasso's *Aminta*, George Peele's *The Old Wife's Tale*, Puteanus' *Comus*, John Fletcher's *The Faithful Shepherdess*, Jonson's *Pleasure Reconciled to Virtue*, and Aurelian Townshend's *Tempe Restored*. But the process of trying to identify literary sources for Milton's masque does not serve to explain why he wrote this particular masque for this particular family at this time.

2. The person who did, ultimately, offer Lady Elizabeth Audley a home was Alice, the Countess Dowager of Derby. This seventy-two-year-old grandmother of both Lady Elizabeth Audley (Castlehaven's daughter-in-law *and* stepdaughter) and Lady Alice Egerton (Bridgewater's daughter) was the woman for whom Milton was soon to write *Arcades*. Her reactions to the scandal are described on pp. 214–16.

3. William Riley Parker, *Milton: A Biography* (Oxford, 1968), p. 133.

4. We say these passages are "cut" because they appear both in the Trinity manuscript of *Comus* (which is assumed to have evolved from an earlier version of the masque than that transcribed in the Bridgewater manuscript) and in the editions of *Comus* printed in Milton's lifetime (1637, 1645, and 1673). Apparently neither the Trinity manuscript (which is in Milton's own hand) nor the Bridgewater manuscript is the original version of the masque or even the exact version used for the first performance. Shawcross dates the revised sections of the Trinity manuscript as late as 1637 according to a change in Milton's handwriting, and concludes that the Bridgewater manuscript was not transcribed until the autumn of 1637. For detailed comparisons of the two manuscripts see: John S. Diekhoff's two articles, "The Text of *Comus*, 1634–1645," *PMLA*, LIV (1937), 705–27, and "Critical Activity of the Poetic Mind: John Milton," *PMLA*, LV (1940), 748–63; and John T. Shawcross, "Certain Relationships of the Manuscripts of *Comus*," *Bibliographical Society of America*, LIV (1960), 38–56. Photographic facsimiles of both the Trinity and Bridgewater manuscripts of *Comus* are found

in volume I of Harris Francis Fletcher's edition of John Milton's *Complete Poetical Works* (Urbana, 1943).

5. John S. Diekhoff, "A Maske at Ludlow," in *A Maske at Ludlow: Essays on Milton's "Comus,"* ed. John S. Diekhoff (Cleveland, 1968), p. 6.

6. It is not known whether Milton or his collaborator Lawes was responsible for making the cuts.

7. Line numbers refer to the text of *Comus* in *John Milton: Complete Poems and Major Prose,* ed. Merritt Y. Hughes (New York, 1957).

8. In the Bridgewater manuscript this passage consists of four lines:

> poore ladie thou has need of some refreshinge
> that hast been tired aldaye without repast,
> a timely rest hast wanted. heere fayre Virgin
> this will restore all soon.

This passage was expanded to twelve lines in the Trinity manuscript on an added pasted leaf. It is an instance of an extensive revision Milton made in the text, perhaps after the performance.

9. See figure 1 for a diagram of these family relationships.

10. Aristocratic daughters often married before they were fifteen, Lady Alice Egerton's age when she performed as the virgin in Milton's masque. Nor was a marriage creating a double bond between two aristocratic families unusual. The Earl of Bridgewater, like Castlehaven's son James, married his stepsister.

11. See *State Papers Domestic, Charles I* (hereafter, cited as *S.P.D.*), vol. 175, no. 2. Significantly, the two women in James' family, his stepmother Anne, Countess of Castlehaven, and his wife, Lady Elizabeth Audley, Anne's daughter, appear not to have instigated the charges against the Earl.

12. It is a measure of the high rank Castlehaven's relatives held, and consequently of the embarrassment and shame he must have caused them, that the Countess Dowager of Derby's second husband, Sir Thomas Egerton, had presided as Lord High Steward in 1616 at the trial of those other notorious aristocratic criminals, Sir Robert Car and his wife Frances. These two were accused of poisoning Sir Thomas Overbury in order to suppress tales about their own illicit acts. Their trial exposed the other great English sexual scandal of the early seventeenth century besides Castlehaven's.

13. *The Arraignment and Conviction of Mervin Lord Audley, Earle of Castlehaven . . . on Monday, April 25, 1631* (London, 1642), p. 8. There are at least five printed versions of the trial, dating from 1642 to 1809, the most recent one being that in *Cobbett's Complete Collection of State Trials,* III (London, 1809), cols. 401–18. Manuscript versions of the trial turn up regularly in catalogues of seventeenth-century manuscripts. The five manuscript versions of the trial that I consulted are, therefore, not all the extant versions: MS Ashmolean 824, fols. 21–25; MS Rawlinsoniani. D. 924, fols. 100–18; MS Harleian 738, fols. 25–31; MS Harleian 2194, fols. 73–84; S.P.D., vol. 207. For the purposes of this paper, the five printed versions and the five manuscript versions of the trial I have read do not differ significantly from one another.

14. Ibid., p. 8.

15. *Cobbett's State Trials,* III, col. 412.

16. Ibid.

17. It may even be that although the "younge Lord and Lady" are reported

to have "lived loveingly" together at first, in *MS Ashmolean* 824 (fols. 21–25), Lady Elizabeth was still a virgin when she was first seduced by Skipwith. She married at the age of eleven or twelve and marriages with such young brides were not always immediately consummated. Such a marriage occurred at Harefield in 1623, a year before Anne and Mervyn's own marriage there. The bride and groom, Mervyn's niece and the Countess Dowager of Derby's grandchild, were, respectively, ten and fifteen years old: "By reason of the youth of this couple, the Lord Hastings being then little more than fifteen and his Lady not eleven . . . it was not held convenient they should cohabit together, whereupon he went to Cambridge where he studied for some time in Queen's College, his lady remaining with her father." *H.M.C. Report on the MSS of the late Reginald Rawdon Hastings,* IV (London, 1947), 352–53. It may be that in 1628 Lady Elizabeth and the young Lord Audley were also thought too young to consummate their marriage, the bride being eleven or twelve and the groom seventeen or eighteen. However, their being allowed to live together argues against this possibility.

18. See relevant dates in *Acts of the Privy Council of England,* ed. P. A. Penford, XIV (London, 1964). Though the Earl of Bridgewater was already a member of the Privy Council and of the Council of Wales, he and his family must have welcomed his nomination to the viceregal position of Lord President of the Council of Wales on June 26, 1631, near the height of the family scandal. They must have greatly valued such a sign of respect from the king at that particular moment.

The Earl of Bridgewater did not take up his official residence as Lord President of Wales at Ludlow Castle until October 1633, having had his appointment confirmed in May 1633. (See William Riley Parker, *Milton,* p. 125.) It is assumed that his family did not join him there until 1634. The family's furniture did not leave Ashridge until early July 1634. Was the interval of two years between the nomination of the Earl of Bridgewater to the Lord Presidency and the confirmation of that appointment a normal one? Or was the two-year interval a delay caused by the Earl's own embarrassment or the Privy Council's embarrassment for him because of the family scandal?

19. "On Munday the Sheriffs of London began to build Scaffolds in Westminster Hall, against Munday next, for tryall of the Earle of Castlehaven, there being 27: Lords summoned by writt to be his Judges (whereof all the Lords of the privy Counsell, except the Earles of Exeter & Bridgewater are part)." Letter from Mr. Pory to Sir Thomas Puckering, April 21, 1631, *MS Harleian* 7043, fol. 475.

20. See *S.P.D.,* vol. 189, no. 69; *S.P.D.,* vol. 190, nos. 60 and 68. One reason Charles I may have felt he could not pardon Castlehaven was that he could not afford to outrage public opinion in 1631. Two years before, he had closed Parliament abruptly because its members were attacking his prerogative to raise money as he chose. He had not called a parliament since. Pardoning a shockingly perverted aristocrat at this time would have further outraged people. Besides, as Lawrence Stone points out, sexual scandals involving members of the aristocracy had for too long gone unpunished. The popular association of sexual license with the aristocracy and with the court gained great strength during James I's reign when conventional sexual morals were blatantly absent from the English court. Though Charles' court was considerably more proper with respect

to homosexuality and promiscuity, the court's reputation still suffered. (See Lawrence Stone's invaluable book, *The Crisis of the Aristocracy: 1558–1641* [Oxford, 1965], p. 668.)

21. *S.P.D.*, vol. 189, no. 70.

22. *S.P.D.*, vol. 192, no. 11.

23. The Earl of Bridgewater apparently did not offer to help his stepmother out with the financial burden of caring for Anne and Elizabeth. In August 1631, Alice wrote to the king, this time asking outright for financial "reliefe of their miseries" (*S.P.D.*, vol. 198, no. 18).

24. *S.P.D.*, vol. 192, no. 11.

25. See *Cobbett's State Trials*, III, cols. 419–426.

26. *S.P.D.*, vol. 203, *Sign. Man.* Car. I., vol. xiii, no. 65.

27. *S.P.D.*, vol. 203, no. 100. The missing word is very difficult to make out in the manuscript.

28. In the years 1631 to 1634 Milton lived first in Cambridge, where he received his M.A. in the summer of 1632, and in London at his parents' house. Then, in the winter of 1631–1632 Milton moved with his parents to Hammersmith, a suburb west of London, where they lived until 1635 when they moved to Horton.

29. In the 1645 edition of Milton's poems, *Arcades* is described as "part of an entertainment presented to the Countess Dowager of *Darby* at *Harefield*, by som Noble Persons of her Family, who appear on the Scene in pastoral habit, moving toward the seat of State." It was very likely the success of *Arcades*, with its graceful redefinition of this recently distraught elderly lady as a serene pastoral queen, that led to Milton's being invited, either directly by the family or indirectly by Henry Lawes, to write a masque for Alice's children, the Bridgewaters.

30. Since Lady Mary Egerton, who was Lawes' pupil, married in 1627, Lawes must have started working for the Bridgewaters before 1627. (See William Riley Parker, *Milton*, p. 759.)

In 1637 and in 1653 Lawes recalled his former associations with the Bridgewaters in very grateful terms. He dedicated the 1637 edition of Milton's "mask" to the original Elder Brother, saying that he had "by many favours been long obliged to your most honour'd Parents." Years later, when aid from his former pupils was particularly appreciated, Lawes recalled his earlier relationship with the family in the same tone. Dedicating some of his "Ayres and Dialogues, for one, two, and three voices" to Alice Countess of Carbery (the original Lady) and her sister Mary, Lady Herbert of Cherbury (wife of George Herbert's nephew), he recalled when the pieces had been composed: "most of them being composed when I was employed by your ever honoured parents to attend your ladyships' education in music: who . . . excelled most ladies, especially in Vocall Musick, wherein you were so absolute, that you gave life and honour to all I set and taught you" (*The Poetical Works of John Milton*, ed. Henry John Todd [London, 1842], p. 46). At a time when the prestige of the aristocracy was falling, Lawes had frequent opportunities as a court musician to observe how masques flattered and respected the aristocracy's ideal image of their power and moral authority. Lawes entertained in at least six court masques before his performance in *Comus*: Jonson's *Love's Triumph through Callipolis,* and *Chloridia* (in which both Lawes and Penelope Egerton acted), Townshend's *Albion's Triumph,* and *Tempe Restored* (in which Lady Alice Egerton and her older sister Catherine performed), Shirley's *The Triumph of Peace,* and Carew's *Coelum Britannicum* (in which the two Egerton boys and their cousin Lord Chandos performed).

31. For an example of a diary item, see Dr. John Southcote, "Diary notebook, 1628–1637," in *Catholic Record Society Miscellanea,* I (1905), 107. For examples of news-letters mentioning the Castlehaven affair see Thomas Birch, *The Court and Times of Charles the First: Containing a Series of Historical and Confidential Letters* (London, 1849), II, 106, 118; George W. Johnson, ed., *The Fairfax Correspondence: Memoirs of the Reign of Charles the First* (London, 1848), I, 232–33; and *MS Harleian* 7043, fol. 476.

32. *MS Harleian* 738, fol. 31. This mock epitaph appears in at least one other manuscript, *Additional MS* 5832, fol. 222b.

33. John Fry, *Pieces of Ancient Poetry, from Unpublished Manuscripts and Scarce Books* (Bristol, 1814), p. 11.

34. *MS Eng. poet.* e 97. There are at least two other manuscript versions of the poem: *MS Ashmolean* 47, fols. 88b–89a, and *MS Rawlinsoniani.* A. 346, fols. 141b–142a.

35. *S.P.D.* vol. 207, fol. 47a–47b. It seems likely that the reason no descriptions of Castlehaven, including this lengthy one, were published until after the Civil War had begun, was that until that time the king and the families concerned could suppress such publications.

36. *MS Tanner,* lxxi, fol. 92.

37. Thomas Birch, *The Court and Times of Charles the First,* II, 230–31.